"In his valuable new book, *Core Competencies in Counseling and Psychotherapy: Becoming a Highly Competent and Effective Therapist*, Dr. Len Sperry brings the lists of clinical core competencies alive for therapists and educators alike by providing clear explanations of the competencies' therapeutic contexts, meanings, and importance. In doing so, he helps us move beyond merely being competent to becoming proficient in our understanding and utilization of these clinically critical best practices. Dr. Sperry's contribution to the competency movement in the mental health disciplines is significant because he is able to synthesize the various and sometimes competing clinical competencies together in order to provide us with six integrative core competencies that once again illustrate how the whole is greater than the sum of its parts. In this manner Dr. Sperry's synergistic solution marks a productive step forward, bringing common competencies-based education to the forefront and mapping our journey towards improving the quality of the counseling and psychotherapeutic care we provide."

—**Ron Chenail, PhD**
Professor of Family Therapy, Nova Southeastern University, Florida
Editor-in-Chief, *Journal of Marital and Family Therapy*

"This is a timely, clinically relevant, and highly readable book that lives up to its comprehensive title. Dr. Sperry seamlessly interweaves empirical research, theory, and illustrative clinical vignettes in a highly organized and accessible manner. This compendium will help trainees and experienced therapists of all disciplines and orientations make sense of what it takes to be a highly effective therapist."

—**Hanna Levenson, PhD**
Professor, Wright Institute, Berkeley, California
Author, *Time Limited Dynamic Therapy*

"The ability to perform psychotherapy is an essential competency for the modern mental health professional. Knowing what is going on, what to do, and how to do it, effectively and ethically, is the focus of Dr. Sperry's concisely and clearly written text, *Core Competencies in Counseling and Psychotherapy*. Dr. Sperry's book will be a valuable resource for learners and experienced practitioners because of its balanced coverage of the major modes of psychotherapy and its clear intent to help with acquiring and maintaining professional competencies."

—**Laura Roberts, MD**
Chair of Psychiatry and Behavioral Sciences
Stanford University School of Medicine, California
Editor-in-Chief, *Academic Psychiatry*

"If the art and science of psychotherapy may be likened to a foreign country, Dr. Sperry's text is a kind of Baedeker—a clear and comprehensive guide book to this often challenging territory. Dr. Sperry emphasizes the curative elements common to all major forms of psychotherapy, yet provides detailed descriptions of the individual schools and approaches. The book is pluralistic in its approach, with a broad-based biopsychosocial orientation to treatment, yet avoids the sort of unfocused eclecticism that detracts from less sophisticated texts. Terms are carefully defined; the text is clearly written; and numerous clinical illustrations are provided.

The use of an ongoing case example lends a vivid, narrative thread to the text, and allows the reader to integrate a broad array of data in a more personalized way. Dr. Sperry's text also provides a sound basis for understanding ethno-cultural and ethical issues that arise in the course of treatment. I believe this book will serve as an excellent introductory text for those seeking to achieve competency in psychotherapy, but will also be an elegant 'refresher course' for many experienced practitioners who want to refine their understanding."

—**Ronald Pies, MD**
Professor of Psychiatry, SUNY Upstate Medical University, Syracuse, New York
Clinical Professor of Psychiatry, Tufts University School of Medicine, Boston, Massachusetts
Past editor-in-Chief, *Psychiatric Times*

"Dr. Sperry has masterfully incorporated assessment, therapeutic relationship, intervention, evaluation, termination, and multiculturalism into a tightly integrated series of competencies. This text is both highly scientific and pragmatic for the neophyte and veteran therapist alike, taking therapist development to the next level."

—Craig S. Cashwell, PhD, LPC, NCC, ACS
Professor, School of Education
University of North Carolina at Greensboro

"This book makes the core competencies of therapy practices not only practical but inspiring…and transforms them into ways of thinking and practicing that we can all aspire to master, no matter what our model of practice or stage of career. Great job, Len Sperry!"

—William J. Doherty, PhD
Professor, University of Minnesota
Author, *Soul Searching* and *Family Therapy*

"This volume develops a systematic approach to teaching the three residency-required core competencies in psychotherapy. With the therapeutic relationship always at the core, the author integrates the common, differentiating, and evolving essentials of cognitive-behavioral, psychodynamic, and systemic (a stand-in for supportive) psychotherapies. It is a useful resource for educators designing programs to achieve the core competencies. Experienced clinicians may also find it of value in reviewing basic concepts of the major psychotherapies."

—Norman A. Clemens, MD
Clinical Professor of Psychiatry
Case Western Reserve University School of Medicine, Ohio
Training and Supervising Analyst, Cleveland Psychoanalytic Center
Psychotherapy columns editor, *Journal of Psychiatric Practice*

"*Core Competencies in Counseling and Psychotherapy* is a wonderful companion to Dr. Sperry's excellent book, *Highly Effective Therapy*. Both seasoned therapists and clinicians-in-training—as well as those who prepare clinicians—will find this book a thorough and accessible resource. Used in combination, *Core Competencies* and *Highly Effective Therapy* provide readers with an excellent, in-depth presentation of the knowledge, attitudinal dispositions, and skill sets involved in the core competencies of successful clinical practice."

—Richard E. Watts, PhD, LPC-S
Professor and Director
Center for Research and Doctoral Studies in Counselor Education
Sam Houston State University, Huntsville, Texas

"Len Sperry succinctly and systematically presents the basic competencies of psychotherapy practice based on his extensive experience as a clinician, psychotherapy researcher, and supervisor. Each phase of treatment and dimension of psychotherapy is clearly formulated and enriched with the wisdom that only comes through decades of experience. As a profoundly deep-thinking therapist and scholar, Dr. Sperry proposes a distillation of a true healing process. His conceptualization offers our field a standard for clinical practice against which to hold ourselves and help our clients heal and evolve. The conduct of very fine psychotherapy is made accessible through his clear formulation of clinical competency. Dr. Sperry creates the bedrock for training for a new therapist and, for more seasoned therapists, a place for reflection on further refinement."

—Lisa Miller, PhD
Associate Professor, Clinical Psychology, Teachers College
Columbia University and Columbia University Medical School, New York
Past President, Division 36, American Psychological Association

Core Competencies in Counseling and Psychotherapy

CORE COMPETENCIES IN PSYCHOTHERAPY SERIES

Series Editor
Len Sperry
Florida Atlantic University, Medical College of Wisconsin

Competency represents a paradigm shift in the training and practice of psychotherapy that is already challenging much of what is familiar and comfortable. This series addresses the core competencies common to highly effective psychotherapeutic practice, and includes individual volumes for the most commonly practiced approaches today: cognitive behavior, brief dynamic, and solution-focused therapies, and others.

Core Competencies in Counseling and Psychotherapy

Becoming a Highly Competent and Effective Therapist

LEN SPERRY

Routledge
Taylor & Francis Group
New York   London

Routledge
Taylor & Francis Group
711 Third Avenue
New York, NY 10017

Routledge
Taylor & Francis Group
27 Church Road
Hove, East Sussex BN3 2FA

© 2010 by Taylor and Francis Group, LLC
Routledge is an imprint of Taylor & Francis Group, an Informa business

10 9 8 7 6 5 4 3 2

International Standard Book Number: 978-0-415-95249-1 (Hardback)

Library of Congress Cataloging-in-Publication Data

Sperry, Len.
    Core competencies in counseling and psychotherapy : becoming a highly competent and effective therapist / by Len Sperry.
        p. cm.
    Includes bibliographical references and index.
    ISBN 978-0-415-95249-1 (hardback : alk. paper)
    1. Psychotherapy. I. Title.

RC480.S653 2010
616.89'14--dc22   2010015636

Visit the Taylor & Francis Web site at
http://www.taylorandfrancis.com

and the Routledge Web site at
http://www.routledgementalhealth.com

CONTENTS

SECTION II Core Competency I: Conceptual Foundations

SECTION III   Core Competency 2: Therapeutic Relationship

SECTION IV   Core Competency 3: Intervention Planning

SECTION V   Core Competency 4: Intervention Implementation

SECTION VI Core Competency 5: Intervention Evaluation and Treatment

SECTION VII   Core Competency 6: Cultural and Ethical Sensitivity

SECTION VIII   Conclusion

FOREWORD

Nadine J. Kaslow, PhD, ABPP

As a psychotherapist, clinical intervention researcher, and teacher of the next generation of psychotherapists, I am fascinated reading books such as Sperry's *Core competencies in counseling and psychotherapy: Becoming a highly competent and effective therapist*. After all, we all strive to be the best we can be as clinicians, and a thoughtfully crafted guide is of great relevance to all psychotherapists, regardless of theoretical orientation, experience level, or discipline.

For a decade, I have been deeply immersed in the competencies movement in professional psychology. I chaired the 2002 Competencies Conference: Future Directions in Education and Credentialing, that brought together a cross-national cadre of educators, trainers, and credentialers who delineated the core foundational and functional competencies in professional psychology, outlined strategies for teaching these competencies, and began to articulate strategies for competency assessment (Kaslow, 2004; Kaslow et al., 2004). Since the landmark Competencies Conference, I have been involved with many colleagues in professional psychology in ascertaining the behavioral indicators that serve as benchmarks for competency within each foundational and functional domain across three levels of professional development: readiness for practicum, readiness for internship, and readiness for entry to practice (Fouad et al., 2009). Along with a team of colleagues, we developed guiding principles and recommendations for assessing competence (Kaslow et al., 2007) and created a Competency Assessment Toolkit for Professional Psychology (Kaslow et al., 2009).

I have been interested in considering competencies from both a theoretical and work setting perspective. For example, I have worked closely with other family psychologists to distill the essential components of the foundational and functional competencies that are most relevant to family psychologists and the practice of couple and family psychotherapy (Celano, Smith, & Kaslow, 2010; Kaslow, Celano, & Stanton, 2005). In addition, I have been involved in enumerating competencies for psychologists practicing in academic health centers (Kaslow, Dunn, & Smith, 2008).

Not only do we need to consider the delineation and assessment of competencies, but also a competency-based approach to education and training. Recently, I co-edited with Eugene Farber, PhD, a special issue of *Psychotherapy: Theory, Research, Practice, Training* focused on the role of supervision in ensuring the development of psychotherapy competencies across diverse theoretical perspectives (Farber & Kaslow, 2010) and I myself have been interested in using a competency-based approach to supervision (Kaslow & Bell, 2008). Unfortunately, not all of our trainees are deemed competent and thus we need strategies for use in a training context to foster the development of competence in individuals whose performance is below the developmentally expected benchmarks. To this end, I have collaborated with colleagues interested in students with competence problems and we have outlined proposals for recognizing, assessing, and intervening with problems of professional competence (Kaslow, et al., 2009). The competency-based approach to education and training should occur in tandem with such a framework toward credentialing. To this end, I have co-authored a chapter on a competency-based approach to board certification through the American Board of Professional Psychology (Kaslow & Ingram, 2009).

Given my active engagement in the competencies movement, I read with great interest Sperry's *Core competencies in counseling and psychotherapy: Becoming a highly competent and effective therapist*, which is written in a very lucid fashion. This text sets the stage for the reader by providing a comprehensive review of the competencies movement in which the psychotherapy competency is embedded. Then each of the core competencies associated with the psychotherapy competency is delineated in turn. The competencies selected are in keeping with the current state of our knowledge base and include conceptual foundation, relationship building and maintenance, intervention planning, intervention implementation, intervention evaluation and termination, and culturally and ethically sensitivity practice. The choice of these core competencies reflects a combining of what have been deemed foundational competencies (e.g., relationship, cultural and ethical sensitivity) and what have been labeled essential components of the intervention competency (e.g., intervention planning, intervention implementation, intervention evaluation) in other frameworks. The addition of conceptual framework is new to this model, but is consistent with the emphasis placed on case conceptualization when competencies have been articulated associated with interventions conducted in accord with specific theoretical approaches (Celano et al., 2010).

The strength of the chapter on the conceptual foundations competency (Core Competency 1) is that it considers conceptualization from multiple

theoretical perspectives. The same is true for the chapter on relationship building, one element of the therapeutic relationship competency (Core Competency 2). However, what is also noteworthy about this chapter is the presentation of an integrative view of the therapeutic alliance and how such an alliance can be forged, enhanced, and utilized effectively to promote therapeutic change. It is valuable that the next chapter addresses maintaining an effective therapeutic relationship, another element of the therapeutic relationship competency, which is just as critical as forming such a deep and meaningful connection. The essential elements of maintaining an effective therapeutic relationship that are elucidated are recognizing and resolving resistance and ambivalence, recognizing and resolving transferences and countertransferences, and recognizing and repairing alliance ruptures. Particular attention is paid to creative strategies for addressing the treatment interfering factors that impede therapeutic progress.

The next section focuses on the third core competency, namely, intervention planning. The first two chapters in this section address case conceptualization as it relates to both assessment and intervention. There is no question that effective treatments are based on insightful case conceptualizations that emerge following a comprehensive diagnostic, theory-based, and pattern-based assessment, the steps of which are outlined. The in-depth review of case conceptualization and treatment planning addresses four key elements that are articulated in a very understandable fashion: diagnostic formulation, clinical formulation, cultural formulation, and treatment formulation. An excellent example is offered that helps to elucidate the key points in this chapter.

The fourth core competency is intervention implementation and to underscore the necessity of implementing interventions effectively for positive results to be obtained, there are four chapters in this section. The first one provides a general implementation strategy, whereas the subsequent three chapters address intervention implementation from different theoretical frameworks: dynamic, cognitive behavioral, and systemic. The three general implementation strategy competencies that are emphasized are establishing a treatment focus, maintaining a treatment focus, and recognizing and resolving therapy interfering factors. Very concrete and specific implementation strategies are enumerated for each of the specific theoretical models.

Intervention evaluation and termination is the fifth core competency and thus there are separate chapters on outcome assessment and termination. In the current zeitgeist, in which accountability is essential, it is imperative that practitioners demonstrate the effectiveness of their interventions. Such accountability is expected by consumers of services and funders of services. Evaluation of treatment progress helps the therapist-client system to modify treatment in an ongoing fashion to ensure that it is optimally effective. Outcome measures at the completion of the intervention help all relevant parties ascertain the extent to which the treatment was a success and what future progress may need to be made. The author provides a very practitioner-friendly approach to outcomes assessment and the case example offered helps to flesh out the key points. As Sperry aptly notes, termination is both an event and a process and typically clinicians have insufficient education and training regarding this element of the therapeutic process. To help practitioners better master this phase of treatment, two essential competencies associated with termination are discussed: maintaining treatment gains and preparing for termination. Ways in which termination may be handled in accord with diverse theoretical perspectives are highlighted and a case example illustrates the termination process.

The final competency is cultural and ethical sensitivity and there are chapters on each of these foundational competencies as related to psychotherapy and counseling. Developing effective cultural formulations and planning culturally sensitive interventions are highlighted, and multiple interesting and engaging case vignettes are presented. To elucidate the construct of ethical sensitivity as related to the psychotherapy and counseling competency, consideration is given to making ethically sound decisions and practicing in an ethically sensitive manner. This discussion is guided by three ethical perspectives that range on a continuum from the view that ethics and professional practice are inextricably interwoven to the notion that the two are only tangentially related. An engaging case illustration of providing ethically sensitive treatment appears at the close of the chapter.

The final section of the book underscores the importance of life-long learning and continued professional development, emphasizing such key foundational competencies as self-reflection. It is an indisputable fact that for us to continue to grow and develop as clinicians, we must continually engage in the learning process, and learn from our clients, colleagues, supervisors/consultations, and knowledgeable people in the field. Sperry is one such knowledgeable person and this book will no doubt foster the professional development process in all who choose to read it.

PREFACE

Competency is the new buzz word in psychotherapy training and practice today. It is not just another approach, technique, or training method; it is considerably different and represents a paradigm shift in therapy training and practice. Arguably, it is already challenging much of what it is familiar and comfortable. For instance, requirement standards are beginning to be replaced with competency standards, core competencies are replacing core curriculums, and competency-based licensure is not far off. This shift has already been felt in the accreditation arena, as psychiatry training programs now require that trainees demonstrate competency in at least three psychotherapy approaches. Training programs in clinical psychology programs have solidly embraced competencies, and marital and family therapy and professional counseling programs are poised to follow suit. Because competencies involve knowledge, skill, and attitudinal components, competency-based education is very different in how it is taught, learned, and evaluated. Not surprisingly, models of instruction and supervision must necessarily change.

The emergence of competencies on the center stage of training and practice reflects several societal trends, among them the demand for professional accountability and evidence-based practice. Fortunately, the expectation that therapists demonstrate the effectiveness of their therapeutic work parallels the recent upsurge in treatment outcomes research. A few books are already in print that endeavor to provide trainees and practitioners with a taste of what the "competency movement" and the "culture of competency" are about and how training and clinical practice are already changing to meet these challenges.

It is in this context that *Core Competencies in Counseling and Psychotherapy* appears. It addresses the core competencies common to the effective practice of all psychotherapeutic approaches, and it includes the most commonly used intervention competencies of the cognitive–behavioral, psychodynamic, and systemic approaches, particularly solution-focused therapy.

Core Competencies is a companion volume to *Highly Effective Therapy: Developing Essential Clinical Competencies in Counseling and Psychotherapy*, recently published by Routledge. The books are intended to be used together. Whereas *Highly Effective Therapy* primarily focused on the skill component of 20 clinical competencies, *Core Competencies* focuses primarily on the knowledge and attitudinal components of the same competencies, and secondarily on the skill component. Accordingly, *Core Competencies* provides a theoretical and research-based framework that will aid therapists in applying these competencies in their own practice. It begins with a panoramic view of the meaning of competency and its wide-ranging impact on training and practice. Then, in subsequent chapters each of the core competencies and related supporting competencies are described and illustrated with clinical case material.

Rather than being an encyclopedic compendium of psychotherapy theory and research or a cookbook of methods and techniques, *Core Competencies* is intended as a highly readable and easily accessible book to enhance the knowledge, attitudes, and skills of clinicians—both novice and experienced—in all the mental health specialties. This book will be of great value to both practicing clinicians and trainees in counseling, counseling psychology, clinical psychology, marital and family therapy, social work, and psychiatry training programs as a basic or supplementary text in a variety of psychotherapy courses.

Section I

Introduction

1

Competencies in Counseling and Psychotherapy
An Overview

In this current era of accountability and evidence-based practice, it should come as no surprise that the training and practice of psychotherapy is expected to become increasingly accountability-based, and specifically competency-based. At the same time, it is becoming less acceptable to practice psychotherapy that is standards-based, just as it is harder to justify standards-based training. In fact, core competency-based training is increasingly expected and soon will be required. In the past few years, the mental health disciplines of psychology, marriage and family therapy, psychiatry, and professional counseling have embraced the "competency movement" and its culture of competency. This chapter provides a brief introduction to competency and competency-based practice and training and overviews what is to come in subsequent chapters.

The chapter begins with a discussion of definition of terms such as *competence, competencies,* and *capability.* Then, it describes the competency movement in the mental health disciplines and their efforts to change training and practice patterns. The six core competencies that are focus of this book are then briefly introduced. Finally, the interrelatedness of the six core competencies is highlighted.

DEFINITION OF TERMS

Competence and Competency

Competence and *competency* are closely related terms. Whereas some use the terms interchangeably, others differentiate them wherein competence refers to the potential or capacity to perform and competency means the actual performance or demonstration of that capacity. In this book, the terms will be used interchangeably.

Here are some common ways in which these terms are described and defined. Competence involves a broad spectrum of personal and professional capacities relative to a given external standard or requirement. Among these are the capacity for critical thinking, analysis, and professional judgment in assessing a situation and making clinical decisions based on that assessment. Furthermore, competence is the capacity to evaluate and modify one's decisions, as appropriate, through reflective practice (Kaslow, 2004). Another aspect of competence is that it is a "state of sufficiency relative to the specific performance or training requirements within the given setting which such abilities are exercised" (Falender & Shafranske, 2004, p. 5). Sufficiency refers to adequacy and quality of one's performance "relative to an external standard, and it is assumed that competence can always be enhanced" (Falender & Shafranske, 2004, p. 22).

Competence is also described as "the habitual and judicious use of communication, knowledge, technical skills, clinical reasoning, emotions, values, and reflection in daily practice for the benefit of the individual and the community being served" (Epstein & Hundert, 2002, p. 26). Competencies "refer to knowledge, skills, and attitudes, and their integration. Competencies are interactive clusters of integrative knowledge of concepts and procedures, skills and abilities, behaviors and strategies, attitudes/beliefs/values, dispositions and personal characteristics, self perceptions, and motivations that enable a person to fully perform a task with a wide range of outcomes" (Kaslow, 2009, p. 2). Furthermore, competencies are reflected in the quality of clinical performance, can be evaluated against professional standards, and can be developed or enhanced through professional training and personal growth (Kaslow, 2004). Ideally, training should provide an integrated learning experience in which knowledge, skills, and attitudes interact to become clinical competencies.

Five themes or dimensions seem to emerge from these various definitions and descriptions of a competency: (1) capacity, (2) integration of knowledge, skills, and attitudes, (3) for the benefit of others, (4) evaluated against a professional standard, and (5) enhanced through training and reflection. Accordingly, the definition of competency used in this book includes these dimensions: Competency is the capacity to integrate knowledge, skills, and attitudes reflected in the quality of clinical practice that benefits others, which can be evaluated by professional standards and be developed and enhanced through professional training and reflection.

Competency Versus Skill

Too often the terms *competency* and *skill* are used synonymously. Although there is some similarity, they are notable different. As described earlier, a clinical competency is composed of knowledge, skills, and attitudes components which are necessary for professional practice. On the other hand, a skill is simply a capacity that can be acquired by training but does not have knowledge or attitudinal components and does not have an external standard to evaluate its sufficiency. In short, besides being more encompassing than a skill, a competency refers to the collection of skills, knowledge, and attitudes required to perform a task to a minimum standard. Training programs and supervision that focus only on skills and skill training are problematic. After all, being highly skilled is useless if a clinician lacks the attitude or resolve to utilize those skills for a client's well-being.

The construct of empathy can be used to illustrate how a competency is more than a skill or skill set. In addition to clinicians, others can and do exhibit empathy, for example, salespersons and psychopaths. Defined as a competency, empathy has three components: empathy knowledge (knowledge), empathy communication skills (skill), and empathic stance (attitude). The presence of all three components is involved in what is called "therapeutic empathy." So what is the empathic stance? This component refers to an attitude of benevolence and a desire to promote the client's well-being. Consequently, for empathy to become therapeutic empathy, the therapist must respond and act out of a stance of benevolence, interest, and respect toward clients (Thwaites & Bennett-Levy, 2007). Effective and successful clinicians exhibit therapeutic empathy and would be considered empathically competent.

Defined as a skill, empathy involves empathy communication skills. Sales personnel who have developed the skill of empathic communication can be quite successful because of their newfound capacity to effectively "read" and respond to customers. Arguably, they are less likely to be successful if they also possess an empathic stance. The reason is that sales personnel who are, in fact, concerned about a customer's well-being are less likely to use empathic influence to sell customers items that are unnecessary or harmful. In short, successful sales personnel are not likely to be empathically competent. Similarly, clinicians who engage in sexual misconduct with clients fail to demonstrate a lack of empathic stance by their harmful, nonbenevolent behavior. Although such clinicians may have mastered the skill of empathy, their behavior would characterize them as empathically incompetent (Sperry, 2010).

Capability

Capability is "the extent to which competent individuals adapt their skills, generate new knowledge and continue to improve their performance. The confluence of competence and lifelong learning is capability" (Kaslow, 2009, p. 4). In this book, capability is the conviction that energizes individuals to do and be their best; it is a striving to achieve more than the minimal or required level of competency. It is also the capacity to adapt competencies to new or changing circumstances while continually expanding knowledge and improving performance. With regard to psychotherapy, it involves striving to become an expert or master therapist (Skovholt & Jennings, 2004). Chapter 15 further extends this discussion.

Table 1.1 summarizes these various definitions.

THE COMPETENCY MOVEMENT IN THE MENTAL HEALTH DISCIPLINES

Competency as an idea and ideal dates from at least the time of the medieval guilds when apprentices worked under the guidance of a master in order to achieve competency in a given craft or trade. Yet, it has only been since the 1960s that the current emphasis on competencies in the professions has evolved into what can be called the "competency movement." A seminal article by David McClelland, titled "Testing for Competence Rather than Intelligence" (McClelland, 1973), led to his being dubbed the father of the competency movement (J. Miller, Todahl, & Platt, 2010).

6

Table 1.1 Definitions

Competency	The capacity to integrate knowledge, skills, and attitudes reflected in the quality of clinical practice that benefits others, which can be evaluated by professional standards and developed and enhanced through professional training and reflection
Skill	A capacity that has been acquired by training and that lacks knowledge and attitudinal components
Capability	The attitude to strive to achieve more than the minimal or required level of competency and the capacity to adapt competencies to new or changing circumstances while continually expanding knowledge and improving performance

Since then, efforts to shift health care, including mental heath care, to a competency-based training and practice model have been under way. Medicine was the first health care discipline to require competency-based training, and initial efforts to incorporate competency-based training are also under way in the mental health disciplines of psychiatry, clinical psychology, addiction counseling, psychiatric nursing, psychiatric rehabilitation, and, to a lesser extent, social work. The Institute of Medicine (2003) has urged the health and mental health disciplines to develop a well-defined set of core competencies for clinical practice, both within and among the disciplines. Because mental health care is largely a team effort involving individuals from different disciplines, the Institute of Medicine deemed it essential that various health care disciplines achieve some consensus about common competencies necessary for effective, efficient, and accountable care. At this point in time, the efforts of the various mental health disciplines have been largely independent, resulting in what has been called a "patchwork quilt of initiatives" (Hoge, Paris, Adger, Collins, Finn, et al., 2005, p. 594). Nevertheless, the initiatives of these mental health disciplines have been dubbed the "competency movement" (Gehart, 2010, p. 4).

Five Mental Health Disciplines

This section briefly describes the efforts of this "movement" to establish competencies for psychotherapy training and practice, particularly among five mental health disciplines: psychiatry, psychology, marriage and family therapy, social work, and counseling. Each will be described in the order in which progress has occurred in the implementation of competency-based training. Although it may first appear that there is little commonality among the seemingly "patchwork" efforts of these organizations, there is, in fact, considerable commonality.

Psychiatry

Of the mental health disciplines, psychiatry appears to have been the first to initiate the development and implementation of psychotherapy competencies, notably with the requirement that trainees demonstrate specific competencies. Psychiatric training in the United States is governed by the Psychiatry Residency Review Committee (RRC) of the Accreditation Council for Graduate Medical Education (ACGME, 2007), whereas the American Psychiatric Association is its primary membership and advocacy organization (Mellman & Beresin, 2003). Since January 2001, the RRC has required that all psychiatry trainees demonstrate competencies in five specific psychotherapy approaches and related competencies (Mellman & Beresin, 2003). For a number of reasons, this requirement was reduced to three approaches in July 2007: cognitive–behavioral therapy (CBT), psychodynamic therapy, and supportive therapy (Plakun, Sudak, & Goldberg, 2009). The American Psychiatric Association Commission on Psychotherapy by Psychiatrists (COPP) has reconceptualized these three therapy approaches and their competencies into one integrative approach called the Y-model. It is called that because of its resemblance in structure to the letter Y (Plakun et al., 2009). The stem of the Y represents the core competencies common to all therapy approaches, while the branches or forks of the Y represent the specialized competencies of CBT and psychodynamic therapy. Supportive therapy is treatment that focuses primarily to relieve symptoms or "supports" the client to live with them rather than to change personality structures. Because it is conceptualized as largely composed of skills and competencies common to all therapies, supportive therapy is represented in the stem of the Y. The core factors and

8

competencies considered common to all psychotherapies identified by the COPP and delineated by Plakun (2008) include the following:

Relationship: Establish and maintain a therapeutic alliance.

Intervention Planning: Identify dysfunction patterns and develop a clinical formulation.

Intervention Implementation: Utilize specific CBT and psychodynamic interventions.

Ethical and Cultural Sensitivity: Attend to boundaries, confidentiality, and other ethical considerations.

Psychology

An ongoing initiative of the American Psychological Association (APA) has been to shift professional training in psychology from a core curriculum model to a core competency model of learning. More specifically, the shift has been a move toward measuring trainee learning outcomes. These outcomes have been articulated as core competencies, which serve as a primary focus of the education and training process (P. Nelson, 2007). Recently, APA's Assessment of Competency Benchmarks Work Group (ACBWG) has identified 15 core foundational and functional competencies for psychology (Fouad, Grus, Hatcher, Kaslow, Hutchings, et al., 2009). Another group, the National Council of Schools and Programs of Professional Psychology (NCSPP) has also developed a set of seven competencies for the professional practice of psychology: relationship, assessment, intervention, research and evaluation, consultation and education, management and supervision, and diversity (Kenkel & Peterson, 2009). Both ACBWG and NCSPP recognize that competencies have knowledge, skill, and attitudinal components, the so-called KSAs. Among the competencies identified by both groups that are specifically related to psychotherapy are the following:

Relationship: Develop effective relationships.

Intervention Planning: Conduct assessment; develop case conceptualizations and design interventions.

Intervention Implementation: Implement evidence-based interventions.

Intervention Evaluation: Evaluate treatment progress and modify planning as indicated.

Ethical and Cultural Sensitivity: Be sensitive to cultural diversity and knowledgeable of ethical and legal standards and policies.

9

Each of the core competencies is defined in terms of its essential components, which are delineated for specific training levels. APA specifies three such training levels: readiness for practicum, readiness for internship, and readiness for entry to independent practice (complete doctoral degree for NCSPP), with progressively more complex thresholds for each level. In addition, behavioral anchors are provided for each training level that demonstrate the expected knowledge, skill sets, and attitudinal threshold for competent performance for that level of training. These anchors specify increasing levels of independence at successive developmental levels.

An example of these three developmental levels and their competency thresholds is illustrated for the core competency of intervention planning. Readiness for entrance into the first practicum experience would be demonstrated by a basic understanding of the relationship between assessment and intervention. By contrast, readiness for entrance into the internship experience would be demonstrated by the capacity to formulate and conceptualize clinical cases and plan interventions utilizing at least one consistent theoretical orientation. Finally, entry into independent practice would be demonstrated by independent intervention planning, including conceptualization and intervention planning specific to a given case and its context (Fouad et al., 2009). Attitudinal thresholds include "appreciation for complexity and ambiguity of clinical problems" for beginning a practicum, "deepened appreciation of client's life experiences" for beginning an internship, and "realistic sense of what is possible in therapy and one's own ability/limitations to create change" for completing a doctoral degree (Binder & Wechsler, 2009, p. 109).

The APA has contributed much to the development of core competencies in psychotherapy by articulating definitions of terms and distinguishing competencies for each of the three levels of training. Both ACBWG and NCSPP have articulated behavioral anchors for the essential components of each core competencies, making assessment of a trainee's or provider's competence possible. Finally, both have addressed the competency of evaluating treatment progress and modifying treatment as indicated—that is, part of the core competency of intervention evaluation.

Marital and Family Therapy
The American Association of Marriage and Family Therapy (AAMFT) created a Core Competency Task Force (CCTF) to define the domains of

knowledge and requisite skills and those characteristics that predispose the therapist for success in those domains (AAMFT, 2002). Two years later, AAMFT disseminated a list of 128 competencies, which were divided into six core competency domains (AAMFT, 2004; T. Nelson, Chenail, Alexander, Crane, Johnson, et al., 2007). Gehart (2010) has since elaborated some of these competencies. Among these are the following:

Relationship: Admission to treatment; establishing and maintaining appropriate and productive therapeutic alliances with clients
Intervention Planning: Clinical assessment and diagnosis; treatment planning and case management—developing a plan of care
Intervention Implementation: Therapeutic interventions—effecting change in the therapy session
Ethical and Cultural Sensitivity: Legal issues, ethics, and standards— understanding the legal and ethical aspects of practice

The contribution of CCTF to psychotherapy competencies is significant, particularly with regard to therapy involving couples and families. It is interesting to note that relationship and therapeutic alliance appears to be a subordinate competency to admission to treatment, whereas relationship is considered a core competency for other mental health disciplines. Furthermore, AAMFT demonstrated its commitment to mainlining competency-based training by establishing a Beta-Test Group of eight universities in 2005 to experiment with strategies for adopting the core competencies as well as evaluating trainee competency by developing various assessment tools and methods.

Counseling

The accrediting arm of the American Counseling Association—the Council for Accreditation of Counseling and Related Educational Programs (CACREP)—has also developed a list of competency-based standards specified in terms of knowledge, skills, and practices (CACREP, 2009). Starting with the CACREP standards, Engels, Minton, Ray, and associates (2010) have articulated a comprehensive list and description of competencies and learner outcomes for several areas of professional counseling, including clinical mental health counseling, addiction counseling, marriage, couple, family, and relationship counseling, and child counseling. Competencies and specific performance guidelines were articulated for each professional practice area. These performance guidelines are framed as markers of the demonstration of a particular competency.

The competencies relevant to psychotherapy for the area of clinical mental health counseling according to Engels and associates (2010) include the following:

Relationship: Establish and facilitate constructive, safe, and ethical relationships with clients.

Intervention Planning: Engage in comprehensive biopsychosocial assessment and appraisal strategies; develop and implement appropriate case conceptualizations and diagnostic-based treatment programs.

Ethical and Cultural Sensitivity: Maintain appropriate ethical, legal, and professional behavior.

This competency-focused articulation of CACREP standards is a remarkable accomplishment for the discipline of professional counseling. Presumably, competencies regarding intervention implementation and intervention evaluation will be forthcoming.

Social Work

The National Association of Social Workers is the membership organization for social work practice, and the Council on Social Work Education (CSWE) is its accrediting body. Because social work does not focus solely on mental health, CSWE does not prescribe any particular curriculum for teaching psychotherapy or counseling (CSWE, 2004). Accordingly, specific psychotherapy competencies have yet to be developed by the accrediting body. Nevertheless, individual graduate social work programs, particularly those that emphasize psychotherapy, are likely to develop or adapt such core competencies.

Progress on Adoption of Competency-Based Training

Currently, there is little or no published research on the extent to which mental health disciplines have fared in introducing competency-based training in their educational programs. However, there is at least one national study that addresses the matter, albeit indirectly. A cross-sectional survey of a probability sample of all accredited training programs in psychiatry, psychology, and social work in the United States was undertaken to determine the nature of psychotherapy training and the extent to which the training involved evidence-based therapy (EBT). Survey results indicate that psychiatry programs provide the most required coursework and clinical supervision and that CBT was the EBT most frequently offered among the three disciplines (Weissman, Verdeli, Gameroff, Bledsoe, Betts, et al., 2006).

Commonality on Core Competencies

A closer look at the independent efforts by the mental health disciplines reveals that there is considerable overlap among the core competencies espoused by these groups regarding the most basic or core competencies involving psychotherapy. These core competencies are *relationship, intervention planning, intervention implementation, intervention evaluation, and cultural and ethical sensitivity*. To these we will add a sixth, *conceptual foundations*, which is implicit in all the disciplines. Conceptual foundations refers to the basic theoretical orientation that informs the therapist's clinical work with clients.

CORE COMPETENCIES IN COUNSELING AND PSYCHOTHERAPY

This section briefly overviews the six core competencies and their supporting essential clinical competencies. The core competencies are detailed in Chapters 2 through 14, along with a description of the related essential clinical competencies. These clinical competencies are described in more detail and illustrated with clinical case material and session transcriptions in *Highly Effective Therapy: Developing Essential Clinical Competencies in Counseling and Psychotherapy* (Sperry, 2010).

1. Conceptual Foundation

Clinicians typically utilize a systematic conceptual framework to understand and guide the treatment process. This framework is often a basic theoretical orientation or treatment approach. Even though clinicians may consider themselves eclectic, research suggests that they rely on a favored theoretical orientation to aid their clinical thinking and decisions (Binder, 2004). This core competency consists of one essential clinical competency: Apply a conceptual map to understand and direct the therapeutic process. This conceptual framework serves as a "map" for understanding the

13

general processes of normal growth and development, deviations from it (psychopathology), and the process of remediation and change (psychotherapy). More specifically, this conceptual map aids the clinician with the other core competencies: building and maintaining a therapeutic relationship, along with planning, implementing, and evaluating therapeutic interventions in a culturally and ethically sensitive manner.

2. Relationship Building and Maintenance

Competent therapy requires that an effective therapeutic relationship, also called a therapeutic alliance, be established and maintained. An effective therapeutic relationship is important because it fosters a bond of trust between client and therapist and a mutual agreement about the goals, roles, and method of the treatment process. Equally important is that an effective therapeutic alliance is associated with positive treatment outcomes (Orlinsky, Ronnestad, & Willutzi, 2004). This core competency consists of five essential competencies. Two of these clinical competencies are involved in relationship building: (1) establish a positive relationship or therapeutic alliance and (2) assess readiness and foster treatment-promoting behaviors. The remaining three are involved in relationship maintenance: (3) recognize and resolve resistance and ambivalence, (4) recognize and repair alliance ruptures and strains, and (5) recognize and resolve transference and countertransference. Thus, whereas engaging the client in the treatment process (relationship building) is a challenge, keeping the client engaged and reducing premature termination (maintaining the relationship) can be even more challenging.

3. Intervention Planning

Competent therapy also requires competency in intervention planning. Intervention planning is a broad core competency usually involving assessment, diagnosis, case conceptualization, and treatment planning (Spruill, Rozensky, Stigall, Vaquez, Bingham, et al., 2004). When required, a written report summarizing this information (e.g., a clinical case report or initial evaluation report) is another component of intervention planning. This core competency consists of five essential clinical competencies: (1) perform a comprehensive diagnostic assessment, (2) develop an accurate *DSM–IV–TR* diagnosis, (3) develop an effective clinical case formulation, (4) develop an effective treatment plan, and (5) draft an integrative clinical case report.

14

4. Intervention Implementation

In addition, competent therapy requires that the clinician be skilled in tailoring interventions to client needs, expectations, and circumstances while implementing the treatment plan. It also requires that the clinician establish and maintain a treatment focus while dealing with treatment-interfering factors (Sperry, 2010). Utilizing intervention modalities, strategies, and tactics and methods from differing therapeutic approaches to achieve specific treatment targets and goals also assumes a minimum level of clinician competence in implementing them. Accordingly, this core competency consists of three essential clinical competencies: (1) establish a treatment focus, (2) maintain the treatment focus, and (3) recognize and resolve treatment-interfering factors. These are general competencies; specific interventions can be specified for the cognitive, dynamic, and systemic approaches.

5. Intervention Evaluation and Termination

Furthermore, competent therapy requires the capacity for evaluating treatment and preparing the client for termination. Ongoing assessment or monitoring of treatment progress is necessary to not only evaluate effectiveness but to modify and refocus treatment. Research demonstrates that ongoing monitoring of the treatment process significantly increases clinical outcomes, especially when client feedback is formally elicited (Anker, Duncan, & Sparks, 2009). Preparation for planned termination includes a plan to prevent relapse or setbacks. Unfortunately, this core competency has been underplayed in the curricula of too many training programs. This core competency consists of two essential clinical competencies: (1) monitor progress and modify treatment accordingly and (2) evaluate progress and prepare clients for termination.

6. Culturally and Ethically Sensitive Practice

Finally, competent therapy requires the clinician's capacity to practice in a culturally and ethically sensitive manner. Until recently, clinicians have been exhorted to be culturally sensitive and culturally competent without having received much guidance in how to practice in that manner. Such practice requires the capacity to develop a cultural formulation and then plan and implement interventions consistent with that formulation (Sperry, 2010). Similarly, ethically sensitive practice requires the competence to recognize ethical issues and dilemmas and to foster

15

confidentiality and informed consent and avoid conflict of interests. This core competency consists of three essential clinical competencies: develop an effective cultural formulation, plan and implement tailored and culturally sensitive interventions, and make ethically sensitive decisions.

INTERRELATIONSHIP OF SIX CORE COMPETENCIES

The practice of competent therapy requires each of these six core competencies. They are not a random set of competencies. Instead, they are highly interrelated. This section describes this interrelationship with a metaphor and a visual depiction.

Journey Metaphor

To illustrate their interrelationship, imagine the process of psychotherapy as a journey involving at least two individuals. A journey is an intentional endeavor with the purpose of achieving some kind of meaningful personal change or outcome. As such, it differs from other travel activities such as a business trip or vacation in which meaningful personal change is not intended. Here is how aspects of the journey (core competencies) relate to the corresponding intentional behaviors involved.

1.	*Conceptual Foundation:*	View the journey as a vehicle for achieving personal change.
2.	*Relationship:*	Find a suitable traveling companion, one who is experienced and can serve as a guide (clinician).
3.	*Intervention Planning:*	Consider destination, time frames, and personal resources; then map the territory, including obstacles and opportunities that are likely to be encountered.
4.	*Intervention Implementation:*	Outfit the trip and embark on the journey.
5.	*Evaluation and Termination:*	Track progress and arrive at the destination.
6.	*Cultural and Ethical Sensitivity:*	Act with respect, integrity, and to promote well-being.

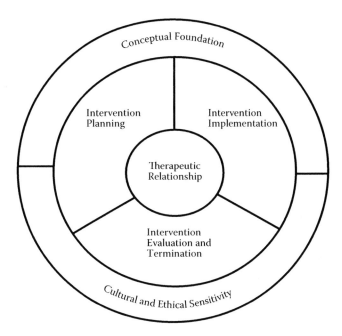

Figure 1.1 Relationship of the Core Competencies.

Visual Representation

Figure 1.1 visually depicts the interrelationship of the six core competencies. Note the centrality of relationship building and maintenance, meaning that it both influences and is influenced by the other core competencies. Surrounding it is the middle circle representing the basic intervention processes of psychotherapy: planning, implementation intervention, and intervention evaluation and termination. The outer circle includes conceptual foundation as well as culturally and ethically sensitive practice, which influence the other core competencies in the inner circles.

CONCLUDING NOTE

This chapter introduced competency and competency-based practice and training. It began with definitions of key constructs, including competence and competencies, skill, and capability. In contrast to skills and

skills training, competencies and competency training include knowledge, skill, and attitudinal components, whereas skills training has no
attitudinal component and often a limited or no knowledge component.
There is also an attitudinal component in a capability, and it energizes
a clinician to do and be his or her best. This attitudinal component of
competency and capability is further discussed in Chapter 15. There is
growing "competency movement" within the mental health disciplines
and there is considerable commonality among them regarding the core
competencies of psychotherapy. Six such core competencies have been
identified and are the main focus of this book.

Section II

Core Competency I:
Conceptual Foundations

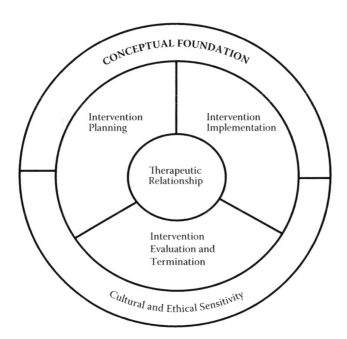

2

Conceptual Foundations

It has been said that there is one requisite clinical competency to which all other clinical competencies are anchored. That requisite competency is a theoretical framework or map "of personality, psychopathy, and therapeutic process" (Binder, 2004, p. 26). First, therapists need a theoretical understanding of the normal process of development and functioning, that is, a theory of personality. Second, therapists need a theory of how functioning goes awry and becomes maladaptive, that is, a theory of psychopathology. Third, therapists need a theory of how maladaptive processes can be changed, that is, a theory of therapeutic processes.

Possessing such a theoretical framework guides what and how a therapist observes and collects client information, how that information is conceptualized, and how the interventions based on that conceptualization are planned, implemented, and evaluated. "Therapists must have a conscious cognitive map or working model of the immediate therapeutic situation, including just enough theory to comprehend the problem context and design intervention strategies, but not so much as to get in the way of attunement to the patient and spontaneous reactions to the changing context" (Binder, 2004, p. 27).

Although therapists may consider themselves eclectic in orientation, research indicates that all therapists espouse at least one basic theoretical orientation that informs their understanding of personality, psychopathology, and the therapeutic process. This cognitive map also serves to guide their therapeutic efforts in a consistent, confident, and effective manner (Binder, 2004). This chapter provides a brief overview of three of the most commonly practiced theoretical orientations in the United States: dynamic, cognitive–behavioral, and systemic approaches. Each is described in terms of its assumptions or premises, its basic theory and methods. It also describes the "conceptual map" of each approach with regard to personality, psychopathology, and the therapeutic process.

COMPETENCY OF APPLYING A CONCEPTUAL MAP

The following essential clinical competency is associated with the core competency of conceptual foundation.

Apply a Conceptual Map to Understand and Direct the Therapeutic Process

This competency involves the capacity to utilize a theoretical understanding and conceptual map of personality, psychopathy, and the therapeutic processes to assess, conceptualize, plan, and implement a course of therapy in a consistent and effective manner.

The "Tri-Y Model"

Chapter 1 briefly described a novel integrative framework, the "Y-model," for visually representing the psychiatry requirement that trainees demonstrate competency in three psychotherapy approaches (Plakun et al., 2009). It is named for the letter Y in which the "stem" represents the core competencies common to all therapy approaches (including supportive therapy) while one "branch" represents the specialized competencies of cognitive–behavioral therapy (CBT) and the other "branch" represents specialized competencies of the dynamic therapies.

Because individuals experiencing severe and chronic mental disorders are commonly treated with medication and supportive therapy, requiring psychiatrists to be competent in supportive therapy makes good sense. However, this requirement makes less sense for nonmedical therapists who are less likely to work with this patient population and because these therapists are more likely to have involvement with couples and families, even if only in consultation. Thus, training in systemic approaches makes

22

more sense. Today, the CBT, dynamic, and systemic (particularly solution-focused therapy) approaches are commonly practiced in the United States and much of the Western world. Accordingly, these three approaches are represented in this book. This chapter focuses on the foundational elements of each, while Chapters 8 through 10 focus on selective CBT, dynamic, and systemic intervention competencies. These three approaches can be visually represented as the Tri-Y model, in which the core competencies of psychotherapy are represented in the stem, and the CBT, dynamic, and systemic approaches are represented in the three branches (Figure 2.1).

DYNAMIC APPROACHES

Dynamic refers to psychological theories that view thoughts, feelings, and behaviors as the manifestation of inner or unconscious drives and processes and their interaction. Dynamic is used in this book to represent a broad category of approaches that encompass psychoanalysis and

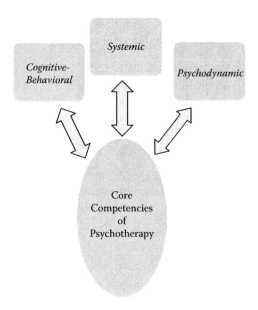

Figure 2.1 "Tri-Y Model": Relationship of Three Therapy Approaches to Core Competencies.

other psychoanalytic and psychodynamic therapies. Generally speaking, dynamic therapies endeavor to bring unconscious material and processes into full consciousness so individuals can gain more control over their lives. These therapies have their origins in psychoanalysis and stem from the work of Sigmund Freud and others who have made major contributions and reformulations to Freud's original theory. These reformulations include ego psychology, object relations theory, self psychology, and the interpersonally oriented dynamics therapies, including time-limited dynamic psychotherapy. Although there are important differences in both theory and practice among these different approaches, they share certain common principles (Blagys & Hilsenroth, 2000; Gabbard, 2004). These include the following:

1. **Unconscious.** Much of mental life involves and is influenced by unconscious processes.
2. **Resistance.** The exploration of resistance, including ambivalence to change, and defenses is a focus of therapy.
3. **Transference.** The exploration of transference, including the reenactment of the past in response to the therapist.
4. **Symptoms and behavior.** Symptoms and behavior serve multiple functions, which are determined by complex and usually unconscious forces.
5. **Exploration.** Therapy emphasizes exploration of basic assumptions about self and the world and/or maladaptive relational patterns rather than simply focusing on symptom relief.

The Evolution of Dynamic Therapy

Dynamic therapy has evolved considerably since Sigmund Freud's time. Five phases of this evolution can be identified. These phases, also called psychologies (Pine, 2003), can be summarized with the key terms *drive, ego, object, self,* and *relationship.* This section briefly describes each of these phases.

Drive: Classical Psychoanalysis
The first drive-based dynamic approach is called classical psychoanalysis and was developed by Freud (1940). In classical psychoanalysis, the analysand (client) verbalizes thoughts, free associations, fantasies, and dreams, from which the analyst (therapist) identifies the unconscious

conflicts causing the client's symptoms and characterological issues, which include unconscious aspects of the therapeutic alliance. The analyst's interventions include confrontation, clarification, interpretation, and working through the process by which a new awareness generalizes to other aspects of the client's life.

Drive: Psychoanalytic Psychotherapy
Another drive-based dynamic approach is psychoanalytic psychotherapy. It is a modified form of classical psychoanalysis that is more widely practiced than classical psychoanalysis today. It is less intense and less concerned with major changes in the client's personality structure and focuses on the client's current concerns and the way these concerns relate to early conflicts.

Ego: Ego Psychology
Ego psychology evolved out of Freud's later thinking and was the dominant form of psychoanalysis practiced until the 1970s. Freud's daughter, Anna Freud, played a significant role in its development (Freud, 1936). It focuses on the ego's normal and pathological development and its adaptation to reality. Unlike the focus on libidinal and aggressive impulses of classical psychoanalysis, ego psychology focuses directly on the ego and its defenses. Through clarifying, confronting, and interpreting the client's commonly used defense mechanisms, the goal is to assist the client in gaining control over these mechanisms.

Object: Object Relations
Since the 1970s, major reformulations of psychoanalysis have emerged. Among these was object relations theory, which emphasizes interpersonal relations especially between mother and child. Melanie Klein was a key architect of this approach (Klein, 1975). Object refers to a significant other who is the object of another's feelings or intentions. Relations refers to interpersonal relations and to the residues of past relationships that affect a person in the present. Object relations theory focuses on internal images or representations of the self and other and their manifestation in interpersonal situations. This therapy focuses on the ways the client projects previous object relationships into the relationship with the therapist. The goal is to assist clients in resolving the pathological qualities of past relationships through the corrective emotional experience. While some interpretation and confrontation may be involved, the working through of

the original pathological components of the patient's emotional world and the objects is the primary intervention strategy.

Self: Self Psychology
Another reformulation, initiated by Heinz Kohut, was self psychology, which emphasizes the development of a stable and cohesive or integrated sense of self through empathic contacts with significant others, that is, self-objects (Kohut, 1977). Self-objects meet the developing self's needs for mirroring, idealization, and twinship, and serve to strengthen the developing self. Treatment proceeds through transmuting internalizations in which the client gradually internalizes the self-object functions provided by the therapist.

Relationship: Relationally Oriented Dynamic Therapies
There are also some reformulations based on relational themes. Interpersonal psychoanalysis emphasizes the nuances of interpersonal interactions, especially the way in which individuals protect themselves from anxiety by establishing collusive interactions with others. Relational psychoanalysis combines interpersonal psychoanalysis, object relations theory, and intersubjective theory. Relational psychoanalysis emphasizes how the individual's personality is shaped by both real and imagined relationships with others and how these relationship patterns are reenacted in the interactions between therapist and client.

Time-limited dynamic psychotherapy (TLDP) is a brief, relationally oriented dynamic therapy that was originally developed for clients with chronic, pervasive, dysfunctional ways of relating to others (Strupp & Binder, 1984). TLDP is influenced by attachment, object relations, interpersonal, experiential, cognitive–behavioral, and system approaches (Levenson, 1995). It focuses primarily on changing cyclic maladaptive relational patterns rather than on symptom reduction per se. The therapist identifies the client's cyclical maladaptive pattern, which consists of inflexible, self-defeating expectations and behaviors and negative self-appraisals that lead to maladaptive interactions (Binder, 2004). TLDP has two therapeutic goals: new experiences and new understandings. In the course of treatment, the therapist provides clients the opportunity to disconfirm their interpersonal schemas, promoting a corrective emotional–interpersonal experience.

The focus of treatment is derived from the client's cyclical maladaptive pattern, which becomes a blueprint for the treatment in that it provides a problem description and goals, a guide for interventions, and a means of anticipating transference reenactments and understanding counter-transferential reactions (Binder, 2004). Treatment is based on a therapeutic strategy, and intervention based on various theoretical orientations is utilized to facilitate the treatment goals.

Basically, this approach assumes that over the course of their lives, clients have unintentionally developed self-perpetuating, maladaptive patterns of relating to others and that these patterns underlie their present problems. The therapist's role is to use the therapeutic alliance to facilitate in clients a new experience of relating, which allows them to break their maladaptive pattern and thereby resolve their presenting problem (Levenson, 1995).

Dynamic Perspective on Personality, Psychopathology, and Psychotherapeutic Process

Personality
From an object relations perspective, personality is viewed in terms of interactional structures, that is, self-object representations, resulting from the internalization of particular interpersonal experiences. Early factors such as temperament influence interactional styles, just as later internalizations can modify these internal structures. These internalizations approximate what actually occurs when interpersonal stress is minimal, but when such stress is significant (i.e., when a person experiences trauma), perceptual and cognitive functions are impaired and distortions of interpersonal occurrences are internalized and can have a significant effect on personality development. Unlike classical psychoanalysis, which holds that personality is crystalized by the end of the Oedipal phase of development, TLDP considers personality to be dynamically changing as it interacts with others (Levenson, 1995; Strupp & Binder, 1984).

Psychopathology
Disturbances in adult interpersonal relatedness typically stem from faulty relationship patterns with early caregivers. These early experiences result in dysfunctional mental representations—also called mental models or schemas—which are maintained in the present (Binder, 2004). These mental models engender maladaptive pattern interpersonal interactions or relationship styles that are reflected in symptoms and occupational and interpersonal distress and dissatisfaction.

27

Psychotherapeutic Process

The client's maladaptive interpersonal patterns are reenacted in therapy, and the therapist will be influenced by the client's enactment and will reciprocate. Thus, treatment is focused on modifying both the mental model and the maladaptive interpersonal pattern. This central focus on interactions distinguishes this from other psychoanalytic approaches that emphasize personality reconstruction (Levenson, 1995).

COGNITIVE–BEHAVIORAL THERAPIES

Cognitive–behavioral therapy (CBT) is a category of psychotherapeutic approaches that emphasize the role of cognitions in feelings and behavior. There are several approaches to CBT, including behavior therapy, cognitive therapy, schema therapy, dialectic behavior therapy, cognitive–behavioral analysis system of psychotherapy (CBASP), and mindfulness-based cognitive therapy.

Common Characteristics

Although there are differences among these approaches, they all share a number of common characteristics. Based on an empirical review of the literature, the following factors were found to characterize the commonalities shared by all CBT approaches (Blagys & Hilsenroth, 2002).

1. **Focus on cognitive and behavioral factors.** A basic premise of CBT is that clients' emotions and behavior are influenced by their beliefs or thoughts. Because most emotional and behavioral reactions are learned, the goal of therapy is to help clients unlearn unwanted responses and to learn a new way of responding. By evaluating, challenging, and modifying maladaptive beliefs and behaviors, clients are able to gain control over problems previously believed to be insurmountable.

2. **Direct session activity.** CBT is a directive approach in which therapists typically direct session activity by setting an agenda, deciding and planning in advance what will be discussed during the session, and actively directing discussion of specific topics and tasks. Cognitive–behavioral therapists also endeavor to stimulate and engage clients in the treatment process and these decisions.

3. **Teach skills.** Because CBT is also a psychoeducational approach, cognitive–behavioral therapists teach clients skills to help them cope more effectively with problematic situations. Dealing directly with skill deficits and excesses is central to clients achieving and maintaining treatment gains.
4. **Provide information.** Cognitive–behavioral therapists also discuss the explicit rationale for their treatment and the specific techniques being used. They may provide clients with detailed information (e.g., books or handouts) to orient clients to the treatment process, to increase their confidence in treatment, and to enhance their ability to cope with problematic situations.
5. **Use homework and between-session activities.** Homework and between-session activities are a central feature of CBT. Such activities provide clients the opportunity to practice skills learned in sessions and transfer gains made in treatment to their everyday lives. Such activities can also foster and maintain symptom reduction.
6. **Emphasize present and future experiences**. CBT focuses on the impact clients' present maladaptive thoughts have on their current and future functioning. In addition, skills learned in therapy are designed to promote more effective future functioning.

The Evolution of CBT

The term *cognitive–behavioral therapy* came into usage about 30 years ago. It evolved from both cognitive and behavioral traditions in psychotherapy. A useful way of understanding this evolution is in terms of what has been called the "three waves" of CBT (Hayes, Follette, & Linehan, 2004).

First Wave
The first wave emphasized traditional behavior therapy, which focused on replacing problematic behaviors with constructive ones through classical conditioning and reinforcement techniques. Joseph Wolpe pioneered classical conditioning, particularly systematic desensitization (Wolpe, 1990). Traditional behavior therapy was a technical, problem-focused, present-centered approach that was markedly different than psychoanalysis, client-centered therapy, and similar approaches of that era that emphasized the therapeutic relationship and the feelings and inner world of the client.

Second Wave
The second wave involved the incorporation of the cognitive therapies, which focused on modifying problematic feelings and behaviors by changing the thoughts that cause and perpetuate them (A. T. Beck, Rush, Shaw, & Emery, 1979; Ellis, 1962; Meichenbaum, 1977). The incorporation of cognitive and behavioral therapies in the 1970s was not initially a cordial or conflict-free union, but today most cognitive therapists incorporate key behavioral interventions and most behavior therapists recognize the role of clients' beliefs about the consequences of their behaviors (Gilbert & Leahy, 2007). The fact that both were problem-focused and scientifically based therapies has helped foster this union, resulting in CBT becoming the most commonly practiced treatment method in the United States since the late 1980s.

Third Wave
The third wave involves the reformulation of conventional CBT approaches, which were based on a modernist paradigm or perspective. In contrast, third wave approaches tend to be more influenced by the postmodern perspective. Accordingly, treatment tends to be more experiential and indirect and utilizes techniques such as mindfulness, dialectics, acceptance, values, and spirituality (Hayes et al., 2004). More specifically, third wave approaches are characterized by "letting go of the attempts at problem solving, and instead standing back to see what it feels like to see the problems through the lens of non-reactivity, and to bring a kindly awareness to the difficulty" (Segal, Williams, Teasdale, & Williams, 2004, p. 55). Unlike the first and second wave approaches, third wave approaches emphasize second-order change (i.e., basic change in structure and/or function) and are based on contextual assumptions, including the primacy of the therapeutic relationship.

Behavior Therapy

Behavior therapy is a treatment approach based on the assumption that behavioral (including emotional) problems are learned responses to the environment and can be unlearned (Wolpe, 1990). Traditional behavior therapy focuses only on observable behavior, and so mental processes are ignored. Thus, instead of uncovering and understanding the unconscious processes that underlie maladaptive behavior, behavioral therapists assist clients in directly modifying the maladaptive behavior or developing a new, adaptive behavior. Basic to behavior therapy is the ABC model of behavioral analysis, which describes the temporal sequence of a problematic behavior in terms of its *antecedents* (stimulus situation that cues or triggers behavior), *behaviors* (the problematic behavior itself), and *consequences* (reinforcement contingencies that follow the behavior; Goldfried & Davison, 1994). Three types of behavior problems can be identified from this analysis: behavior excesses, deficits, or inappropriateness. Core concepts of behavior therapy include respondent and operant conditioning and positive and negative reinforcement.

Various strategies are utilized in promoting the desired (new or modified) behavior. Contingency management involves efforts to shape the consequences of a behavior so that a desired behavior is reinforced and the undesired ones are extinguished, while shaping is the process of reinforcing the client's successive approximation of the desired behavior. Rehearsal involves practicing the desired behavior. In addition, therapeutic interventions, such as skill training, exposure, response prevention, emotional processing, flooding, systematic desensitization, and homework, are used to achieve specific therapeutic outcomes (Goldfried & Davison, 1994).

Cognitive Therapies

Cognitive therapies arose as a response to the supposed shortcomings of psychoanalysis. The cognitive therapies view emotional difficulties as associated with clients' irrational beliefs— as in rational emotive behavior therapy (Ellis, 1962; Ellis & Harper, 1997)—or maladaptive automatic thoughts and beliefs, as in cognitive therapy (A. T. Beck et al., 1979; J. Beck, 1995). Four major categories of irrational beliefs described in rational emotive behavior therapy are demanding, catastrophizing, overgeneralizing, and copping out (Ellis, 1962). Instead of listing specific maladaptive beliefs, A. T. Beck emphasized that individuals operate from core schemas, which are a network of core beliefs about self, other people, and the world that are learned early in life. He described automatic thoughts as instantaneous, habitual thoughts that affect an individual's moods and behavior.

Cognitive therapists foster change in clients by assisting them to be more aware of their maladaptive thoughts and beliefs and their problematic impact, and to replace these problematic thoughts with more adaptive ones. A variety of interventions are utilized in the cognitive therapies, particularly cognitive restructuring, which is a broad method including disputation, guided discovery, Socratic questioning, examining the evidence, reattribution, and cognitive rehearsal (Wright, Basco, & Thase, 2006).

Schema Therapy

Schema therapy is a derivation of cognitive therapy that was developed primarily for personality-disordered clients who failed to respond adequately to cognitive therapy (Young, 1999). Schema therapy is a broad, integrative model that has commonalities with object relations therapy, experiential therapy, dialectic behavior therapy, and interpersonal therapy, as well as cognitive therapy and other forms of CBT. Despite these similarities, schema therapy differs from these approaches with regard to the nature of the therapy relationship, the general style and stance of the therapist, and the degree of therapist activity and directiveness (Young, Klosko, & Weishaar, 2003). Basic to schema therapy are early maladaptive schemas that emerge from aversive childhood experiences such as abuse, neglect, and trauma in early life and lead to maladaptive or unhealthy life patterns.

The basic goals of schema therapy are the following: identify early maladaptive schemas, validate the client's unmet emotional needs, change maladaptive schemas to more functional ones, promote more functional life patterns and coping styles, and provide an environment for learning adaptive skills. Schema therapy requires considerable training and experience to practice it appropriately and effectively.

Dialectic Behavior Therapy

Dialectic behavior therapy (DBT) was developed for the treatment of borderline personality disorder (Linehan, 1993) but has recently been modified and extended for use with other personality disorders as well as Axis I or symptom disorders such as mood disorders, anxiety disorders, eating disorders, and substance use disorders (Marra, 2005). DBT is an outgrowth of behavior therapy but is less cognitive than traditional CBT, as DBT assumes that cognitions are less important than affect regulation.

Four primary modes of treatment are noted in DBT: individual therapy, skills training in a group, telephone contact, and therapist consultation. Following an initial period of pretreatment, involving assessment, commitment, and orientation to therapy, DBT focuses on specific targets for stages, which are arranged in a definite hierarchy of relative importance. These include decreasing suicidal behaviors, decreasing therapy-interfering behaviors, decreasing behaviors that interfere with the quality of life, increasing behavioral skills, decreasing behaviors related to post-traumatic stress, improving self-esteem, and individual targets negotiated with the client. The core strategies in DBT are validation and problem solving. Attempts to facilitate change are surrounded by interventions that validate the client's behavior and responses in relation to the client's current life situation and demonstrate an understanding of their difficulties and suffering. Problem solving focuses on the establishment of necessary skills. Other treatment modalities include contingency management, cognitive therapy, exposure-based therapies, and medication.

Cognitive–Behavioral Analysis System of Psychotherapy

Cognitive–behavioral analysis system of psychotherapy (CBASP) is a form of CBT that was developed by McCullough (2000). Basic to this approach is a situational analysis that combines behavioral, cognitive, and interpersonal methods to help clients focus on the consequences of their behavior and to use problem solving to resolve both personal and interpersonal difficulties. CBASP was initially targeted for the treatment of clients with chronic depression. The basic premise of CBASP is that clients can be helped to discover why they did not obtain a desired outcome by evaluating their problematic thoughts and behaviors.

The overall goal of CBASP treatment is to identify the discrepancy between what clients want to happen in a particular situation and what has happened or is actually happening. There are two phases in CBASP treatment: elicitation and remediation. The elicitation phase consists of a detailed situational analysis. During the remediation phase, behaviors and interpretations or cognitions are targeted for change and revised so that the client's new behaviors and cognitions will contribute and result in their desired outcome. Each of the client's interpretations of the situation is assessed to determine whether it helped or hindered the achievement of the desired outcome. Next, each of the client's behaviors is similarly analyzed to determine whether or not it helped or hindered in the attainment of the desired outcome.

33

Mindfulness-Based Cognitive Therapy

Mindfulness can be defined as paying attention in a particular way, that is intentional, in the present moment, and nonjudgmental (Kabat-Zinn, 1994). This awareness is based on an attitude of acceptance of personal experience that involves a commitment to living fully in the present moment. Mindfulness-based cognitive therapy is an adjunctive or stand-alone form of treatment that emphasizes changing the awareness of, and relation to, thoughts rather than changing thought content. It offers clients a different way of living with and experiencing emotional pain and distress. The assumption is that cultivating a detached attitude toward negative thinking provides one with the skills to prevent escalation of negative thinking at times of potential relapse. Clients engage in various formal meditation practices designed to increase moment-by-moment nonjudgmental awareness of physical sensations, thoughts, and feelings. Assigned homework includes practicing these exercises along with exercises designed to integrate application of awareness skills into daily life. Specific prevention strategies derived from traditional cognitive therapy methods are incorporated in the later weeks of the program.

Cognitive–Behavioral Perspective on Personality, Psychopathology, and Psychotherapeutic Process

Personality
Personality is shaped by innate dispositions—particularly cognitive schemas and temperament—interacting with environment. These schemas develop early in life from personal experiences and identification with significant others and are reinforced by further learning experiences which then influence the formation of specific beliefs, values, and attitudes. In short, the constraints of one's neurobiology and personal learning determine how one develops and responds.

Psychopathology
There are multiple causes of psychological distress, including neurobiological vulnerability, learning history, and schemas. Psychological distress is experienced when situations are perceived as threatening, and a set of cognitive, emotional, motivational, and behavioral schemas are

34

activated and may be expressed as symptoms and functional impairment. Specifically, such distress leads to interpretations that are selective, egocentric, and rigid, and results in impaired cognitive processes, including distorted thinking, poor concentration, and faulty recall. Maladaptive or negative behaviors (deficits or excesses) further reinforce maladaptive cognitions.

Psychotherapeutic Process
CBT is a problem-focused, here-and-now approach that endeavors to modify maladaptive cognitions and behaviors using a variety of cognitive and behavioral methods to change thinking, mood, and behavior. Because behavior is learned, negative behavior can be unlearned while new behaviors can be learned. The mark of successful treatment is healthier ways of thinking and behaving.

SYSTEMIC APPROACHES

Many of the preceding individual therapeutic approaches have been adapted for use with couples and families. Nevertheless, the need for specialized approaches that address the unique dynamics of couple and family resulted in the development of family systems or systemic approaches. This section will introduce the concept of systems and then briefly describe three systemic approaches: structural, strategic, and solution-focused.

Systems Concepts

Couples and families are more than a collection of individual spouses or individual family members. They are members of a couple system or family system. Such relational systems are characterized by emotional interconnectedness, structures (repetitive pattern of family interactions or transactions that determine how members relate to each other and are regulated by power hierarchies, control, and expectations), boundaries (emotional and structural barriers that protect and enhance member well-being), subsystems (smaller systemic groups within the larger system such as spousal, parent, and sibling subsystems), homeostatic mechanisms (factors that maintain equilibrium in the system), alliances (explicit and positive bonds between members), coalitions (an alliance of two members against a third), and family rules that reflect interaction patterns that maintain homeostasis (Gehart, 2010).

Structural Therapy

A systemic approach is based on the assumption that family structures arise in order to maintain problems in a family system and that dysfunctional families lack sufficient organization to cope with external and internal problems. According to Salvador Minuchin, a key figure in this approach, the therapist role is to attend to a family's structures or repetitive communication and transaction patterns and effect positive change by endeavoring to shift these patterns (Minuchin & Fishman, 1981). Three phases of treatment are noted. The first is to join the family and accommodate to their style. The second is to map the family structures, boundaries, alliances, and hierarchies, and the third is to intervene to transform these structures to diminish symptoms (Minuchin & Nichols, 1993).

Typically, therapists alternate between the second and third phases several times, revising and refining the map and hypotheses about family functioning until problems are sufficiently addressed and resolved. Interventions include systemic reframing, enactments, boundary making, challenging the family's worldview, intensity and crisis inductions, unbalancing, and expanding family truths and realities.

Strategic Therapy

A systemic approach is based on the premise that families are rule-governed systems and that the presenting problem serves a necessary function for the family. There are three schools or models identified with this approach: Mental Research Institute, Milan model, and the Washington School of Jay Haley. This discussion emphasizes Haley's approach. (Haley, 1984; Haley & Richeport-Haley, 2007). Symptoms are considered to be system-maintaining, and destructive ongoing cycles of interaction can prevent the couple or family from achieving its basic purposes. The therapist's role is to plan interventions in which directives and other strategies are utilized in an effort to realign the family system in order to resolve the presenting problem. Basic interventions strategies include directives, paradoxical directive, reframing, prescribing the symptom, pretend techniques, restraining changes, ordeals, metaphor for tasks, and the devil's pact (Haley, 1984).

Solution-Focused Approaches

Among the various systemic approaches, solution-focused therapy (SFT) is one of the most commonly used approaches throughout the world, particularly in the United States. Unlike most of the other approaches identified in this chapter, SFT is based on a postmodern perspective of the therapeutic process (de Shazer, 1985), as it is closely related to a version called solution-oriented therapy (O'Hanlon & Weiner-Davis, 1989). It is based on two premises: Change is constant and inevitable, and therapy should focus on what is possible and changeable rather than what is impossible. In recognition of this premise, one of the codevelopers of solution-oriented therapy, O'Hanlon (O'Hanlon & Beadle, 1999), has recently changed the name to possibility therapy.

SFT views the solutions clients are using as their real problem rather than the presenting problem itself. Thus, SFT focuses on solutions and strengths rather than on problems. In this approach, meanings are negotiable, and thus the goal of therapy is to choose meanings that will lead to change. SFT focuses on clarifying clients' goals, identifying exceptions that can make a difference to the client's problems, and then enhancing solutions. Interventions include deconstructing, doing something different, overcoming the urge, focusing on past successes, scaling, and addressing the miracle question (de Shazer, 1985, 1988).

Systemic Perspective on Personality, Psychopathology, and Psychotherapeutic Process

Personality
This approach does not posit a theory of personality development or how individuals come to be the way they are. However, it does posit that individuals are unique and so are their problems and symptoms. In line with the approach's social constructivist philosophy, clients are understood to be experts on their own lives, and they have the strengths and resources necessary to resolve any difficulties.

Psychopathology
This approach does not recognize pathology and refuses to pathologize individuals or assign diagnoses. Rather, problems are understood to arise when clients continue to apply solutions that do not work rather than solutions that do work.

Psychotherapeutic Process

This is a brief form of therapy that lasts only as long as necessary to get the client on track toward his or her goals. Goals do not need to be achieved for treatment to be finished; rather, the treatment is finished when the client is satisfied with changing direction and understanding what is needed to change, even without therapy. This approach holds that change constantly happens, that small changes lead to big changes, and that solutions may not seem related to problems.

Table 2.1 summarizes the conceptual maps of the three approaches.

CONCLUDING NOTE

This chapter began with the therapist's need for a theoretical understanding and the capacity to utilize such a cognitive map in guiding the therapeutic process. This cognitive map also serves to guide the therapist's efforts in a consistent, confident, and effective manner. This competency is a requisite to all of the other core competencies and essential clinical competencies described in this book.

Case of Geri

Throughout subsequent chapters, readers will follow an ongoing case example that illustrates the various core competencies and essential clinical competencies. Some brief background information on the client, her presenting problem, and the reason for referral are presented here.[*]

Geri R. is a 35-year-old female administrative assistant of African American descent. She is single, lives alone, and was referred by her company's human resources director for evaluation and treatment following a 3-week onset of depressed mood. Other symptoms included loss of energy, markedly diminished interest, insomnia, difficulty concentrating, and increasing social isolation. She had not shown up for work for 4 days; her absence prompted the referral. The planned addition of another senior executive led Geri's supervisor to discuss a promotion wherein Geri would be transferred out of a relatively close-knit work team where she had been for 16 years, and had been an administrative assistant for 6 years, to become the new senior administrative assistant for the newly hired vice president of sales.

---

[*] Discussions paraphrased from diagnostic interview presented in Sperry's *Highly Effective Therapy* (New York: Routledge).

Table 2.1 Core Concepts of the Common Psychotherapy Approaches

Approach	Personality Development	Psychopathology	Psychotherapy
CBT	Personality is shaped by innate dispositions—particularly cognitive schemas & temperament interacting with environment	Result of maladaptive cognitions, schemas, and/or behavior patterns, including deficits or excesses	Recognize and modify maladaptive cognitions, schemas, and/or behavior patterns to be more functional
Dynamic	Self-object representations result from internalization of interpersonal experiences (object relations); personality is crystalized after Oedipal phase (psychoanalysis) but viewed as dynamically changing as it interacts with others (TLDP)	Result of defensive reactions to anxiety, maladaptive schemas, or object representations related to childhood experiences or cyclic maladaptive relationship patterns	Insight, corrective emotional experiences, resolution of conflict areas and defense mechanisms used, reworking personality structures related to childhood conflicts or self-objects/schemas
Systemic	Clients are understood to be experts on their own lives and have the strengths and resources necessary to resolve their difficulties (SFT)	Result of dysfunction patterns of family boundaries, power, intimacy, schemas, rules, skill deficits, narratives, or solutions	Reestablish more functional boundaries, schemas, narratives, rules, or power and skills in problem-solving strategies/solutions

Section III

Core Competency 2: Therapeutic Relationship

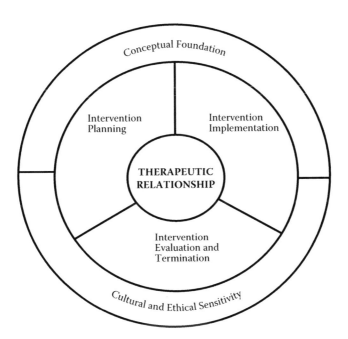

Conceptual Foundation

Intervention Planning

Intervention Implementation

THERAPEUTIC RELATIONSHIP

Intervention Evaluation and Termination

Cultural and Ethical Sensitivity

3

Relationship Building

Effective therapy typically begins with the establishment of an effective therapeutic relationship, also called a therapeutic alliance. The therapeutic alliance can have a profound effect on the treatment process and outcomes. Research consistently demonstrates that the therapeutic relationship is the best predictor of therapeutic outcome (Horvath & Symonds, 1991; Orlinsky, Grawe, & Parks, 1994; Orlinsky, Ronnestad, & Willutzi, 2004). In a meta-analysis, Horvath and Symonds (1991) found that treatment outcomes were clearly a function of the therapeutic alliance rather than of the length or type of treatment. They also found that collaboration and negotiation of mutually agreeable goals and plans were essential to treatment success. Yet, trainees and beginning therapists are often unaware of the importance of the therapeutic alliance. Often, this is because their training did not emphasize the clinical value and utility of effective therapeutic alliances. Instead, some graduate programs focus heavily on counseling microskills, whereas other programs emphasize empirically supported treatments. Even though microskills and empirically supported treatments have some impact on treatment outcomes, without an effective therapeutic alliance, the best treatment interventions are unlikely to succeed. Accordingly, this core competency is one of the first and most important competencies for therapists to develop. Its centrality among the other core competencies is highlighted throughout this book.

This chapter discusses several aspects of therapeutic alliance, including its development, an integrative view of the alliance, and therapist attributes and skills in developing therapeutic alliances. Next, it describes the challenge of developing a therapeutic alliance with difficult clients. It then shifts to treatment-promoting factors, beginning with readiness for change. The stages of the readiness for change model are briefly described as well as some markers for assessing readiness. Next, it describes common factors, that is, nonspecific curative factors that are common to all forms of psychotherapy. Treatment-promoting factors and strategies are also described.

Finally, a case example illustrating key points of this discussion is provided.

COMPETENCIES OF ESTABLISHING AN EFFECTIVE THERAPEUTIC ALLIANCE

This chapter addresses two essential clinical competencies of establishing or building an effective therapeutic relationship, which is associated with the core competency of intervention planning.

Establish an Effective Therapeutic Alliance

This competency involves the capacity to form an effective therapeutic alliance that is sensitive to the client's needs, expectations, and explanatory model; that engenders trust and hope in the therapist and therapy process; and that engages the client in the treatment process.

Assess Readiness and Foster Treatment-Promoting Factors

This competency involves the capacity to accurately identify the client's motivation and readiness for change as well as to effectively foster treatment factors that will promote and facilitate the treatment process.

ESTABLISHING AN EFFECTIVE THERAPEUTIC RELATIONSHIP

The therapeutic alliance begins with first contact between client and therapist and continues until the last contact. Although initial interactions are especially important, as first impressions usually are, the development of the therapeutic alliance is intertwined with all aspects of the treatment process and evolves and changes over time. An effective therapeutic alliance may develop as quickly as the first session but must be in place by the fifth session if treatment is to be successful (Orlinsky et al., 2004). Needless to say, every client–therapist contact, either positive or negative, influences the development and maintenance of the therapist alliance.

THERAPEUTIC APPROACHES

Cognitive–Behavioral Approaches

Increasingly, cognitive–behavioral therapy (CBT), particularly cognitive therapy, considers that "a sound therapeutic alliance" (J. Beck, 1995) is a basic principle and essential for effective treatment outcomes. It is considered a collaborative endeavor with specific expectations for client and therapist. The client is expected to report their thoughts, feelings, and behaviors that occur in various situations. The therapist is expected to set the agenda, develop a plan for treatment, implement it, and maintain a treatment focus (Ledley, Marx, & Heimberg, 2005). The therapist's role is to educate the client about the link between thoughts and feelings and serve as a guide in the change process (Gilbert & Leahy, 2005). Clients are also expected to share responsibility for setting the agenda for the session, provide feedback to the therapist, and complete between-session homework (Ledley et al., 2005). Unlike the dynamic therapies, the therapeutic relationship in CBT was viewed, early on, primarily as a secondary mechanism that facilitated change rather than as the primary mechanism of change. This necessary but secondary role of the therapeutic relationship remained the prevailing perspective for some time. "Specific problems in forming, maintaining, understanding and dealing with ruptures in the therapeutic relationship were rarely addressed ... at least until the advent of cognitive therapies' exploration of personality disorders" (Gilbert & Leahy, 2005, p. 5).

Recently, challenges, such as working with personality-disordered individuals, have prompted CBT to expand its perspective on the therapeutic alliance to a point where it is now closer to the dynamic approaches, particularly to the interpersonally oriented dynamic therapies. Three stages of the therapeutic relationship are now identified in CBT: establishing a relationship, developing the relationship, and then maintaining it (Hardy, Cahill, & Barkham, 2007). In the first stage, building positive

45

expectations of therapy—both with regard to outcome as well as to what is expected of both client and therapist—is necessary as is developing clients' intentions and motivations for change. Hardy, Cahill, and Barkham (2007) cite research indicating that higher expectations predict positive outcomes of CBT. Once clients have hope that therapy will help and they are motivated to change, the therapist turns to the second stage, developing the relationship, which involves promoting client openness to the process, trust in the therapist, and commitment to working with the therapist. In the third stage, maintaining the relationship, the goal is "continued satisfaction with the relationship; a productive and positive working alliance; increased ability for clients to express their emotions and to experience a changing view of self with others" (Hardy et al., 2007, p. 31). It also includes dealing with threats to the therapeutic alliance, such as negative feelings of the therapist (e.g., countertransference and client resistance and hostility), or relationship challenges such as ruptures and misunderstandings. In short, a shift is occurring in CBT. Before a collaborative therapeutic relationship was established to facilitate the change, it was considered a secondary mechanism, whereas now the relationship is increasingly viewed as a primary mechanism as is changing maladaptive beliefs and behaviors.

Dynamic Approaches

Clients seek help from a professional therapist who is viewed as an expert or as a participant-observer who is expected to be trustworthy. In relationally oriented approaches such as time-limited dynamic psychotherapy, the client is "expected to come to each session prepared to talk candidly about any topic that ... is relevant to the agreed-upon problems focus. ... The therapist's role is to offer his or her attention and expertise for the purpose of facilitating a therapeutically productive dialogue. This goal is accomplished through a variety of interventions, including observations, questions, and interpretations" (Binder, 2004, p. 40). In order for client and therapist to collaborate effectively, a therapeutic alliance is established and maintained.

> The therapeutic alliance involves an explicit agreement between therapist and patient to collaborate on working toward the resolution of the patient's problems. This collaboration is based on an agreement, sometimes achieved through negotiation, about the goals of therapy and the

tasks required of each party to reach these goals. At least equally important, the alliance is based on an emotional bond of liking and trust. … [and] derives primarily from the real relationship between patient and therapist although it may be augmented by positive transference and countertransference. (Binder, 2004, p. 40)

Therapists anticipate and work to resolve resistance such as transference–countertransference enactments and ruptures in the therapeutic alliance. Ideally, an effective therapeutic alliance is continually maintained. The reality is that strains or ruptures of the alliance may occur in briefer forms of dynamic therapy. Such ruptures are manifestations of "prepotent maladaptive patterns of interaction, i.e., transference and countertransference responses" (Binder, 2004, p. 40).

This perspective on the therapeutic relationship reflects a paradigm shift that is occurring within dynamic thinking and practice. The shift is away from a focus on drive reduction as the basis for personality development and functioning and toward a focus on the process of forming interpersonal relationships. In fact, many dynamic approaches "are becoming less drive-oriented and more relational for various cultural, social, clinical and scientific reasons" (Levenson, 1995, p. 31). This shift is reflected in the roles and expectations of therapists and clients. In the traditional perspective, the therapist was viewed as an expert and an objective translator and interpreter who attempted to maintain neutrality, whereas in the interpersonal view, the therapist is viewed as a participant-observer or even as a total participant and for which neutrality is an impossible position. In the traditional perspective, the client was viewed as a reactive recipient of the therapeutic process, whereas in the interpersonal view, the client is viewed as an active construer of his or her own interpersonal world (Levenson, 1995).

Accordingly, therapeutic relationship is generally viewed to be a safe environment (also called a holding environment) in which to explore the client's inner and interpersonal world, to clarify repetitive or cyclic maladaptive patterns, and to deal with transference's expression of these patterns. Because it is assumed that the therapist will become hooked in to reenacting maladaptive relational patterns with the client, the therapy process focuses largely on these transference enactments, and their resolution can result in a corrective emotional experience. In short, the therapeutic alliance in dynamic approaches is the principal mechanism for change.

Systemic Approaches

For the most part, the systemic approaches have de-emphasized or ignored the role of therapeutic relationship factors in the therapy process. Instead, the systemic approaches have primarily emphasized problem solving and resolution. In fact, one of the ways in which the systemic therapies, as a whole, distinguished themselves from individual therapy approaches was to focus on effecting change quickly—change that was largely therapist-centered. This required therapists, particularly those practicing structural family therapy and strategic therapy, to assume the role of expert and direc-tor. "Historically, as problem resolution received more attention, some sys-temic therapists have in fact paid insufficient attention to the therapeutic alliance" (Quick, 2008, p. 85). Nevertheless, Quick adds that although the therapeutic alliance is not directly addressed in some descriptions of the systemic approaches, "a focus on joining with the client has always been present" (p. 85). As pointed out in Chapter 1, the Association of Marriage and Family Therapy (AAMFT) has specified six core competencies or domains, but the therapeutic alliance is not one of them. However, it is one of the 20 listed competencies subsumed under the first core competency or domain: admission to treatment (AAMFT, 2004).

One systemic that focus directly on the therapeutic alliance is emo-tionally focused therapy (Johnson, 2004). In emotionally focused therapy, which is largely a couples therapy approach, empathic attunement is cen-tral to developing the relationship. With it, the therapist attunes to each partner's emotions in order to connect or join with their emotional worlds. The therapist also continually monitors the alliance with each partner in order to maintain a strong affect bond and sense of safety for both part-ners (Johnson, 2004).

A set of approaches that are relatively sensitive to the therapeutic relationship are the solution-focused therapies. Like other postmodern systemic approaches that emphasize client strengths and optimism, the therapeutic relationship is important in the solution-focused therapies. Not surprisingly, the use of reflection and reflection of feelings in devel-oping the therapeutic relationship are advocated (O'Hanlon & Beadle, 1999). This intervention is similar but different from the client-centered reflection process in that it delimits the problematic feeling, thought, or behavior by reflecting a time, context, or relational limit. The purpose of this is to define the problem in more solvable terms and to create hope and optimism. For example, if a client describes how her husband got angry at her "for no reason," a client-centered reflection might be "You did not feel understood by him," whereas a solution-focused reflection might be "You did not feel understood by your husband yesterday."

In the solution-focused approaches, the therapist functions as a participant-observer. Clients are understood to be experts on their lives while therapists support and encourage clients' movement to finding and implementing solutions. Unlike other approaches that view resistance negatively, solution-focused therapy views it as the client's unique way of cooperating with the therapist—that is, providing information that can help them work toward their goals (de Shazer, 1985). This view of resistance, which can involve the therapeutic relationship, is discussed further in Chapter 4.

In short, in their focus on problem resolution, the systemic approaches have largely de-emphasized the role of therapeutic relationship factors in the therapy process. Depending on the particular systemic approach, the therapist serves as a family consultant, director, or participant-observer and joins with and/or challenges the family structures, boundaries, rules, and relations.

Table 3.1 provides a capsule summary of these three perspectives on the therapeutic relationship.

AN INTEGRATIVE VIEW OF THE THERAPEUTIC ALLIANCE

The preceding section reviewed the perspectives of three common therapeutic approaches to the therapeutic relationship. It is noteworthy that these three perspectives have evolved over time. An integrative view of the therapeutic alliance emerged which operationalizes the therapeutic alliance in terms of three factors: bond, goals, and tasks (Bordin, 1979). Another way of saying this is that an effective therapeutic alliance involves a "meeting of hearts" (bond) and a "meeting of minds" (goals and tasks) between clinician and client.

Important to the formation of a strong therapeutic bond is that clients feel understood, safe, and hopeful. It also means that they are more likely to take the risk of disclosing painful affects and intimate details of their lives, as well as risk thinking, feeling, and acting in more adaptive and healthier ways. Besides the therapeutic bond, clinicians need to attend to mutually agreed upon therapeutic goals and tasks or methods. This entails recognition of the client's explanatory model and expectations for treatment goals and methods and the way treatment will be provided (Sperry, 2010; Sperry,

Table 3.1 Therapeutic Relationship Considerations Among Therapeutic Approaches

Approach	Relationship Considerations
CBT	Historically, the primary purpose of the therapeutic relationship was to develop a collaboration with the client to facilitate the primary goal of therapy: identifying and changing maladaptive beliefs and behaviors. The therapist's role was to educate clients about the link between thoughts, feelings, and behaviors, help identify maladaptive patterns of beliefs and behaviors and change them, and serve as a guide to change. Now, there is a broadened view of the therapeutic alliance in which it is at least an equal factor in the process of change.
Dynamic	The therapeutic relationship is considered the principal mechanism for change, meaning that as therapist and client work to resolve transference enactments that arise from early maladaptive relational patterns, the client experiences change. A historical shift occurred in the therapist role from that of expert and objective, neutral interpreter to that of participant-observer in TLDP and other brief dynamic approaches. Similarly, the client role has shifted from reactive recipient to active construer and participant in the process.
Systemic	Many systemic approaches underplay the role of the therapeutic alliance. Depending on the particular systemic approach, the therapist serves as a family consultant, director, or participant observer and joins with and/or challenges the family structures, boundaries, rules, and relations. By contrast, the solution-focused approaches are more likely to directly foster the therapeutic alliance.

Carlson, & Kjos, 2003). Such expectations are influenced by cultural factors and norms. Among some cultures, it is customary for family members to accompany the designated client to appointments. Because there may be the unspoken expectation that family members be included in the treatment process, effective clinicians will inquire about such expectations. Similarly, there may be "silent expectations" about the type of intervention utilized. Sometimes, the silent expectation is that healing requires some measure of touch or contact. Some clients prefer action-oriented approaches over strictly talk-oriented approaches. In short, an effective therapeutic alliance involves a "meeting of hearts" and a "meeting of minds" between clinician and client. The basic constructs involved in developing an effective therapeutic alliance are defined and elaborated in Table 3.2.

Table 3.2 Description of Factors Influencing the Therapeutic Alliance

Factor	Description
Bond	Bond is the affective quality of the relationship between therapist and client. It reflects how the client feels understood, respected, valued, and cared for. The more the first nine attributes and skills described earlier are present in the relationship, the better the bond. A positive therapeutic bond reflects "a meeting of hearts."
Goals	Goals are the targets toward which an intervention is directed. For instance, achieving insight and a corrective emotional experience are two basic goals of time-limited dynamic psychotherapy.
Tasks	Tasks are the in-therapy and between-session behaviors and activities that the client must engage in to benefit from the treatment. For example, an important task in CBT might be to engage in a behavioral rehearsal role plan in session or to complete a mutually agreed upon homework activity between sessions.
Explanatory model	Explanatory model or causal explanation is the client's theory or best guess of what causes or accounts for their presenting problems whether symptom or impaired functioning. It is akin to the therapist's case conceptualization.
Treatment expectations	Treatment expectations are what the client wants and anticipates of treatment, both its process and outcomes. It involves the role and responsibilities the client expects the therapist will assume, as well as the role and responsibilities the client is willing to assume in the treatment process. Expectations flow from the client's explanatory model. For example, if a client believes his or her panic attacks result from a chemical imbalance in the brain, the client may expect that treatment will consist of medication to correct the imbalance.

(continued)

51

Table 3.2 Description of Factors Influencing the Therapeutic Alliance (Continued)

Factor	Description
Client–therapist negotiation	Negotiation is a reciprocal communication process between client and therapist for arriving at a mutual agreement about treatment goals and tasks. To the extent that treatment goals and tasks offered by the therapist are consistent with the client's explanation and expectations, the client is likely to agree and collaborate with treatment. However, if the therapist's treatment goals and tasks do not match the client's explanation and expectations, the client's agreement and collaboration in the treatment process is unlikely, and noncompliance is the result. For this reason, negotiation plays a central role in achieving a mutually agreed treatment plan, the result of which is a "meeting of the minds."

Therapist and Therapeutic Alliance

Clinical lore holds that therapists who embody the core conditions of effective treatment, empathy, respect, and acceptance (Rogers, 1961), and who demonstrate active listening and responding, facilitate the development of an effective alliance. In such a relationship, clients will feel accepted, supported, and valued and will believe that their therapist cares about them and is worthy of their trust. As a result, they become hopeful and confident that treatment will be successful.

Research has validated some of the clinical lore of the therapist's contribution to the alliance, but it does not support Rogers's claim that the three core conditions are the necessary *and* sufficient conditions for therapeutic change (Norcross, 2002). However, there is increasing support for the premise that specific therapist attributes and skill sets are positively related to an effective therapeutic alliance (Orlinsky et al., 2004). Therapists in an effective alliance present in a warm and friendly manner and are confident and experienced. They are interested in and respectful toward the client, and they relate with honesty, trustworthiness, and openness. During treatment, they remain alert and flexible and provide a safe environment in which clients can discuss their issues. They are supportive, use active and reflective listening, affirm the client's experience, and demonstrate an empathic understanding of each client's situation.

Furthermore, they attend to the clients' experiences and facilitate the expression of affect to enable a deep exploration of concerns. Finally, they provide accurate interpretations of the client's behavior and are active in treatment and draw attention to past therapeutic successes (Ackerman & Hillensroth, 2003; Orlinsky et al., 1994; Orlinsky et al., 2004). Another key therapist variable that fosters an effective therapeutic alliance is clinician credibility. It is described here and further discussed in Chapter 13.

Clinician Credibility

Clinician credibility is a complex phenomenon that involves all of the preceding therapist attributes. It is defined as the client's perception that the therapist is trustworthy and effective based on how the therapist instills faith, confidence, and hope in the client (Sue & Zane, 1987). In other words, credibility involves the elements of trustworthiness and effectiveness. Trustworthiness has already been described. The second element is a perceived sense of therapist effectiveness and interpersonal influence—that is, the use of expertise and power to foster self-awareness and constructive change. Clients recognize such influence when therapists show they are competent, have a clear sense of direction, give structure to the sessions, and empower and affirm clients by encouraging and fostering client change in sessions and between sessions. Credibility must be achieved in the early sessions for the client to remain in treatment long enough to gain therapeutic benefit. Finally, clinician credibility is emphasized in the treatment of culturally diverse clients (Paniagua, 2005).

Developing a Therapeutic Alliance with Difficult Clients

Developing an effective therapeutic alliance is more of a challenge with certain clients. Because personality disorders are associated with significant impairment in interpersonal relationships, special issues and problems arise in the formation of a therapeutic alliance in the treatment of clients with these disorders. In particular, clients with narcissistic, borderline, and paranoid personality traits are likely to have troubled interpersonal attitudes and behaviors that will complicate the patient's engagement with the therapist. Whereas a strong positive therapeutic alliance is predictive of more successful treatment outcomes, strains and ruptures in the alliance may lead to premature termination of treatment. Therefore, therapists need to consider the client's characteristic way of relating in order to select appropriate interventions to effectively retain and involve the patient in treatment. Research has shown not only the importance of building an alliance but also that this alliance is vital in the earliest phase of treatment (Bender, 2005).

Because the Axis II clusters of *DSM* (*Diagnostic and Statistical Manual of Mental Disorders*) do not adequately capture the complexity of character pathology, therapists need to consider which aspects of a client's personality pathology are dominant at the moment in considering salient elements of the therapeutic alliance.

Clients with Cluster A personality disorders (schizotypal, schizoid, and paranoid personality disorders) tend to present with profound impairment in interpersonal relationships. Whereas responding empathically and endeavoring to get acquainted and close is acceptable to most clients, clients in this cluster are more likely to fear and distrust therapists who respond in this manner. Coming across as too warm or caring initially is threatening to these clients. Rather proceed slowly and expect to be tested by them.

Clients with Cluster B "dramatic" personality disorders (antisocial, borderline, histrionic, and narcissistic) tend to push the limits. Consequently, therapists need to exercise great care to avoid crossing inappropriate lines in a quest to build an alliance with patients with one of these disorders.

Clients with Cluster C "anxious/fearful" personality disorders (avoidant, dependent, and obsessive-compulsive personality disorders) tend to be emotionally inhibited and averse to interpersonal conflict. Some, particularly those with avoidant personality disorder, are sensitive to rejection and will test the therapist's trustworthiness, often in the beginning. These patients frequently feel guilty and internalize blame for situations even when there is none, a tendency that may facilitate alliance building because the patients are willing to take some responsibility for their dilemma and may engage somewhat more readily with the therapist to sort it out, compared with patients with more severe Cluster A or B diagnoses (Bender, 2005).

ASSESSING READINESS AND FOSTERING TREATMENT-PROMOTING FACTORS

While developing an effective therapeutic relationship, the therapist needs to consider the various treatment factors that can promote or impede the treatment process as well as progress in therapy. This means that the therapist must attend to such critical factors as the client's readiness for change, capacity for collaboration, expectations, and other treatment-promoting factors.

Stages of Readiness for Change

Prochaska, DiClementi, and Norcross (1992) found that individuals who change their behaviors, on their own or with a therapist's help, typically proceed through five stages of change. The stages are precontemplation, contemplation, preparation, action, and maintenance. This stage model is quite useful in understanding and predicting client change across a wide array of client concerns in psychotherapy.

A preliminary assessment of readiness for change can be extremely valuable and useful in treatment planning. Since most clients cycle in and out of these stages several times before achieving their goals, it is helpful to gauge the current stage during the initial session and to monitor movement of these stages. Ideally, the client enters therapy at the preparation or action stage, which means that treatment outcomes will be predictably positive. When the client enters at the precontemplative or contemplative stage, the therapist's primary task is to tailor treatment in order to move the client toward the action stage.

Readiness is typically assessed through observation or interview. Markers, by stage, to elicit or observe when assessing readiness include the following:

Precontemplation	The client does not consider his or her behavior to be a problem and/or does not currently consider making any change.
Contemplation	The client is considering that his or her behavior may be a problem and contemplates, that is, seriously considers, making a change *within the next 6 months.*
Preparation:	The client has made a commitment to change a behavior considered problematic and intends to make the change soon. The client can have a specific plan or a target date set for change *within a month.*
Action	The client is already making changes and is considered to be *in this stage for up to 6 months* from the start of the initial change.
Maintenance	The client works to stabilize the new change and prevent a return of the problem behavior. (Prochaska et al., 1992)

Interventions to Optimize Readiness for Change

The treatment implications of the concept of readiness for change are immense. Several strategies for fostering readiness have been proposed, implemented, and researched. Currently, motivational interviewing has become a useful strategy. The following outline, adapted from S. Miller, Duncan, and Hubble (1997), indicates some of the targets for motivational interviewing and suggests other possible interventions.

Stage	Interventions
Precontemplation	1. Explore the client's explanatory model.
	2. Suggest the client think about the situation from another perspective.
	3. Provide education and information.
Contemplation	1. Encourage the client to think about making changes.
	2. Suggest an observational task (e.g., what happens to make the situation better or worse).
	3. Join with the client's ambivalence to action with a "go slow" directive.
Preparation	1. Offer several viable treatment options.
	2. Invite the client to choose from among these options.
Action	1. Elicit details of the client's successful efforts.
	2. Reinforce those efforts and encourage other efforts.
Maintenance	1. Support the client's successful efforts.
	2. Predict relapse and setbacks.
	3. Help the client make contingency plans.

COMMON FACTORS IN PSYCHOTHERAPY

Based on his review of several psychotherapy outcome research studies, Michael Lambert (1992) proposed that there are four common factors or curative elements central to all forms of psychotherapy: (1) client resources; (2) therapeutic relationship; (3) intervention strategies and tactics; and (4) faith, hope, and expectancy.

Client Resources

Clients come for therapy with symptoms, conflicts, and predicaments, but they also come with certain resources that contribute to the outcome of therapy. Also called "extra-therapeutic factors," client resources refer to those factors, both internal and external, which the client brings to therapy, that foster treatment progress irrespective of participation in the treatment process. Internal resources include the client's readiness for change, coping skills and social skills, resilience, psychological mindedness, courage, and past history of success in change efforts. External resources include the client's social support system, access to treatment, financial resources, and even fortuitous events. The presence of such client resources is estimated to account for about 40% of improvement that occurs in any treatment (Lambert, 1992).

Therapeutic Relationship

The therapeutic alliance or relationship is the context in which the process of therapy is experienced and enacted. It is estimated that about 30% of the variance in psychotherapy outcome is due to relationship factors (Lambert, 1992). It appears that when clients feel understood, safe, and hopeful, they are more likely to risk disclosing painful affects and intimate details of their lives, as well as risk thinking, feeling, and acting in more adaptive and healthier ways.

Intervention Strategies and Tactics

A defining feature of psychotherapeutic approaches is a unique set of intervention strategies and tactics such as interpretation, free association, confrontation, cognitive restructuring, empty chair technique, desensitization, finding exceptions, and reframing. Despite the emphasis on specific intervention strategies and tactics, the overall impact of specific intervention on the outcome of treatment is rather minimal, accounting for only about 15% of the variance in psychotherapy outcome (Lambert, 1992).

Expectancy

The remaining 15% of the variance of psychotherapy is attributed to a phenomenon known as the expectancy effect or faith factor, meaning that the client's belief in the treatment and in the clinician who provides the treatment has healing or curative power (Lambert, 1992). Related to this belief is the expectation that therapy will mobilize hope, facilitate improvement, and reverse the client's demoralization (Frank & Frank, 1991). When the clinician instills hope and the belief that the treatment will likely work, verbally and nonverbally, improvement and positive treatment outcomes tend to occur.

Treatment-Promoting Factors and Strategies

Lack of treatment progress typically reflects treatment-interfering behaviors, which are behaviors that clients bring to bear and that impede the progress of therapy (Linehan, 1993). A broader designation is "treatment-interfering factors," which also includes client-interfering behaviors, therapist factors, client–therapist relationship factors, and treatment factors. The other side of treatment-interfering factors is "treatment-promoting factors."

Treatment-promoting factors include a range of client factors, therapist factors, client–therapist relationship factors, and intervention factors that promote progress in therapy (Sperry, 2010; Sperry, Carlson, et al., 2003). Because therapeutic alliance considerations are central in the treatment process and outcomes, it behooves the therapist to actively promote the alliance and related treatment processes.

There are several treatment-promoting strategies that will be identified here. Of these strategies, eliciting a client's explanatory model is critical. The client's explanation inevitably provides invaluable information to the therapist. As will be noted in Chapter 5, eliciting the explanatory model is essential in developing an accurate case conceptualization. This strategy also has immense clinical value for the therapeutic alliance. The fact that the therapist takes the time to inquire about the client's explanatory model (also called etiology beliefs) and then discusses with the client the clinician's own explanation (the therapist's clinical formulation) can have a profound bearing on the therapeutic alliance and on the treatment process and outcomes. Often this discussion involves education and negotiation to increase the degree of similarity between the two explanations. Clinical experience indicates that the closer the similarity is, the better the therapeutic alliance and treatment outcomes will be.

Although research does not find that an actual similarity must exist, it does show that if the client perceives that there is a similarity of explanations or etiology beliefs, the therapeutic process and outcome are improved. Specifically, it was found that when there was a perceived similarity of explanations, the therapist was perceived as credible, clients felt they were understood by their therapist, they were satisfied with the therapeutic orientation used by the therapist, and they were also satisfied with the therapeutic process in general (Atkinson, Worthington, Dana, & Good, 1991).

Another strategy for enhancing the therapeutic alliance is eliciting and being responsive to client preferences regarding treatment modalities and methods (Vollmer, Grote, Lange, & Walter, 2009). Recent research shows that attending to client preferences for the type of treatment positively affects the outcomes of treatment. A meta-analysis reviewed data from over 2,300 clients across 26 studies and compared treatment outcome differences between clients matched to a preferred treatment and clients not matched to a preferred treatment. The findings indicate a small but significant effect in favor of clients who received a preferred treatment (Swift & Callahan, 2009). These strategies are summarized in Table 3.3.

CLINICAL EXAMPLE: FOSTERING AN EFFECTIVE THERAPEUTIC ALLIANCE

This clinical example involves the case of Geri.[*] It highlights her explanatory model, treatment expectations, and preferences for therapist characteristics and treatment modalities, methods, and focus. Geri brings the following treatment-promoting factors or resources to therapy. She is intelligent, loyal to her employer, and has worked at the same job for 12 years, which suggests she can sustain commitments. Despite her pattern of social insolation and distrust of others, she maintains contact with a paternal aunt, implicitly trusts one coworker, and cares for her dog. Her level of readiness for treatment appears to be between the contemplative and the preparation stage of change. Her explanatory model of her illness is that her depression is the result of stresses at work as well as a chemical imbalance in her brain.

Her expectations for therapy are consistent with her explanatory model, and thus she believes she needs medication. Her goal for treatment would be symptom relief and a better way of handling work-related stressors. Thus, a combination of medication and therapy that focuses on solving problems rather than exploring feelings is her preference. Because of her fear of others, especially in group settings, she is initially resistant

---

[*] Discussions paraphrased from diagnostic interview presented in Sperry's *Highly Effective Therapy* (New York: Routledge).

Table 3.3 Treatment Factors and Promotion Strategies

Factor	Description
THERAPEUTIC ALLIANCE	
Bond	Client's preferences for therapist characteristics: gender, language, ethnicity, religion, sexual orientation
Goals	Client's preferences for therapist approach: active/take charge, quiet/passive, expressive/warm
Explanatory model	Client's explanatory model: symptoms/problem caused by bad luck, God's will, interpersonal conflict, trauma, unrealistic expectations, unmet needs, no will power, chemical imbalance in brain, illness, etc.
Treatment expectations	Client's expected treatment outcomes: symptom relief, increased functioning, improved health or well-being, personality change, relationship change, etc. Client's preferences for type of therapy: CBT, dynamic, humanistic or person-centered, problem-focused, solution-focused, 12 step or addictions counseling, Christian counseling, etc. Client's expectation of roles and responsibility for change: Continuum: therapist is responsible<————————> client is responsible

Tasks	Client's preferences for treatment modality: individual therapy, couples, family, or group sessions
	Client's preferences for between-session therapy tasks: undertaking mutually agreed upon tasks, monitoring thoughts, feelings, dreams, etc., reading self-help books or watching self-help movies
CLIENT RESOURCES	Engage client's internal and external resources to optimize the client's engagement and commitment to the treatment relationship and treatment process
INTERVENTION	Tailor interventions to client need, capacity, and expectations
EXPECTANCY-FAITH FACTOR	Increase expectancy for positive treatment outcomes, reverse demoralization, and trigger the faith factor

to involvement in a psychoeducation group or group therapy. Her preference is for a therapist who will be somewhat active but always supportive and nonjudgmental.

Given her avoidant personality structure, it is likely that she will have difficulty discussing personal matters with therapists and other clients in group settings. Individuals with this personality structure commonly "test" and provoke others, therapists and clients (in both individual and group settings), into criticizing her for changing or canceling appointments at the last minute or being late. They tend to procrastinate, avoid feelings, and otherwise "test" the therapist's trustability.

CONCLUDING NOTE

The therapeutic alliance can and does have a profound effect on treatment process and outcomes. The chapter described an expanded view of the therapeutic alliance, which encompasses the client's explanatory model and treatment expectations, in addition to the three basic parameters of therapeutic bond, goals, and tasks. The chapter emphasized necessity for the therapist and client to endeavor to discuss these five parameters in order to achieve a meeting of hearts and mind. In a subsequent chapter (Chapter 11), an ultrashort assessment device, the Session Rating Scale, will be described that fosters this discussion of the therapeutic alliance in each session. In the next chapter, clinical competencies related to maintaining an effective therapeutic alliance are described.

4

Relationship Maintenance

Because of its impact on the treatment process and outcomes, establishing an effective therapeutic relationship is a critical challenge for the therapist. As noted in the previous chapter, a specific set of competencies and skills is necessary for developing such a relationship. Maintaining an effective therapeutic relationship is an equally critical therapeutic challenge for therapists, and it too requires a specific set of specific competencies and skills. Needless to say, therapist competency and capability in dealing with these challenges and impasses are essential to the competent practice of psychotherapy. This chapter addresses these impasses and their corresponding clinical competencies.

Just as there are "treatment-promoting factors" as described in Chapter 3, there are also "treatment-interfering factors." Treatment-interfering factors, also called impasses, are factors that arise within and between sessions that impede the progress of therapy. This chapter deals directly with three specific interfering factors in the client–therapist relationship: (1) resistance and ambivalence, (2) alliance ruptures, and (3) transference–countertransference enactments. Chapter 7 describes other treatment interfering factors. Each of these factors and strategies for resolving them are discussed in separate sections. Finally, a case example illustrates the recognition and resolution of one of these interfering factors.

COMPETENCIES OF MAINTAINING EFFECTIVE THERAPEUTIC RELATIONSHIPS

The essential clinical competencies of the core competency of maintaining an effective therapeutic relationship associated with the core competency of relationship building and maintenance are the following:

Recognize and Resolve Resistance and Ambivalence

This competency involves the capacity to accurately identify indicators of client resistance and/or ambivalence in a clinical context as well as to effectively resolve the resistance or ambivalence, which results in maintaining and enhancing the therapeutic relationship.

Recognize and Resolve Transferences and Countertransferences

This competency involves the capacity to accurately identify indicators of transference and countertransference, including transference enactments, as well as to effectively resolve such enactments, which results in maintaining and enhancing the therapeutic relationship.

Recognize and Repair Alliance Ruptures

This competency involves the capacity to accurately identify indicators of alliance ruptures and strains as well as to effectively resolve such ruptures and strains, which results in maintaining and enhancing the therapeutic relationship.

RECOGNIZING AND RESOLVING RESISTANCE AND AMBIVALENCE

Resistance to change, including resistance to the therapeutic relationship, is a problem that complicates psychotherapy, particularly for trainees. In fact, resistance is one of the most important yet least understood concepts in psychotherapy. Because therapeutic approaches have differing views of it and there has been no integrative theory of resistance, there has been little to guide the work of psychotherapists (Engle & Arkowitz, 2006).

Understanding why clients don't change is a complex issue. Because change is associated with a sense of unpredictability and uncontrollability, it is often resisted, whereas non-change is perceived as relatively safe (Arkowitz, Westra, Miller, & Rollnick, 2007).

As previously noted, widely differing views of resistance are espoused by various treatment approaches (Engle & Arkowitz, 2006). These differences are particularly observable in the way in which resistance is manifested, the way it is understood and explained, and the way in which specific interventions are utilized to modify or resolve it. This section briefly describes the phenomenon of resistance from the dynamic, cognitive–behavioral, and systemic perspectives. Each of the approaches is described in terms of manifestation, explanation, and management. An integrative perspective, which incorporates many of these features, is then presented.

Cognitive–Behavioral Approaches

Manifestation

Across the spectrum of cognitive and behavioral approaches, resistance is described quite broadly and likely to be referred to as "roadblocks" or "impediments" than as resistance (Freeman & McCluskey, 2005). Resistance may involve any of the various therapy-interfering behaviors. Among these is noncompliance both within the session and between sessions, particularly homework whether it involves monitoring thoughts and feelings, social skills practice, or enacting a relational task. Resisting homework is probably the most common form of resistance seen in cognitive–behavioral (CBT) approaches (Kazantzis, 2005).

Explanation

Resistance, for the more cognitively oriented CBT approaches, can result from a client's faulty beliefs or schemas, or from client rigidity or poor impulse control. Other reasons include inadequacy of a therapist's case conceptualization, negative therapist attitude or lack of skills, and problematic therapist–client relationship. In the more behaviorally oriented CBT approaches, resistance may result from the inappropriate or inadequate use of reinforcers, reinforcing behaviors that conflict with therapy goals, or unrealistic expectations of change.

Management
In the more cognitively oriented CBT approaches, resolving resistance typically involves assisting clients in modifying the beliefs and schemas that underlie their resistance. It might involve structuring homework such that clients are more likely to complete it. In the more behaviorally oriented CBT approaches, managing resistance typically involves changing the activating stimuli and reinforcers that maintain the client's noncompliance.

Dynamic Approaches

Manifestation
Across many of the psychodynamic approaches, resistance is viewed as behaviors that avoid painful insights or awareness. As such, resistance is reflected in ego defense mechanisms such as projection, denial, or repression (Gabbard, 1999). Particularly, in the interpersonal dynamic approaches, resistance is manifest in ongoing, repetitive, and maladaptive interpersonal patterns. It commonly manifests in the therapeutic alliance as alliance ruptures and transference–countertransference enactments (Binder, 2004).

Explanation
The postulated explanation or reason for resistance varies by the dynamic approach. For instance, in the classical and ego psychology approaches, resistance results in anxiety reduction in that there is an avoidance of insights or awareness into one's unconscious drives. In contrast, unconscious pathogenic beliefs maintain and engender resistance (Weiss, 1994). In general, however, it may be that the client's fear of change is the likely explanation for resistance.

Management
The corrective or treatment of resistance differs. In most dynamic approaches, the intervention of choice is the interpretation of the defensive, avoidant, or repetitive patterns and behavior. In more relationally oriented dynamic approaches, resistance is likely to be resolved as a result of the therapist not enacting early negative patterns but instead facilitating a corrective emotional experience. In therapeutically processing such situations, the client can experience a corrective emotional experience and thereby question the need to engage in resistant patterns.

Systemic Approaches

Manifestation

Across the various family and systemic approaches, resistance is variously described. It may range from resisting changes in family rules or structures, to changes in specific symptoms of a family member. Manifestations of resistance include noncompliance with therapy, hostility, attempts to control the therapeutic process, as well as ongoing dysfunctional family interaction patterns. In contrast, in the solution-focused therapies, the concept of resistance is absent, as all of a client's or client system's behavior and language are considered to be "cooperation" (de Shazer, 1985).

Explanation

Most of the systemic approaches understand resistance to result from fear of change or because of systemic maintenance of the status quo. In contrast, in the solution-focused therapies, where clients are viewed as always "cooperating" with the therapist, it is the therapist's task to discover and follow the client's idiosyncratic way of cooperating.

Management

Depending on the particular systemic approach, specific tactics are utilized to manage or resolve resistance. For example, in structural and strategic approaches, resistance is reframed or paradoxical interventions are utilized, such as prescribing the symptom. In other approaches, the therapist enters the family system and challenges the resistance, or therapist directives are employed. In contrast, in the solution-focused therapies, resistance is not to be managed or resolved. Rather, by recognizing this unique pattern, the therapist can pace responses accordingly, which can enhance client cooperation (de Shazer, 1985). Table 4.1 summarizes these approaches.

Integrative Perspective on Resistance

An integrative perspective for understanding and working with resistance has been proposed by Engle and Arkowitz (2006). The basic premise of this perspective is that resistance is less commonly manifested as outright refusal by a client, while ambivalence is the more common presentation. Ambivalence is typically manifested as defensive avoidance or a repetitive pattern of interpersonal behaviors that cause distress or result in limited gratification. This type of resistance is described as "resistant

Table 4.1 Perspective on Resistance of Three Therapeutic Approaches

Approach	Manifestation	Explanation	Management
CBT	Noncompliance with homework: monitoring thoughts and feelings, practicing social skills, engaging in agreed upon enactments, etc.	Faulty beliefs/ schemas; poor impulse control; inappropriate use of reinforcers; unrealistic treatment goals	Correct maladaptive beliefs/schemas; change stimuli/ reinforce behavior that maintains compliance; modify treatment goals
Dynamic	Defense mechanisms of repression, denial, and projection; resisting efforts to change cyclic maladaptive relational patterns	Reduction of anxiety by avoidance of painful insights; fear of change; unconscious pathogenic beliefs that maintain symptoms; secondary gain	Interpret defenses and avoidance behavior and interpersonal patterns; enable client to experience a corrective emotional experience
Systemic	Hostility; attempts to control sessions; unwillingness to perform between-session tasks; repetitive maladaptive family patterns; *Solution-focused therapy:* Resistance is really the client's unique way of cooperating	Maintain status quo; fear of change; *Solution-focused therapy:* Don't attempt to manage resistance but instead recognize the client's unique way of cooperating	Reframe resistance; use paradoxical interventions; *Solution-focused therapy:* Assess client expectations and pace responses accordingly to enhance cooperation

ambivalence" (Engle & Arkowitz, 2006). It reflects discrepancies among self-schemas relevant to change, that is, schemas associated with movement toward change and those associated with movement away from change. Most often, clients are not fully aware of their self-schemas and the discrepancies among them that cause resistant ambivalence (Arkowitz et al., 2007).

Because resistant ambivalence is also an interpersonal phenomenon, it is best understood in the interpersonal context in which it occurs. When it occurs in a therapeutic setting, it is essential that the therapist view it as a temporary state rather than a personality trait. Resistant ambivalence is operative when the following elements are observed:

1. The client believes or agrees that the anticipated change is in his or her own best interest.
2. The client has sufficient information and the capacity to make the change happen.
3. The client demonstrates initial movement toward change with words and other behaviors.
4. The client, at the same time, demonstrates movement away from change with words and other behaviors.
5. The client experiences a negative emotional reaction to the failure to change. (Engle & Arkowitz, 2006)

To effectively resolve ambivalence, two therapeutic interventions are recommended: the two-chair approach and motivational interviewing. A third intervention strategy utilized with ambivalence resistance is solution-focused therapy. The first two interventions are briefly described here.

Strategies for Resolving Ambivalent Resistance

Two-Chair Approach

The two-chair approach, which has its roots in Gestalt therapy, has recently been adapted by Greenberg (Greenberg & Watson, 2006) for the resolution of resistant ambivalence. This approach presumes that each individual has at least two selves or voices that coexist and often conflict. Utilizing this approach, the therapist endeavors to create a dialogue between the two discrepant selves of the client regarding change. In the so-called conflict split, one self advocates for change, while the other self struggles against making a change. In the therapy session, the client is invited to participate in a dialogue in which each self occupies a separate chair (Engle &

Arkowitz, 2006). The therapist's role is to facilitate dialogue between the differing selves. The self that struggles against change typically operates outside of the client's awareness; thus, the client requires the therapist's assistance to foster greater awareness such that a productive dialogue can develop and possibly lead to change.

Motivational Interviewing

Although acceptance of the status quo is a reasonable outcome in the two-chair approach, motivational interviewing is more focused on moving the client toward change. Motivational interviewing utilizes a number of interventions to resolve ambivalent resistance, among them decisional balance, value–behavior discrepancies, and development and reinforcement of "change talk" (W. Miller & Rollnick, 2002). With the decisional balance method, the client is encouraged to list the pros and cons of change. With the value–behavior discrepancies method, the therapist subtly uses reflections of the client's own values and behaviors to help move him or her toward change. For example, the therapist might say: "You really want to be a good mother, but your drinking interferes with that desire." Such reflections point out the inconsistency of what the client desires to happen and what actually happens, and are a powerful cognitive dissonance, which the client feels compelled to resolve, at least to some degree. Therapists can also develop and reinforce "change talk," which further tips the decisional balance toward change. Change talk is particularly important because it indicates that the client is in the process of schema change. Accordingly, the therapist would listen for and then reinforce the client's change talk. It is important to note that the therapist's role in motivational interviewing is that of consultant rather than as change agent, in that the client is the final decision maker in the change enterprise.

RECOGNIZING AND RESOLVING TRANSFERENCES AND COUNTERTRANSFERENCES

The quality of the therapeutic alliance is the foundation upon which all other therapeutic endeavors are based. In addition to conditions that facilitate the development and maintenance of an effective therapeutic alliance, there are also conditions that militate against its development and maintenance. This section focuses on one set of these conditions—transference and countertransference—that can and do interfere with the therapeutic relationship as well as therapeutic outcomes. It first describes transference, countertransference, and their enactments, and then describes a strategy for resolving such enactments.

Past experiences with relationships affect subsequent relationships, and seldom are individuals consciously aware that they "transfer" feelings and thoughts from past relationships onto current ones. In addition to transferring feelings and thoughts, expectations to act in certain ways are also transferred. Thus, a college student may meet a professor for the first time and react to that professor with the same or similar set of thoughts, feelings, and expectations that she had for her high school biology teacher. She may be surprised and even experience slight confusion when the professor is friendlier but more academically demanding than she expected. This confusion is because transference and countertransference are interpersonal distortions that often do not fit present role expectations (Good & Beitman, 2006).

Just as there are active elements like trust and collaboration in current relationships, there are also active elements of past relationships that both clients and therapists bring to the client–therapist relationship. It is these active elements of past relationships that can negatively impact the treatment process. Transference is such an element. Transference is a phenomenon in which clients inaccurately transfer thoughts, feelings, and expectations about past interpersonal experiences onto their current relationship with their therapist. These distortions tend to be considerably potent and can negatively impact the process of therapy (Good & Beitman, 2006). Transference can be either positive or negative. It is a form of reenactment of the client's old and familiar pattern of relating, a pattern that often involves "unfinished business." In this reenactment, clients demonstrate how they felt in the past when they were treated in a particular manner. Transference typically occurs when a therapist—often inadvertently—says or does something that triggers the client's unfinished business.

Countertransference is a similar phenomenon in which clinicians inadvertently and inaccurately transfer thoughts, feelings, and expectations from past experiences onto clients. Similarly, these distortions can impact the treatment process. Countertransference can be positive or negative. An increasing consensus among clinicians from the various therapeutic orientations is that countertransference can be a useful source of information about the client (Gabbard, 1999).

71

Transference–Countertransference Enactments

Whereas in the past, transference and countertransference were considered "separate" phenomena, today an increasing number of researchers and clinicians consider transference and countertransference as best understood from a relational perspective or model (Safran & Muran, 2000). The emphasis in this model is not on the client as in the past, but on the interaction between client and therapist. In this view, both client and therapist are viewed as participants who *cocreate enactments* that represent configurations of transference and countertransference. Both client and therapist have roles in the transference reenactment. The client's role is to respond, while the therapist's role is to trigger and shape that response. In other words, transference has two aspects. The first is the client and the client's past, and the second is the interpersonal dynamic between therapist and client. Thus, transference involves "the here-and-now experience of the client with the therapist who has a role in eliciting and shaping the transference" (Ornstein & Ganzer, 2005, p. 567). For example, a client who was raised by a mother who alternated between being emotionally distant and angry and abusive may be reluctant to disclose and discuss feelings in therapy. When encouraged by the therapist to discuss feelings, the client may react by becoming aloof and withdrawn or by becoming irritated and angry.

Recognizing Transference and Countertransference

Manifestations of transference and countertransference are relatively common in therapeutic settings. They are more likely to be expressed in long-term therapies that emphasize feelings and unconscious dynamics than in briefer therapies that focus on here-and-now issues (Binder, 2004; Gabbard, 1999). As previously noted, transference and countertransference can be either positive or negative. It behooves therapists to recognize the signs or indicators of both.

Transference and countertransference are interrelated or reciprocating phenomena. Typically, a client's negative transference triggers a therapist's negative countertransference. Although there are many types of such enactments, two are quite common. The first involves the experience of being exasperated with a client's reactions, as when clients expect therapists to punish them for enacting unfinished business. The second involves experiences of being sexually attracted to, or "falling in love" with, a particular client.

Dealing with Transference–Countertransference Enactments

Unfortunately, recognizing and resolving transference and countertransference issues do not appear to be a priority in the didactic portion of therapy training programs today. Unless a trainee initiates the discussion, transference and countertransference may not come up in supervision either. Based on the conviction that effectively dealing with transference and countertransference enactments is essential for trainees to practice therapy competently, this section and subsequent case material discuss and illustrate these clinical issues. Because therapists can too easily get blindsided by transference–countertransference enactments, it is critical to deal with these concerns proactively and directly.

Various methods of managing transference have been proposed. For instance, Gelso and Hayes (2007) provide a research-based set of strategies for preventing such acting out as well as for managing the therapist's internal countertransferential reactions. The strategies are self-insight; self-integration, that is, possession of a healthy character structure; empathy; anxiety management; and conceptualizing ability, that is, use of theory to grasp the patient's dynamics in the therapeutic relationship. Of these, self-insight and self-integration are critical for the therapist in gaining greater self-understanding of the treatment situation in which the countertransference arose, including client–therapist boundary issues. Self-insight and self-integration are also necessary for the therapist's work on his or her own psychological health, and for managing and effectively using the therapist's own internal reactions. The therapist's level of self-integration plays a pivotal role in whether countertransference is acted out or utilized therapeutically. It is axiomatic that resolution or completion of unfinished business is a prerequisite for a therapist to provide optimal therapeutic assistance to clients. Focused reflection and clinical supervision are two common ways of understanding and managing, although personal therapy may be necessary when countertransference is a chronic problem (Gelso & Hayes, 2007).

These methods can be very helpful in dealing with transference and countertransference after they have occurred. But there are proactive, here-and-now strategies for dealing with transference enactments as they arise in a particular session. The strategy described here not only addresses and resolves the immediate transference enactment but also effects a corrective emotional experience, that is, experiencing the client–therapist interaction in a way that reverses or changes the maladaptive pattern underlying the transference enactment (Levenson, 1995).

This strategy involves five steps. Essentially, the therapist would (1) indicate that the emotionally charged situation likely reflects a past transference experience; (2) encourage the client to recall how a significant other, usually a parent, reacted to the client in the *past* emotionally charged context; (3) ask the client to describe how the therapist reacted in the *present* to him or her; (4) assist the client to compare and contrast the therapist's behavior with that of the significant other; and (5) validate the client's resulting corrective emotional experience. Others have described somewhat similar strategies (McCullough, 2005). This strategy is illustrated in the case example near the end of the chapter.

RECOGNIZING AND REPAIRING ALLIANCE RUPTURES

This section emphasizes another formidable difficulty or impasse in maintaining a therapeutic relationship: alliance strains and ruptures. Such strains and ruptures can and do occur in all forms of therapy. They are briefly described as well as some strategies for resolving this threat to the therapeutic alliance and a major cause of premature termination.

Therapeutic Alliance Rupture and Strains

As previously described, the integrative view of the therapeutic alliance involves three interdependent variables: (1) an agreement on the therapeutic tasks, (2) an agreement on goals, and (3) the quality of the interpersonal bond between therapist and client (Bordin, 1979). An effective therapeutic alliance is a relationship that is mutual and collaborative. Alliance ruptures are basically tensions or breakdowns in the collaborative relationship between client and therapist. Safran, Muran, Samstag, and Stevens (2002) conceptualize ruptures as either disagreements about the tasks and goals of treatment or as *strains* in the therapeutic bond.

Transferences and countertransferences, particularly negative ones, can significantly strain and even rupture the therapeutic *bond*. Such ruptures often begin as transference–countertransference enactments between client and therapist (Samstag, Muran, & Safran, 2003). For instance, a client will enact a difficult or traumatic early experience and then try to hook the therapist into playing a role that conforms to the client's early experience. To the extent that the therapist unwittingly gets hooked and enacts this role, an alliance rupture results (Safran & Muran, 2000). Nevertheless, such a rupture can often be repaired if the therapist recognizes his or her contribution to it and then helps resolve the enactment, resulting in a corrective emotional experience. In other words, ruptures are breaches in relatedness and negative fluctuations in the quality of the relationship between therapist and client (Safran & Muran, 2000).

Ruptures vary in intensity, duration, and frequency depending on the nature of the particular therapist–client relationship. Intensity can range from relatively minor (i.e., a "strain") to major breakdowns in understanding and communication (i.e., a "rupture"). When the rupture is extreme, the client may directly manifest negative sentiments toward the therapist or even terminate therapy prematurely. Where the rupture is mild, only minor fluctuations in the quality of alliance are manifest, but they may be difficult to detect (Safran & Muran, 2000).

Differentiating Alliance Rupture From Resistance and Related Terms

Clinicians, particularly those in training, may question the validity of the concept of alliance strains and ruptures and often consider them as synonymous with resistance. A strong case can be made that ruptures are different from resistance. Basically, an alliance rupture is defined as a tension or breakdown in the *collaborative relationship* between client and therapist (Samstag et al., 2003).

> The interpersonal nature of alliance ruptures distinguishes the term from other definitions of impasses that emphasize either patient characteristics (e.g., resistance, negative transferences) or therapist characteristics (e.g., empathic failure, counter transference reaction). In other words, a rupture is not a phenomenon that is located exclusively within the patient or caused exclusively by the therapist. Instead, a rupture is an *interactive process* that includes these kinds of defensive experiences as they play out within the context of each particular therapeutic relationship. (Samstag et al., 2003, p. 188)

The Experience of Alliance Ruptures

How often do strains and ruptures occur? Until relatively recently, the construct "alliance strains and ruptures" was of interest primarily to those with a dynamic orientation. Today, there is increasing interest in this phenomenon, and most orientations recognize it. This suggests that alliance strains and ruptures are not rare. But how common are they? Some estimate that alliance strains and ruptures occur more commonly than therapists realize. Research "indicates that it is rare to have more than a session or two without some minor strain in the alliance, and that therapists often fail to see ruptures experienced by patients" (Safran & Muran, 2000, p. 234). It should be noted that this research involved only relational therapy, the approach advocated by these authors. Other advocates of relational-oriented dynamic therapy disagree with Safran and Muran and contribute its occurrence to a function of the type of client and the context, i.e., type and length of therapy (Binder, 2004).

Which clients are most likely to be involved in alliance strains and ruptures? The most likely are clients who present for therapy with a deep-seated, pervasive mistrust and pessimism of others and who have a history of ongoing relational problems, including multiple relationships, separations, and divorce. The least likely are clients who present for therapy with a history of parents and caretakers who modeled adequate or healthy relationships, have a somewhat optimistic view of others, and have been relatively successful in close, interpersonal relationships. There are also clients who present for therapy with negative views of others but have experienced some level of success in interpersonal relationships; this suggests that they have the some capacity and some interpersonal skills and are likely to be less vulnerable to alliance strains and ruptures than those with pervasive mistrust and no success in interpersonal relationships. Another factor is the therapist. Therapists with a demeanor perceived by the client as trusting, caring, and consistent are more likely to maintain effective therapeutic alliances and are less likely to activate alliance strains and ruptures than therapists who do not demonstrate this demeanor (Good & Beitman, 2006).

In what therapeutic contexts are alliance strains and ruptures likely to occur? It appears the type and length of therapy play a role in the expression of strains and ruptures. Such strains and ruptures can occur in all forms of therapy, and different therapeutic approaches and tasks are at risk for inducing characteristic types of alliance ruptures. For instance, the more active, directive approaches, such as behavior therapy or Gestalt therapy, are more likely to induce ruptures stemming from the client's feeling that they are being controlled. Experiential approaches, which emphasize moment-by-moment tracking and exploration of client experiences, are at risk for inducing feelings of being invaded. On the other hand, interpretative and dynamic approaches, with their emphasis on explanation, can lead clients to feel that their life experience is reduced to a compulsive pattern. Although different forms of therapy may be at risk for different kinds of alliance ruptures, the task of working through them is common to all (Safran & Muran, 2000; Samstag et al., 2003).

When alliance ruptures are expressed, they are most likely to occur in long-term psychotherapies but less often in time-limited therapy because of its brevity. This observation is consistent with the view that transference enactments are a common cause or precipitant of alliance ruptures. Furthermore, it is speculated that when a client's maladaptive relationships are the treatment focus, relatively brief therapeutic relationships may not last long enough for those relational problems outside the therapeutic context to significantly impact the therapeutic alliance (Binder, 2004).

Differing Views of the Cause of Alliance Ruptures

Dynamic Therapies

Dynamic therapies, particularly interpersonally oriented ones, consider alliance strains and ruptures as conflicts that develop from the interaction of therapist and client, where each brings their unconscious ways of relating to create the problematic interaction. In this perspective, it is believed that alliance ruptures are synonymous with transference enactments (Safran & Muran, 2000), although these enactments are less likely to occur in time-limited therapy because there is not always sufficient time for these enactments to occur (Binder, 2004). When present, these strains and ruptures can occur in the initial, middle, or final phases of therapy. In fact, termination is considered the ultimate alliance rupture, providing an invaluable opportunity to deal with the critical issues of acceptance, loneliness, separation, and loss (Ochoa & Muran, 2008).

Experiential Therapies

In the experiential therapies, particularly emotionally focused therapy, ruptures and strains are presumed to result from breakdowns in the agreement between clients and therapists regarding collaboration on the goals and tasks of therapy during the early and middle phases of treatment. Because of their focus on emotional experience rather than on the content of client problems, experiential therapists tend to be acutely aware of the alliance with their clients on a moment-to-moment basis. Thus, they quickly recognize these phenomena. Strains and ruptures develop in the initial phase of treatment when clients have difficulty turning inward to their experiences, when they withdraw or constrict energy, or when they question the value of the experiential focus in helping them to achieve their goals. In the middle phase of treatment, strains and ruptures occur because of a breakdown in trust and collaboration, often reflecting perceived power differences in the therapeutic situation. Or, they may occur because of lack of agreement on tasks, typically when clients refuse to engage in certain therapeutic tasks (Watson & Greenberg, 2000).

Cognitive–Behavioral Therapies

Traditionally, problems in the therapeutic relationship, including strains and ruptures, are presumed to occur in CBT as a result of the client's cognitive distortions (Ochoa & Muran, 2008). However, Judith Beck (2005) acknowledges that therapists may also have a role in alliance difficulties. She notes that these alliance difficulties "may have a practical basis (the therapist is interrupting too much or too abruptly), a psychological basis (the patient has interfering beliefs such as: 'If my therapist doesn't give me 100%, it means she doesn't care'), or both" (p. 64). That being said, the protocol or format Beck offers for dealing with alliance strains and ruptures is focused primarily on cognitive distortions: elicit cognitive distortions, help the client test the validity of these distorted cognitions, identify and modify dysfunctional assumptions, and evaluate these assumptions in the contexts of other relationships.

Types of Alliance Ruptures

Two categories of alliance rupture have been specified. The first category is called *withdrawal rupture*. In this type, clients avoid or limit their participation and collaboration with treatment (Safran & Muran, 2000). Signs of withdrawal expressed by clients include denying obvious emotions, giving minimal responses, or providing overly detailed descriptions of situations. Other observable signs are rationalizing, intellectualizing, shifting topics often, and talking more about others than about themselves.

The second category is called *confrontation rupture*. In this type, clients express frustration or question or lash out at the therapist (Safran & Muran, 2000). Signs of frustration expressed by clients include complaints about the therapist's questions, responses, or abilities. Other observable signs include clients questioning their need for therapy, their lack of progress, or the therapeutic tasks or interventions being utilized.

Strategies for Resolving Alliance Ruptures

There are a number of strategies for repairing alliance ruptures. These include therapeutic processing, supervision, role-playing, the two-chair technique (Watson & Greenberg, 2000), and meta-communication. One way of developing skill in metacommunication is reflective writing. Ruptures can be addressed either directly or indirectly. Chapter 6 "Recognize and Repair Alliance Ruptures" in *Highly Effective Therapy* (Sperry, 2010) provides three extended examples of strategies for repairing alliance ruptures.

EXAMPLE: MAINTAINING THE THERAPEUTIC ALLIANCE

This example involves the case of Geri and illustrates the resolution of a transference–countertransference enactment. Recall that Geri had previously described her father as a critical and demanding individual. As a child, Geri was convinced that she could not meet her father's expectations for high grades and social success. She reported that although he never physically nor sexually abused her, he verbally and emotionally abused her when she made mistakes, got less than perfect grades, kept gaining weight, and was introverted rather than extroverted and not socially involved with family and friends. Based on this relational history, Geri's male therapist anticipated that negative transference enactments were likely to arise in the course of treatment. Accordingly, he intentionally related to her in a nonjudgmental, nondemanding manner. Nevertheless, in the beginning of treatment she changed her appointment times and came late for her second and third sessions. The first time she was late, the therapist refrained from any comments and continued to extend respect and a nonjudgmental attitude. When she came in late for the third session, she was silent for about 3 minutes. When asked what was happening inside, she became tearful and said she expected the therapist "to lay into" her for being late and rescheduling appointments. When asked to elaborate, she said she expected the therapist to be angry and critical of her for "screwing up." Guided by the strategy for resolving transference enactments, the therapist indicated that he was not in any way angry at her and suggested that her reaction might well reflect past relationships. He then encouraged Geri to recall persons from her past who reacted to her for coming late or screwing up. Geri immediately indicated that is how her father reacted and how she responded with fear, tears, and running out of the room. Then the therapist asked Geri to describe how he (the therapist) had reacted in the present to her. She indicated that he did not make an issue of her being late and was calm, respectful, and nonjudgmental. When asked to contrast the therapist's behavior with that of her father, Geri gasped and said there was a night and day difference, and began to cry, saying, "Don't worry, these are tears of joy." Finally, the therapist validated Geri's experience, referring to it as a corrective emotional experience.

Basically, Geri had enacted unfinished business, but it was a much different cognitive and emotional experience than she had had with her father. The therapist was not surprised by or unprepared for the transference enactment, and in therapeutically processing it, the likelihood of premature termination was decreased and the therapeutic process was greatly facilitated.

CONCLUDING NOTE

This chapter has focused on three specific interfering factors or roadblocks or impediments to an effective therapeutic alliance and their corresponding essential competencies. Needless to say, the therapist's capacity to competently resolve these client–therapist interfering factors is a requisite for competent and effective clinical practice.

Section IV

Core Competency 3: Intervention Planning

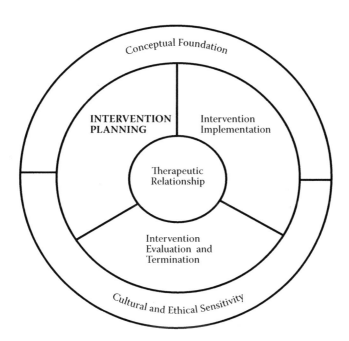

Conceptual Foundation

INTERVENTION PLANNING

Intervention Implementation

Therapeutic Relationship

Intervention Evaluation and Termination

Cultural and Ethical Sensitivity

5

Case Conceptualization and Assessment

In the late 1980s and early 1990s, trainees and clinicians seldom, if ever, talked about case conceptualization, and very few developed and implemented them. Twenty years later, the situation is markedly different, as the case conceptualization is increasingly associated with competent, quality mental health practice. Basically, a case conceptualization is a method and process of summarizing seemingly diverse clinical information about a client into a brief, coherent statement or "map," which elucidates the client's basic pattern and which serves to guide the treatment process from first contact to termination. The capacity to develop and utilize a case conceptualization is now considered an essential clinical competency associated with the core competency of intervention planning. Assessment is integrally related to case conceptualization. In fact, the assessment process itself is guided by the case conceptualization. The case conceptualization is based on an assessment, particularly a comprehensive assessment. Needless to say, performing a comprehensive assessment is also an essential clinical competency associated with the core competency of intervention planning.

This chapter begins by defining *case conceptualization* and its functions. It distinguishes three levels of competency with regard to case conceptualizations and then introduces four components of a case conceptualization: diagnostic formulation, clinical formulation, cultural formulation, and treatment formulation. Along the way, it describes three roles and three types of conceptualizations and the role of inductive and deductive reasoning in its development. Finally, it addresses assessment, emphasizing the importance of a comprehensive assessment, including diagnostic assessment, theory-based assessment, and pattern-based assessment.

ASSESSMENT COMPETENCY AND INTERVENTION PLANNING

This chapter addresses the essential clinical competency of performing a comprehensive assessment, which is associated with the core competency of intervention planning.

Perform a Comprehensive Assessment

This competency involves the capacity to undertake a broad assessment of the client and context that will serve as the basis for the diagnostic formulation component of the case conceptualization.

CASE CONCEPTUALIZATION: DEFINITION AND FUNCTIONS

Case conceptualizations provide clinicians with a coherent treatment strategy for planning and focusing treatment interventions in order to increase the likelihood of achieving treatment goals. Although many therapists develop conceptualizations to guide their practice, not all therapists explicitly articulate these conceptualizations. There are a number of reasons for developing and articulating a case conceptualization, but the most cogent reason is that a conceptualization enables therapists to experience a sense of confidence in their work (Hill, 2005). Hill (2005) believes that this confidence is then communicated to the client, which strengthens the client's trust and the belief that the therapist has a credible plan, and that therapy can and will make a difference. In other words, an effective case conceptualization increases "clinician credibility" (Sue & Zane, 1987).

A case conceptualization is defined in this book as a clinical strategy for obtaining and organizing information about a client, explaining the client's situation and maladaptive patterns, guiding and focusing treatment, anticipating challenges and roadblocks, and preparing for successful termination (Sperry, 2010). This definition highlights interrelated functions when the case conceptualization is understood as a clinical strategy. These five functions are the following:

1. *Obtaining and organizing:* The case conceptualization process begins with the first client contact and formulating tentative hypotheses about the client's presentation, expectations, and dynamics. These hypotheses are continually tested out while performing an integrative assessment guided by a search for patterns—maladaptive patterns—in the client's current and past life with regard to precipitant, predisposing, and perpetuating factors.

2. *Explaining:* As the contours of the client's maladaptive pattern comes into focus and hypotheses are refined, a diagnostic, clinical, and cultural formulation emerges. Within these formulations is a likely explanation of the factors that account for the client's reactions in the past, the present, and the future without treatment. This explanation also provides a rationale for treatment that is tailored to the client's needs, expectations, culture, and personality dynamics.

3. *Guiding and focusing treatment:* Based on this explanation, a treatment formulation emerges, including strategies for specifying treatment targets and for focusing and implementing treatment strategies.

4. *Anticipating obstacles and challenges:* The test of an effective case conceptualization is its viability in predicting the obstacles and challenges throughout the stages of therapy, particularly those involving resistance, ambivalence, alliance ruptures, and transference enactments.

5. *Preparing for termination:* The case conceptualization also assists therapists in recognizing when the most important therapy goals and treatment targets have been addressed and in identifying when and how to prepare for termination. (Cucciare & O'Donohue, 2008)

Roles in Developing a Case Conceptualization

Three roles are related to the five functions and four components of a case conceptualization. The point of specifying these roles is that the therapist must actively engage in different types of thinking and energy in developing a clinically useful case conceptualization. Although some therapists might find one role is easier or more natural for them, all three roles must be adequately performed to develop a clinically useful case conceptualization. Another reason for specifying these three roles is that only one of these roles, the investigator role, seems to be operative in many if not most books, book chapters, and articles on case conceptualizations. Not surprisingly, the functions and components of such case conceptualizations are limited. These three roles are briefly described here.

Investigator
The metaphor of investigative journalist, detective, private investigator, *CSI* investigator, or medium aptly characterizes this role. Whether it is Sherlock Holmes, Monk, Columbo, Gil Grissom (*CSI*), or Allison DuBois (*Medium*), all of these investigators are able to answer the "what happened?" and "why did it happen?" questions that are central to solving a murder mystery and other crimes. These questions are equally important in developing a clinically useful case conceptualization, particularly the diagnostic formulation, clinical formulation, and cultural formulation.

Travel Planner
The metaphor of travel planner nicely captures the role of specifying a destination and a plan for getting there. Typically, this involves routes, an annotated map or an AAA TripTik travel planner, and a compass, functions that are now served by a GPS (global positioning system). A clinically useful case conceptualization provides the therapist with treatment goals (destination), treatment focus, treatment strategy, and treatment plan (map) for achieving those goals.

Forecaster
The metaphor of forecaster is a useful characterization of this role whether it be a weather forecast or a business or market forecast. The forecaster is able to base future predictions on both past factors or performance and future factors or performance. A clinically useful case conceptualization should provide the therapist with reasonably accurate predictions of the kind of obstacles and challenges that are likely to be encountered in the various phases of treatment, including resistances, ambivalence, alliance ruptures, and transference–countertransference issues, as well as

CASE CONCEPTUALIZATION AND ASSESSMENT

Table 5.1   Roles, Functions, and Components in Case Conceptualizations

Roles	Functions	Components
Investigator	Obtaining and organizing	Diagnostic formulation
	Explaining	Clinical formulation
		Cultural formulation
Travel planner	Guiding and focusing treatment	Treatment formulation
Forecaster	Anticipating obstacles/challenges	Treatment formulation
	Preparing for termination	

anticipating the ease or difficulty that the client will have with termination. Table 5.1 visually depicts these factors and their relationships.

Deductive and Inductive Reasoning in Case Conceptualization

Deductive and inductive reasoning are two reasoning processes that are central to completing an assessment and a case conceptualization (Sperry, 2005a). This section describes both of these processes.

Deductive Reasoning

Deductive reasoning involves reasoning from the general to the specific. This type of reasoning is essential in doing a diagnostic assessment as well as completing the diagnostic formulation component of the case conceptualization. Accordingly, arriving at a diagnosis based on criteria from the *Diagnostic and Statistical Manual of Mental Disorders (DSM)* is an example of deductive reasoning. It is a process that involves collecting data about symptomatic distress and impaired functioning, ordering these data into criteria, and matching these criteria to a single diagnostic category. In other words, the diagnosis (the general) provides order and meaning to symptoms matching criteria (the specifics). For instance, a client who presents with the following symptoms would likely receive the diagnosis of social anxiety disorder: (1) marked fear of exposure to the possible scrutiny of others, (2) avoidance of situations in which such scrutiny may occur, (3) marked fear of exposure to unfamiliar people, (4) respond with intense anxiety or panic when facing such exposure, (5) recognition that their fear is excessive and irrational, and (6) become socially isolative as a consequence of the fear. On the other hand, generalized anxiety or panic disorder might be considered if only symptoms (4) and (5) were noted. If just symptoms (1) and (6) were noted the diagnosis of social phobia could

87

be considered but so could schizoid personality. However, if all six symptoms are present, only the diagnosis of social phobia would be warranted from the perspective of *DSM–IV–TR* (American Psychiatric Association, 2000). The more data available about symptoms and functioning, the easier it is to reach a conclusion, that is, a diagnostic formulation, and the more certain one can be of that conclusion.

Inductive Reasoning

On the other hand, inductive reasoning involves reasoning from the specific to the general. Accordingly, this type of reasoning is essential in the process of developing the clinical, cultural, and treatment formulation components of a case conceptualization. The more data that are available (i.e., symptoms, social and developmental history, etc.), the more complex and difficult it is to develop and feel confident about a clinical formulation. The reason is that deriving a clinical formulation requires inductive reasoning. Unlike deductive reasoning, the inductive reasoning process involves synthesizing from a group of seemingly unrelated bits of data about symptoms, functioning, and history, a single unifying concept or theme that connects all of those disparate data into a meaningful explanation of why the client is experiencing these particular problems in this particular context at this particular time.

The following example illustrates the difficulty of finding a single unifying concept, which is the heart of inductive reasoning. Suppose you are playing a mind game that involves speculation. You will be given a series of clues—in the guise of items—and are asked to offer a series of guesses as to what they ultimately represent. First, you are given an iPod and a phone charger. You speculate their link or commonality is "electronic devices." Then you are given a book of crossword puzzles. Finding a commonality is a bit more challenging, but after a moment's reflection you say "things that entertain and pass the time." Next you receive a map and a bottle of water. The task has become much more difficult, but you suggest a more abstract guess or formulation: "They are all inanimate objects." Two other clues are then given: two parents and three children. It occurs to you that the concept that links all these items together is "family trip." Ten other clues are given, including snacks, sunglasses, and hand wipes, but you keep the same formulation: family trip, because in each instance the clues are consistent with, or confirm, your guess. You win the game because the answer was "family trip."

For many, the prospect of finding a common meaning among 15 or more discrete pieces of data might be daunting and even maddening. That is why having a clinical theoretical framework aids the process of developing a clinical formulation. Not only does a theoretical framework provide a way of meaningfully linking collected data together, it provides a map for eliciting and attending to selected pieces of data while "ignoring" other data. For instance, let's say that the theoretical framework of therapist #1 (an acknowledged master therapist) would have her elicit four pieces of data—parents, child, car, and map—for which the linking theme is "family trip." Compare this to therapist #2 (a beginning counseling practicum student) who, guided by no theoretical framework, collects all 15 pieces of data in no particular order. As is often the case, students and therapists with little or no training or experience in deriving clinical formulations tend to engage in premature closure. Thus, in the illustrated exercise, they might take the first three pieces of data presented and arrive at "things that entertain" as their formulation.

The task of synthesizing disparate pieces of data into a meaning and clinically useful case conceptualization is one that often seems beyond the capacity of many trainees. Whereas it is true that individuals with talent for analytic thinking and synthesis tend to approach the case conceptualization process with ease, ability, although necessary, is not sufficient. Training in case conceptualization is essential. Case conceptualization, particularly clinical formulation, is the requisite skill for effective treatment planning (Eells & Lombart, 2003). This skill is best acquired through didactic instruction, supervision, and continued practice. If training programs fail to provide opportunities for learning to conceptualize cases, and if faculty do not teach and model effective case conceptualization, trainees are less likely to develop effective treatment plans and interventions. The end result is that even though these future therapists might achieve some positive treatment outcomes with some clients, these outcomes will not be as great, nor will as many clients profit from their therapeutic encounters with such trainees and therapists.

Training programs can no longer excuse their failure to teach and foster case conceptualization competencies on the grounds that it is too complex and time consuming. There is convincing evidence to the contrary. Therapists who participated in a 2-hour training session were found to develop more accurate, precise, complex, and comprehensive clinical formulations compared to therapists without such training (Kendjelic & Eells, 2007). Furthermore, incorporating the competency of case conceptualization in a training program provides trainees the opportunity to demonstrate the capacity to integrate theory and practice, which may be the most elusive programmatic goal of therapy training.

Excellence in teaching case conceptualization should be a high priority for training programs, as trainees who have developed some competency in case conceptualization have developed one of the most valuable clinical competencies necessary for effective counseling practice (Falvey, 2001). This has been demonstrated in a growing number of studies. For instance, in comparing the clinical formulations of expert therapists, experienced therapists, and trainees, it was found that those considered expert therapists produced more comprehensive, systematic, complex, and elaborate formulations than experienced therapists or trainees. However, trainees were found to produce better quality clinical formulations than experienced therapists (Eells & Lombart, 2003; Eells, Lombart, Kendjelic, Turner, & Lucas, 2005).

Three Types of Case Conceptualizations

Three general types of case conceptualizations can be described and differentiated. The three are symptom-focused, theory-focused, and client-focused, and each is briefly described in this section.

Symptom-Focused Conceptualizations

This type of conceptualization derives from the medical and behavioral models of human behavior and is favored by managed care organizations and other third-party payers. It identifies symptomatology and functional impairment and then specifies treatment goals and associated interventions for reducing symptoms and increasing functioning. This symptom-focused approach to case conceptualization emphasizes measurable objectives that are stated in behavioral terms. The obvious limitation of this type of conceptualization is its focus on symptoms and its unstated assumption that only the "what" (diagnostic formulation) and "how" (treatment formulation) questions count and that the "why" question (clinical formulation) is unimportant and the answer is not clinically valuable. Such a symptom-focused approach to case conceptualization is believed to engender accountability and positive treatment outcomes because symptom-focused treatment goals are relatively easy to measure and monitor.

From an individual therapy perspective that recognizes individual psychodynamics are essential in understanding and changing behavior, a symptom focus is quite limiting. From a family therapy perspective, the symptom-focused approach is also viewed as limiting. Besides the behavioral family therapy models, systemic approaches have little interest in individual symptoms and tend to view individual symptoms as reflections of larger contextual dynamics. Despite these limitations, many clinics, inpatient, and residential treatment programs require this type of case conceptualization. There are several treatment planning manuals that emphasize this type of conceptualization (e.g., Jongsma, Peterson, & Bruce, 2006).

Theory-Focused Conceptualizations

Besides recognizing symptoms and impaired functioning, theory-focused conceptualizations can provide a compelling explanation for them. This type of conceptualization derives from a therapist's theoretical or therapeutic orientation, and this orientation serves as the basis for treatment goal setting and implementation. Thus, a theory-focused case conceptualization will reflect a dynamically oriented, existential-humanistic oriented, cognitively oriented, or one of many systemic approaches to therapy. Such a conceptualization involves "fitting" a specific theory to a client or client system (family members and/or significant others).

Not surprisingly, from a theory-focused perspective, the "why" question is the most important of the three primary, orienting questions of a case conceptualization (Sperry, 2005a). Beyond a mere description of symptoms and functioning, it is believed that the richness and texture of an individual's, a couple's, or a family's life can be more fully captured by a psychoanalytic, structural, intergenerational, solution-focused, narrative, theoretically guided explanation, (i.e., clinical formulation). Because the various theoretical orientations attend to intrapersonal, relational, cultural, systemic, and other contextual factors, the explanation of the source or cause of reported symptoms can aid both the therapist's and the client's or client system's understanding.

There is considerable value and support for theory-focused conceptualizations. First, trainees and practicing clinicians with specialized training in a given therapeutic orientation have been trained by instructors and supervisors to conceptualize human behavior through the prism of a particular theoretical framework. Thus, developing a clinical formulation can be compelling conceptually but also clinically useful in specifying treatment goals and selecting compatible treatment interventions for achieving goals above and beyond symptom relief.

91

The downside of theory-focused conceptualizations is that they are primarily therapist-centered and may not sufficiently reflect the client's or client system's own conceptualization of the problem or concern. The result can be limited client commitment to the treatment plan and process because the goals and plan are more meaningful to the therapist than the client.

Pattern-Focused Conceptualizations

The pattern-focused type of conceptualization derives primarily from the overall pattern representing the client and factors contributing to the client's distinctive style and mode of action and functioning. The four general factors or dimensions on which this approach to case conceptualization is based are presentation, precipitants or triggers, predisposition, and perpetuants or maintaining factors (Sperry, 2005a, 2010; Sperry, Gudeman, Blackwell, & Faulkner, 1992). In many respects, these four general factors are not unique, and some or all of them can be found in certain cognitive–behavioral approaches (E. Persons, 1989) and certain dynamic approaches (Levenson, 1995). In comparing this pattern-focused approach with theory-based approaches, commonalities are likely to be found with presentation and precipitants, whereas predisposition, or the reason why the client acts and functions in a particular way, will predictably differ based on the specific approach, for example, maladaptive beliefs and behaviors in cognitive–behavioral therapy (CBT) as compared to unconscious processes in dynamic approaches. This approach will be described and illustrated in a subsequent section of this chapter.

COMPETENCE IN CASE CONCEPTUALIZATIONS

Not all case conceptualizations are alike. As with other clinical processes, some case conceptualizations are more clinically useful than others. Anyone who has reviewed client charts quickly realizes that case conceptualizations vary widely in clinical utility from one therapist to another. Research indicates that master therapists develop significantly better conceptualizations than average therapists (Eells et al., 2005). So what does a reasonably competent case conceptualization look like? A highly competent one?

In the descriptions that follow, note that both the highly competent and reasonably competent case conceptualizations address the four case conceptualization components: diagnostic, clinical, cultural, and treatment formulation. In addition, highly effective conceptualizations demonstrate other characteristics. These include treatment focus, intervention strategy, and anticipation of obstacles or roadblocks to effective treatment outcomes. The point is that the more a case conceptualization approximates the characteristics of a highly competent case conceptualization, the more it is likely to facilitate highly effective treatment processes and outcomes.

Highly Competent Case Conceptualizations

A highly competent conceptualization is recognized by the following characteristics. It addresses the "what happened" question (diagnostic formulation statement), the "why did it happen" question (clinical formulation statement), the "what can be done about it" question (treatment formulation statement), and the "what role does culture play" question (cultural formulation statement). In addition, it anticipates treatment "obstacles" (e.g., resistance, transference, noncompliance), it specifies a clearly defined "treatment focus" and "intervention strategy," and it serves as the basis for "tailoring" interventions. It also serves as a guide to making and modifying treatment decisions, as the basis for maintaining an effective therapeutic alliance, and for planning and anticipating issues regarding termination. Finally, there is a high degree of coherence among sections of the written report containing the various components of the case conceptualization (Sperry, 2010). More specifically, this means that the treatment formulation directly reflects the clinical formulation and the diagnostic formulation. Finally, this conceptualization has considerable explanatory power and predictive value.

Reasonably Competent Case Conceptualizations

A reasonably competent conceptualization is recognized by the following characteristics. Like the highly competent conceptualization, it addresses diagnostic, clinical, cultural, and treatment formulation questions. Although there is also a reasonable degree of coherence among sections of the written case conceptualizations and among sections of the written report containing its various components, there are missing elements that are central to the highly competent conceptualization. Typically, whereas treatment goals are included, it is less likely that a clearly identified treatment focus and a treatment strategy are noted. Similarly, how treatment will be tailored to the client and what the obstacles are to achieving treatment targets and goals are less likely to be included. In short, these conceptualizations may have good to excellent explanatory power but little predictive value.

Noncompetent Case Conceptualizations

Conceptualizations in this category are deficient in several respects. First and foremost, such conceptualizations tend to be an extended description of clinical material rather than a clinically useful explanation of it because they failed to address the diagnostic, clinical, treatment, and formulation questions. As a result, treatment goals are unlikely to be sufficiently defined and focused. Because obstacles to achieving these goals are not anticipated, the clinician is likely to be surprised or dismayed with the course of treatment. Premature termination is likely because issues in the therapeutic alliance become problematic. There is also likely to be little or no coherence among sections of the written report containing the conceptualizations. Not surprisingly, this conceptualization has neither explanatory power nor predictive value.

FOUR COMPONENTS OF A CASE CONCEPTUALIZATION

A case conceptualization consists of four components: a diagnostic formulation, a clinical formulation, a cultural formulation, and a treatment formulation (Sperry, 2005a, 2010; Sperry et al., 1992). This section and chapter 6 describe and illustrate the diagnostic, clinical and treatment formulation. It also briefly describes the cultural formulation which will be detailed and illustrated in chapter 13.

Diagnostic Formulation. The diagnostic formulation provides a description of the client's presenting situation and its perpetuants, or triggering factors. It is a phenomenological description as well as a cross-sectional assessment of the client. It answers the "what" question (i.e., "What happened?"). This formulation usually includes a *DSM–IV* diagnosis.

Clinical Formulation. A clinical formulation provides an explanation of the client's presentation. It offers a rationale for the client's symptoms, concerns, functioning, and maladaptive personal and relational patterns. It answers the "why" question (i.e., "Why did it happen?"). The clinical formulation is the central component in a case conceptualization and serves to link the diagnostic and treatment formulations.

Cultural Formulation. A cultural formulation provides an analysis of social and cultural factors on the client's functioning. It answers the "What role does culture play?" question. Besides specifying the clients cultural identity and level of acculturation, it describes the influence and interaction of cultural dynamics with personality dynamics in the client's behavior and functioning.

Treatment Formulation. A treatment formulation provides an explicit blueprint for intervention planning. It is the logical extension of the diagnostic and clinical formulations and answers the "how" question (i.e., "How can it be changed?"). It contains treatment goals, treatment focus, and specific interventions and anticipates challenges and obstacles in achieving those goals.

THE ROLE OF ASSESSMENT IN CASE CONCEPTUALIZATION

Assessment is a prerequisite to developing a case conceptualization, and a comprehensive assessment is essential in developing a competent and clinically useful case conceptualization. Assessment organizes the content of the case conceptualization, focuses treatment goals, clarifies expectations about what can and what needs to change, and then defines the client's and the clinician's roles in the change process (Sim, Gwee, & Bateman, 2005). The irony is that while assessment influences the case conceptualization, at the same time the case conceptualization influences and guides the assessment process.

PERFORM A COMPREHENSIVE ASSESSMENT

A comprehensive assessment serves as the basis for identifying a diagnosis and developing a case conceptualization and treatment targets. Three approaches to such an assessment are diagnostic, theory-based, and pattern-based. An assessment is likely to be more complete or comprehensive if it includes at least two of these approaches.

Diagnostic Assessment

A diagnostic assessment is a focused assessment of the client and the current and developmental context influencing the client. The purpose of this assessment is to discover the answer to the question of what accounts for the client's concerns, distress, and/or diminished functioning for which the client seeks therapeutic assistance. A relatively complete diagnostic assessment interview can often be accomplished within the first 30 to 40 minutes of the initial session between client and therapist. However, the time frame necessary to complete such an evaluation may take considerably longer, depending on the client's previous history and treatment, sense of ease and trust of the clinician, language, and other psychological and cultural factors.

The focus of the diagnostic assessment is to gather information about the client that is clinically relevant to the treatment process and outcomes.

Table 5.2   Components of a Comprehensive Diagnostic Assessment

1. Presenting Problem and Context
2. Mental Status Exam
3. Developmental History, Personal, and Family Dynamics
4. Social History and Cultural Dynamics
5. Health History, Family History, and Previous Mental Health Treatment
6. Client Resources and Treatment-Promoting Factors
7. Explanatory Model, Treatment Expectations, and Treatment Readiness

This includes data on the client's current problems; current functioning and mental status; social, cultural, developmental, and medical history and health behaviors; and, particularly, the expectations and resources the client brings to therapy. Because cultural factors such as cultural identity, level of acculturation, and illness perceptions can influence the treatment process, it is imperative that these factors be identified. Chapter 13 describes and illustrates, in detail, the assessment of these and other cultural factors.

In the past few years, it has become the norm for nonmedical clinicians to collect relevant biological data in addition to psychosocial and cultural data pertaining to the client. For instance, it is important to elicit health history and health behavior data because a client who complains of anxiety symptoms may regularly ingest caffeine and other stimulants that could trigger, exacerbate, or even cause the anxiety symptoms experienced by the client. Similarly, the diagnostic assessment emphasizes client resources, such as the client's coping skills and support system, previous success in making changes, readiness and motivation for change, and treatment expectations. Table 5.2 summarizes key factors of a diagnostic assessment.

Case Example of a Diagnostic Assessment
The mental status examination is a key part of the diagnostic assessment. Following is the summary report of the mental status exam for the case of Geri.

> The client appears her stated age and is appropriately dressed and groomed. She is oriented to person, place, and time and cooperative with the evaluation. Her intelligence, language skills, and ability to abstract appears to be above average, consistent with individuals completing an associate's degree. Her mood is moderately depressed, while her affect is slightly constricted, but appropriate to the situation. No obvious perceptual or cognitive deficits are noted. Her memory for immediate, short-term, and long-term appears to be intact. She denies suicidal and homicidal ideation, intentionality, or plan currently. She does

admit to having had occasional thoughts that she might be better off dead, but dismisses them stating, "I'd never do it because it's against my religious beliefs." Her insight into her current situation is fair, and her judgment is adequate to good. (Sperry, 2010, p. 157)

Theory-Based Assessment

The second assessment approach is theory-based assessment. While diagnostic assessment can be useful in establishing a diagnosis based on grouping a client's symptoms into an ordered pattern that matches *DSM* criteria (American Psychiatric Association, 2000), a diagnosis does not provide an understanding of the client. Neither will the results of such an assessment reveal the personality dynamics or relational dynamics that activated that particular set of symptoms. Nor can a diagnosis indicate why or how these symptoms began when they did or what maintains them. On the other hand, a theory-based assessment can provide such an understanding, and it is for this reason that theory-based assessment is a valuable component of a comprehensive assessment strategy.

The type of information gathered in a theory-based assessment differs depending on the given theoretical orientations. For instance, CBT-based assessment is likely to focus on questions such as "What particular dysfunctional thoughts lead to the client's specific emotional and behavioral problems? How, then, does problematic emotion and behavior feedback into the maintenance of dysfunctional cognition?". Assessing such theory-based information is essential to developing a CBT-based case conceptualization (Ledley et al., 2005).

In psychodynamically oriented approaches, such as time-limited dynamic psychotherapy, the focus of inquiry is more likely to be on eliciting a story or narrative of recurrent maladaptive interpersonal patterns that reflect dysfunctional mental working models and their reenactment in the therapeutic alliance (Strupp & Binder, 1984). Accordingly, identifying the cyclical maladaptive pattern is essential to the dynamic case conceptualization as well as providing a treatment focus (Levenson, 1995).

In contrast to the assessment strategies in CBT and the psychodynamic approaches, the systemic approaches, such as brief strategic therapy and solution-focused therapy, focus assessment primarily on solutions and attempted solutions. Accordingly, they pose questions such as "What have you tried? How did you do that? Exactly what did you say? Did it work?" (Quick, 2008).

Table 5.3   Assessment Considerations Among Therapeutic Approaches

Approach	Focal Considerations
Dynamic	Reenactment of past in present; unconscious conflicts and defense mechanisms; *TLDP: cyclical maladaptive patterns*
Cognitive–behavioral	Automatic thoughts; distorted beliefs; core maladaptive schemas; maladaptive behaviors and faulty learning (relationship of stimulus and consequences); behavioral deficits and excesses; *CBT/CBASP: interpretations and behaviors in terms of actual and desired outcomes*
Systemic	Patterns of couple or family interaction; boundary problems; *SFT: identifying positive exceptions to problems, and client strengths and unique resources*
Integrative	Various behavioral patterns, personality dynamics, and systemic dynamics; Adlerian psychotherapy: early recollections, family constellation, and other indicators of lifestyle convictions *CBT/CBASP, cognitive–behavioral therapy/cognitive–behavioral analysis system of psychotherapy; SFT, solution-focused therapy; TLDP, time-limited dynamic psychotherapy.*

Finally, in an integrative approach such as Adlerian psychotherapy, the focus of assessment is primarily on the identification of lifestyle convictions (i.e., maladaptive beliefs and schemas) and on family patterns. This can be accomplished with such assessment devices as the elicitation of early recollections, family constellation, and other indicators of lifestyle convictions (Dinkmeyer & Sperry, 2000). This information is considered essential to establishing an Adlerian case conceptualization. Table 5.3 identifies the focus considerations in assessment for these theoretical approaches.

Case Example of Theory-Based Assessment

Following is an example of theory-based assessment for the case of Geri. Eliciting early recollections is the primary assessment technique in Adlerian psychology from which a client's lifestyle convictions (i.e., core maladaptive beliefs or schemas) can be derived. Here is a summary of Geri's early recollections.

Her earliest childhood memory involved seeing her infant brother for the first time when he was 4 years old. She recalls her parents had just returned from the hospital. Geri had been frightened staying with her aunt and not knowing where her mother had gone. Her mother lovingly placed her baby brother in Geri's old crib, while Geri's father said that the birth was the happiest day of his life. Geri is told to stop whining and asking questions about the baby and to go outside to play or she would be punished. She remembers running outside crying and hiding in her tree fort until it got dark. She felt frightened and confused. Geri described intense feelings of humiliation and rejection following the birth of a younger brother. A second childhood memory is reported when she was about 7 years old. Geri recalls answering her friend's question about why Geri's father wasn't at church the day before. She said it because he had drunk too much the night before. Geri's mother overheard this and spanked her for being a bad girl and "airing the family laundry in public." Geri ran to her bedroom crying and feeling unloved and hurt for being unjustly punished for answering her friend's question. In short, it appears she experienced her parents' harsh treatment of her after her brother's birth as the nullification of the sense of specialness and nurturance that she had previously enjoyed from her parents. (Sperry, 2010, p. 158)

Pattern-Based Assessment

The third approach to a comprehensive assessment is pattern-based assessment. Unlike diagnostic and theory-based assessments, this type of assessment is based on pattern identification, where pattern refers to the characteristic way of perceiving, thinking, and responding, which is reflected in the client's presentation as well as related precipitants, predispositions, and perpetuants (Sperry, 2005a, 2010; Sperry et al., 1992). A pattern is assessed by identifying the sequence of the client's presenting symptoms, precipitants, and predisposing factors that when activated result in the client's response. By also identifying maintaining factors, the client's basic *modus operandi* or pattern is revealed. A brief description of these four factors is summarized in Table 5.4.

While this map has some similarity with the cognitive–behavioral formulation model (Tarrier & Calam, 2002) and the cyclic maladaptive pattern model (Levenson, 1995; Strupp & Binder, 1984), there are some differences. The primary difference is that unlike the others, this map is neither theory-based nor theory-bound. Another difference and a primary advantage of this assessment approach is that it provides a generic model or map for developing a case conceptualization. As a generic model, it provides a framework in which any theoretical orientation can be incorporated, specifically in providing a theoretically based "explanation" for the client's symptoms and situation (as the predisposing

Table 5.4 Four Factors in Pattern-Based Assessment

Presentation	The client's characteristic response to precipitants; type and severity of symptoms, history, course of illness, diagnosis, and relational behaviors
Precipitant	The triggers or stressors that activate the pattern resulting in the presentation
Predisposition	All the intrapersonal, interpersonal, and systemic factors, including attachment style, biological factors, and trauma, which can render a client vulnerable to maladaptive functioning
Perpetuants	Also referred to as maintaining factors, these are processes by which a client's pattern is reinforced and confirmed by both the client and the client's environment

factor). In other words, all three of the other factors (presentation, precipitant, and perpetuant) are the same; only the predisposing factor differs, irrespective of the theoretical orientation. The advantage of this general model is that trainees and experienced clinicians can relatively easily develop a coherent case conceptualization and pick a best "fit" explanation from the various theoretical approaches in specifying the predisposing factor. Chapter 6 further elucidates and illustrates this model.

Case Example of Pattern-Based Assessment
With regard to the case of Geri, the following is a summary of a pattern-based assessment.

> In terms of *presentation*, Geri presented with depressive symptoms and increased social isolation. The *precipitant* involved Geri's supervisor discussing the possibility of job promotion for Geri. *Relevant predisposition or predisposing factors* included demanding, critical, and emotionally unavailable parents and Geri's anticipation that she would be teased and criticized by a new boss. Specifically, her core beliefs are as follows: Geri's self-view is that she is inadequate and unable to function "normally"' around others. Her worldview is that other people are and will be critical and demanding of her. Thus, her basic life strategy is to stay safe by maintaining distance from others and "testing"' others' trustability. In terms of *perpetuants*, Geri's avoidant, isolative pattern of living alone, her exquisite shyness, and her generalized pattern of isolating herself even when among others serve to maintain and to further reinforce this avoidant pattern.

CONCLUDING NOTE

The capacity to perform a comprehensive assessment and the capacity to develop and utilize a case conceptualization are two essential clinical competencies associated with the core competency of intervention planning. Of the two, this chapter emphasized the comprehensive assessment competency and its importance to case conceptualizations. Yet, the bulk of this chapter was devoted to introducing case conceptualization and its centrality to all the intervention core competencies. It was also noted that training programs have no excuse for not teaching case conceptualizations, as research convincingly demonstrates that even limited formal training fosters the development of this competency. The next chapter will emphasize three components of a case conceptualization: the diagnostic formulation, the clinical formulation, and the treatment formulation.

6

Case Conceptualization and Treatment Planning

Chapter 5 introduced case conceptualization and the role of a comprehensive assessment in developing case conceptualizations. It made the case that training, even brief training, fosters the development of competencies associated with case conceptualizations (Kendjelic & Eells, 2007). It emphasized that irrespective of their theoretical orientation, therapists need to develop an understanding of their clients' problems, personality, and pathology. It was noted that case conceptualizations assist therapists in choosing treatment strategies and interventions that guide treatment. Even though some therapists develop conceptualizations that guide their practice with specific clients, it was not expected that these conceptualizations would be explicitly articulated in a written document or report. Increasingly, such written reports are being expected of all therapists, including those in training. Finally, it was noted that developing effective case conceptualizations engenders confidence in the therapist, which is then communicated to the client, and which further increases the client's trust and confidence in both the therapist and the therapy; this is called clinician credibility (Sue & Zane, 1987). This confidence is often what leads the client to recovery (Hill, 2005).

The chapter continues the discussion of case conceptualization begun in Chapter 5, by describing and illustrating three of the four components of a case conceptualization: diagnostic formulation, clinical formulation, and treatment formulation. The remaining component, cultural formulation, requires a detailed assessment of cultural factors and entails different formulation considerations. These factors and considerations are the focus of a separate chapter, Chapter 13.

This chapter begins with a listing of additional clinical competencies associated with intervention planning. Next, it describes and illustrates the diagnostic formulation, the clinical formulation, and the treatment formulation. Then, it briefly describes a clinical case report, which includes the comprehensive assessment and components of the case conceptualization.

CASE CONCEPTUALIZATION AND INTERVENTION PLANNING COMPETENCIES

The previous chapter addressed two essential clinical competencies associated with the core competency of intervention planning. This chapter addresses four additional clinical competencies related to the case conceptualization.

Specify an Accurate Diagnostic Formulation

This competency involves the capacity to specify a descriptive statement about the client's presentation, its precipitants, and its acuity and severity. It often includes applicable *DSM* diagnoses.

Develop an Effective Clinical Formulation

This competency involves the capacity to develop a compelling explanation for the client's presenting problem and maladaptive pattern.

Develop an Effective Treatment Formulation

This competency involves the capacity to develop a coherent intervention or treatment plan, with appropriate treatment goals and treatment focus, and which anticipates likely obstacles and challenges to achieving these treatment goals.

Prepare an Integrative Clinical Case Report

This competency involves the capacity to draft a compelling and coherent clinical report that accurately describes the client's presentation and case conceptualization along with treatment considerations.

SPECIFYING AN ACCURATE DIAGNOSTIC FORMULATION

A diagnostic formulation is a descriptive appraisal about the nature and severity of the client's current presenting symptoms and functioning (Sperry, 2005b). The diagnostic formulation aids the clinician with immediate clinical considerations: Is the client's presentation primarily psychotic, personality-disordered, or neurotic? Is the client's presentation primarily organic or psychogenic in etiology? Is the client's presentation so acute and severe that immediate intervention such as hospitalization or intensive outpatient treatment is needed? The diagnostic formulation is essentially a phenomenological description and cross-sectional assessment of the client. Such a formulation answers the "what" question (i.e., "What happened?"). The diagnostic formulation includes a five-axes *DSM–IV* diagnosis as well as addressies immediate treatment considerations and disposition based on acuity, severity, and concerns about safety issues.

DSM–IV–TR Diagnoses

The *DSM–IV–TR* is the current diagnostic system, consisting of 17 diagnostic categories and accounting for some 300 mental disorders (American Psychiatric Association, 2000). The *DSM–IV–TR* is a five-axes system of diagnosis which reflects a client's biological, psychological, and social functioning. Making a *DSM* diagnosis on Axis I (symptom disorders) and Axis II (personality disorders) involves identifying disorders based on how well the client's symptoms and functioning matches diagnostic criteria for specific *DSM* disorders. Axis III specifies any health condition that may trigger or exacerbate an Axis I disorder. Axis IV is for specifying contributory stressors, and Axis V specifies the client's overall level of functioning on a scale of 1 to 100.

Case Example of a Diagnostic Formulation

The following case example describes what is often contained in a diagnostic formulation statement. For the case of Geri, the diagnostic formulation contains this narrative statement and a five-axes *DSM* diagnosis.

> Geri meets six of the nine criteria for Major Depressive Disorder, Single Episode, Moderate Severity (296.22) in *DSM–IV*. The criteria met include (1) depressed mood most of the day, nearly every day for more than 2 weeks; (2) markedly diminished interest or pleasure, also called anhedonia; (3) weight loss of 10 pounds and appetite loss; (4) insomnia with some early morning awakening; (5) fatigue and low energy; and (6) diminished concentration. She does not meet criteria for recurrent suicidal ideation or for excessive or inappropriate

guilt. Geri also meets four criteria of the seven criteria for Avoidant Personality Disorder: (1) She avoided the job promotion because of fear of criticism and disapproval; (2) she showed restraint within intimate relationships because of fear of being teased and ridiculed; (3) she was preoccupied with being criticized and rejected in social situations; and (4) she views herself as socially inept and personally unappealing (i.e., obese) and inferior to others. In short, Geri's history and initial evaluation were consistent with major depressive episode. In addition, she met criteria for avoidant personality disorder.

DSM-IV-TR Five-Axes Diagnosis

I.   Major Depressive Disorder, Single Episode, Moderate (296.22)
Occupational Problem (V62.2)

II.   Avoidant Personality Disorder (301.82)

III.   None

IV.   Limited support system; job stressor

V.   GAF 54 (at time of initial evaluation); 71 (highest in past 12 months)

DEVELOPING AN EFFECTIVE CLINICAL FORMULATION

By contrast, a clinical formulation is a more explanatory and longitudinal appraisal than the descriptive and cross-sectional appraisal of the diagnostic formulation. Clinical formulations attempt to provide a rationale for the development and maintenance of a client's symptoms and dysfunctional life patterns (Sperry, 2005b). Most clinical formulations are theory-based, meaning the basic explanation is informed by a particular theoretical orientation such as dynamic, cognitive–behavioral, systemic, solution-focused, Adlerian, or other. As is described in a subsequent section, clinical formulations can also reflect a pattern-based or generic model. Clinical formulations answer the "why" question (i.e., "Why did it happen?"). In short, the clinical formulation articulates and integrates the intrapsychic, interpersonal, and systemic dynamics to provide a clinically meaningful explanation of the client's pattern—that is, the predictable style of thinking, feeling, acting, and coping in stressful circumstances— and a statement of the causality of the client's behavior (Sperry et al., 1992). Not surprisingly, the clinical formulation is the central component in a case conceptualization and serves to link the diagnostic and treatment formulations (Cucciare & O'Donohue, 2008).

Essentially, the clinical formulation is an appraisal of the client's predominant predispositions and perpetuants. As such, this formulation is derived largely from the developmental, social, and health histories, which provide clues about likely predisposing factors. Predispositions reflect the client's biological, psychological, and social vulnerabilities. These include specific psychological vulnerabilities, such as a history of trauma, insecure attachment, maladaptive beliefs or schemas, as well as biological vulnerabilities, such as a personal or family history of substance abuse or dependence, other Axis I or Axis II conditions or history of suicide, or deficits in self-management or social skill. For example, it would be important to identify vulnerabilities to depression or panic disorder, or to specific social or environmental factors such as drinking friends or living or working in a place hostile to immigrants.

Perpetuants serve to "protect" or "insulate" the client from symptoms, conflict, or the demands of others. For example, individuals who are shy and sensitive to rejection may gravitate toward living alone because it reduces the likelihood that others will criticize or make interpersonal demands on them. Because the influence of these factors seem to overlap, at times it can be difficult to specify whether a factor is a predisposition or a perpetuant. These might include personal or social skill deficits, hostile work environment, living alone, and negative responses of others.

A pattern is an explanation that links and makes sense of the client's presentation, precipitants, predispositions, and perpetuants. The pattern may be situation-specific but is most often longitudinal. A situation-specific maladaptive pattern is an explanation that is unique to the current situation only. On the other hand, a maladaptive longitudinal pattern, called an "ongoing pattern," is an explanation that is common to the current situation as well as to previous situations. In other words, it reflects a lifelong pattern that can provide a reasonable explanation or set of reasons for the client's situation. A theory-based assessment can inform the search for such an explanation or reasons given that theoretical orientations provide prototypical explanations. Table 6.1 summarizes the explanations associated with the most common theoretical orientations.

Case Example of a Clinical Formulation

Here is a statement of the clinical formulation for the case of Geri. Note that the presentation, precipitants, predisposition, perpetuants, and ongoing pattern are identified in parentheses in the narrative.

> Geri's increased social isolation and depressive symptoms (presentation) seem to be her reaction to the news of an impending job transfer and promotion (precipitant), given her

Table 6.1   Essential Features of Clinical Treatment Formulations

Dynamic Therapy	Personal and/or relational problems or symptoms result from *unconscious conflict* (classical), *defensive reactions* (ego), *faulty object representations* (object relations), *pathogenic schema* (control-mastery), or *cyclic maladaptive patterns* (time-limited dynamic psychotherapy). *The focus of treatment* is on experiential and relational learning to engender new experiences and insight.
Behavior Therapy	Personal and/or relational problems or symptoms result from *faulty learning* or *skill deficits,* which result in *maladaptive behavior patterns* in contrast to normal, adaptive behavior, which is learned through reinforcement and imitation. The *focus of treatment* is to identify (ABC: antecedent–behaviors–consequences), eliminate maladaptive behaviors and patterns, and learn more effective behavior and patterns.
Cognitive Therapy	Personal and/or relational problems or symptoms result from *faulty beliefs* and/or *maladaptive schemas.* The *focus of treatment* is to become aware of limiting automatic thoughts, confront faulty beliefs with contradictory evidence, and develop more adaptive beliefs through various restructuring methods (e.g., Socratic questioning, examining the evidence, reattribution).
CBT	Personal and/or relational problems or symptoms result from *maladaptive behavior patterns* and the *faulty beliefs and maladaptive schemas* that inform them. The *focus of treatment* is to modify both behavior patterns and cognitions using various cognitive and behavioral strategies.
CBASP	Personal and/or relational problems or symptoms result from the *discrepancy between an individual's desired outcome and what actually occurs* because specific thoughts or interpretations and behaviors have gotten in the way of achieving the desired outcome. The *focus of treatment* is to analyze those thoughts and behavior and replace them with thoughts and behavior that can achieve the desired outcome.
Adlerian Therapy	Personal and/or relational problems or symptoms result from *mistaken lifestyle convictions* about self, others, and the world, *which reflect,* in part, *one's family constellation.* The *focus of treatment* is to analyze and process situations involving specific mistaken lifestyle convictions and maladaptive behaviors.
Solution– Focused Therapy	Personal and/or relational problems or symptoms result from *continuing to apply solutions that don't work* rather than solutions that do work. The *focus of treatment* is to find exceptions and implement solutions.

history of avoiding situations in which she might be criticized, rejected, and otherwise harmed (predisposition). Her reaction and predisposition can be understood in light of demanding, critical, and emotionally unavailable parents, strong parental injunctions against making personal and family disclosure to others, and the teasing and criticism of peers. Thus, she came to believe that life was demanding, others were critical and harsh, that she was inadequate, and that it was necessary to socially isolate and conditionally relate to others (ongoing pattern). Given these maladaptive beliefs, her biological vulnerability for depression, her lack of social skills, her tendency to "test" others' trustability, and the resulting life-long pattern of conditionally relating to others, it is not unreasonable to conclude that her current depression and increased isolation were triggered by news of a job promotion, news that others would find uplifting rather than depressing. Although presumably this pattern was adaptive when Geri was a child, it appears to be quite maladaptive now and may negatively impact the treatment process, at least initially. (Sperry, 2010, p. 160)

DEVELOPING AN EFFECTIVE TREATMENT FORMULATION

A treatment formulation follows from a diagnostic and clinical formulation and serves as an explicit blueprint governing treatment interventions. Informed by the answers to the "What happened?" and "Why did it happen?" questions, the answer to the "how" question (i.e., "How can it be changed?") forms the basis of the treatment formulation (Sperry, 2005a). A well-articulated treatment formulation provides treatment goals, a treatment plan, and treatment interventions and anticipates treatment obstacles and challenges. It also should provide a prognosis, that is, a prediction of the likely outcomes of treatment. In short, the treatment formulation is a plan that specifies the goals and targets of treatment along with a strategy for tailoring, focusing, and implementing the treatment goals and targets.

Essential aspects of a treatment formulation are treatment goals and focus, and predictions about obstacles to implementing the plan. This section describes these aspects in more detail.

Treatment Goals and Focus

The treatment focus serves as a guide or action plan for the therapist to achieve the treatment goal. The treatment focus is not the same as the treatment goal but rather derives from it and the theoretical orientation that informs the therapist's work. For instance, if the stated treatment goal is to change certain maladaptive beliefs and the clinician's orientation is CBT, the focus of treatment will likely be to analyze and process situations in which specific maladaptive beliefs are operative (Sperry, 2010).

Predicting Obstacles and Challenges

Anticipating obstacles and challenges to the implementation of the treatment plan is indispensable in achieving treatment success. The test of an effective case conceptualization is its viability in predicting the obstacles and challenges throughout the stages of therapy, particularly those involving resistance, ambivalence, transference enactments, and issues that complicate maintaining treatment gains and preparing for termination (Sperry, 2010).

Case Example of a Treatment Formulation

The following treatment formulation statement for the case of Geri includes these essential aspects of a treatment formulation as well as the specific treatment target and interventions.

Given that this is her first [depressive] episode, that her current GAF is 54, and her baseline GAF is around 71, the degree of severity of the depression would likely be considered "moderate" rather than "severe." Since the probability of suicide is low (i.e., Geri's denial of any suicide ideation as well as religious prohibition), hospitalization is not deemed a necessity at this time. Rather, treatment could be initiated on an outpatient basis.

In terms of readiness for treatment, Geri agreed she was moderately depressed and was willing to collaborate with a combined treatment involving both therapy and medication. When offered an appointment with the clinic's psychiatric consultant for medication evaluation, she refused, saying she was uncomfortable with someone she didn't know. She did agree to meet with her personal physician, Dr. Winston, for such an evaluation later this week. If medication is indicated, Dr. Winston would monitor it; the clinic's psychiatrist agreed to consult with him as needed. Individual outpatient therapy will begin immediately with this counseling intern and will be time-limited psychotherapy. Because Geri does not appear to be particularly psychologically minded and has moderate skill deficits in assertive communication, trust, and friendship skills, she will likely require a more problem-focused, here-and-now psychotherapy. It was also discussed and mutually agreed that a skill-oriented, psychoeducation group was the treatment of choice for increasing her relational and friendship skills and decreasing her social isolation.

Treatment goals include reducing depressive symptoms, increasing interpersonal and friendship skills, and returning to work and establishing a supportive social network there.

The treatment focus will be threefold: (I) reduction of her depressive symptoms and social isolation with medication, social skills training, and behavioral activation strategies; (2) cognitive restructuring of her interfering beliefs of self, others, and the world, as well her coping strategy of shyness, rejection sensitivity, distrust, and isolation from others; (3) collaboration with Geri's work supervisor and the human resources director in order to accommodate Geri's return to a more tolerable work environment. Treatment will be sequenced with CBT beginning immediately. Later, group therapy with a psychoeducational emphasis will be added because of her significant skill deficits in assertive communication, trust, and friendship skill.

Some obstacles and challenges to treatment can be anticipated. Given her avoidant personality structure, ambivalent resistance is likely. It can be anticipated that she will have difficulty discussing personal matters with therapists and that she will "test" and provoke therapists (both individual and group) into criticizing her for changing or canceling appointments at the last minute and being late, and that she'll procrastinate, avoid feelings, and otherwise "test" the therapist's trustability. Once trust in the therapist has been achieved, she is likely to cling to the therapist and treatment, and thus termination may be difficult unless her social support system outside therapy is increased. Furthermore, it is expected that she will have difficulty with self-disclosure in group therapy settings. Transference enactment is another consideration. Given the extent of parental and peer criticism and teasing, it is anticipated that any perceived impatience and verbal or nonverbal indications of criticalness by the therapist will activate early transference.

Geri has agreed to an initial treatment of eight 45-minute individual sessions combining medication and CBT, with the sessions focused on symptom reduction and returning to work. With Geri's signed consent, her job supervisor will be contacted about the necessity of a familiar, trusting social support in order for Geri to return to work. Aware that her pattern of avoidance would make entry into and continuation with group work difficult, the plan is for the individual sessions to serve as a transition into group. (Sperry, 2010, p. 161)

PREPARE AN INTEGRATIVE CLINICAL CASE REPORT

A clinical case report is a clinical document that describes the results of the diagnostic assessment of a client and specifies a plan of treatment consistent with the presenting problem and the case conceptualization (Sperry, 2010). An integrative clinical case report is a clinical case report that is internally consistent, formulation-based, and cogent and coherent. It is an essential competency that trainees and therapists can find considerably challenging. The clinical case report is not simply a document containing the facts of the case or a summary of all the data collected in the diagnostic assessment interview. Instead, it is more like a legal brief, which makes the case for a specific diagnosis, a specific case conceptualization, and a specific treatment plan. Rather than being a nontheoretical description of a client's life and concerns, the clinical case report should be a theoretically informed explanation and tailored treatment prescription. Furthermore, the report should be internally consistent, meaning that the diagnostic formulation and *DSM* diagnoses should directly reflect the presenting problem and be directly addressed in the treatment goals and focus specified in the treatment formulation. Finally, a clinical case report should be a compelling portrait of the client's present, past, and likely future if the treatment plan is accomplished. The portrait description should be sufficiently cogent and detailed so that other clinicians could "pick" the client out of a lineup.

Components of an Integrative Clinical Case Report

Typically, a clinically useful, integrative clinical case report will include the following sections.

1. *Presenting Problem:* Describes presenting symptoms, diminished functioning, and/or concern; addresses the "why now" question; specifies the link between *precipitant(s)* and *presentation*; reflects the clinician's awareness of client personality dynamics on interview process
2. *Mental Status Exam:* Specifies appearance, orientation, language, and intelligence; mood and affect; perceptual and cognitive status; memory; harm potential to self and others; insight; and judgment
3. *Developmental History:* Contains information about parent–child, sibling, and parent–parent relationships; family values; self-management and relational capacity and functioning
4. *Social History and Cultural Dynamics:* Describes school and job performance; social and intimate relationships; acculturation; ethnic and gender identity
5. *Health History and Health Behaviors:* Discusses health status, medical treatment; any previous individual or family therapy; response to medications; substance use or abuse
6. *Client Resources:* Includes previous change efforts, level of readiness and motivation for change, and social support system
7. *Diagnostic Formulation:* Provides a succinct statement that adequately addresses the "what" question; refers to specific *DSM* criteria for Axis I and II, indicated in narrative (optional)

8. DSM-IV-TR *Diagnosis:* Specifies a five-axes diagnosis that accurately reflects the presentation; 5-digit codes are present and appropriate
9. *Clinical Formulation:* Adequately links presentation, precipitant, perpetuants, and predisposing factors in a convincing explanation of "why" the client thinks, feels, and acts (maladaptive pattern) as he or she does in terms of CBT, dynamic, or other theoretical approach
10. *Cultural Formulation:* Identifies level of acculturation, ethnic and gender identification (if relevant); links presentation to culture versus psychological factors; anticipates impact of cultural factors on treatment process
11. *Treatment Formulation:* Specifies a treatment plan that is consistent with clinical formulation; a treatment focus and treatment goals and corresponding treatment interventions; treatment strategy; culturally sensitive interventions, if indicated; predictions of likely obstacles (resistance, transference, alliance ruptures, ambivalence) and other challenges over the phases of treatment

CONCLUDING NOTE

In continuing the discussion of Chapter 5 on the core competency of intervention planning, this chapter emphasized three more clinical competencies associated with intervention planning. It described and illustrated diagnostic formulation, clinical formulation, and treatment formulation, as well as the clinical case report. A key point of both chapters is that the case conceptualization is the central construct and process for understanding not only the core competency of intervention planning but also the core competencies of intervention implementation and intervention evaluation and termination.

Section V

Core Competency 4: Intervention Implementation

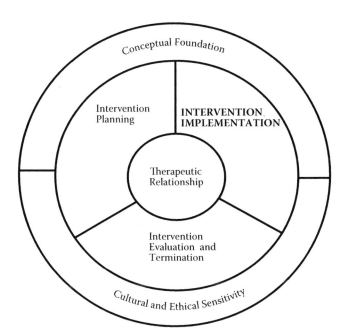

7

General Implementation Strategy

Based on a realistic and appropriate treatment formulation, the clinician's next task is to implement the intervention plan. Presumably, this process is guided by an implementation strategy reflecting the treatment focus. This chapter addresses establishing and maintaining the treatment focus and handling treatment-interfering factors that impede the process of implementation. Basically, a treatment focus is the clinician's central therapeutic emphasis within and across sessions. Guided by the clinician's conceptual map, the treatment focus is analogous to utilizing a spotlight, which illuminates a circumscribed area, rather than a floodlight, which illuminates a broad area. This focus and a therapeutic strategy (i.e., an action plan) guide and give direction in achieving treatment goals. Not surprisingly, focused treatment fosters the therapeutic change process and is associated with positive treatment outcomes (Goldfried, Raue, & Castonguay, 1998). Although establishing such a focus is relatively easy, maintaining it can be quite challenging. Because clients' lives are complex and changing, they will want to discuss and process recent issues and concerns unrelated to the treatment focus. The challenge is for the therapist to "track" the treatment focus and "stay the course" despite digressions from the initial focus. "There is now a convincing body of empirical evidence indicating that therapist ability to track a problem focus consistently is associated with positive treatment outcomes" (Binder, 2004, p. 23). Needless to say, highly competent and effective therapists are considerably better at "staying on track" than are trainees and less effective therapists.

This chapter begins with a brief description of the general implementation strategy competencies, followed by definitions of key terms. It then discusses the essential competencies of establishing and maintaining a treatment focus. Next, it describes treatment focus, treatment goal, and treatment strategy considerations in the three major therapeutic approaches. Then, it describes the competency of recognizing and resolving therapy-interfering factors. Finally, a case example illustrates key points in the chapter.

GENERAL IMPLEMENTATION STRATEGY COMPETENCIES

This chapter addresses three essential clinical competencies associated with the core competency of intervention implementation.

Establish a Treatment Focus

This competency involves the capacity to establish a focus for treatment based on the case conceptualization. The treatment focus, along with the treatment strategy, provides a map and direction for achieving specific treatment goals and treatment targets.

Maintain a Treatment Focus

This competency involves the capacity to maintain the focus for treatment. In the process of tracking this focus, it may be necessary to reestablish it or revise it as indicated.

Recognize and Resolve Therapy-Interfering Factors

This competency involves the capacity to anticipate, recognize, and resolve various client, therapist, client–therapist relationship, and treatment factors that are impediments to treatment progress.

DEFINITION OF KEY TERMS

Following are definitions of key terms relevant to the three general implementation strategy competencies.

Treatment Focus.   Treatment focus is the central therapeutic emphasis of a given therapeutic approach. For example, the therapeutic focus of behavior therapy is changing behavior, whereas the therapeutic focus of cognitive therapy is changing cognitions, whether they be automatic thoughts, beliefs, or schemas.

Treatment Goals.   Treatment goals are the specific outcomes clients wish to achieve in psychotherapy. Such goals are typically mutually agreed upon by client and therapist at the outset but may change over the course of treatment. For example, a basic treatment goal may be to reduce and eventually eliminate depressive symptoms or compulsive checking and counting behaviors.

Treatment Strategy.   A treatment strategy is an action plan involving the use of specific intervention methods to achieve a treatment goal or target. For example, the treatment strategy of behavior therapy is to utilize behavior modification methods, such as response prevention, to achieve the goal of reducing compulsive checking and counting behaviors.

Therapy-Interfering Factors.   Therapy-interfering factors cover a broad range of client, therapist, client–therapist relationship, and treatment factors that are operative both within and between therapy sessions which impede treatment progress. Ambivalence and treatment refusal are examples of treatment-interfering factors.

ESTABLISHING A TREATMENT FOCUS

Why is a treatment focus necessary? For many years, therapists have been trained to give undivided attention to the client's words, feelings, body language, and concerns. Clinical lore has encouraged and supported this view of practice with the dictum "follow the client's lead," which means that the clinician should provide a nondirective and nonevaluative environment, show interest and respond empathically to whatever the client wants to talk about, and refrain from giving advice. This viewpoint is more attuned to the open-ended, long-term approach to therapy of yesterday than it is to the accountability-based, time-limited therapy that third-party payers are currently willing to authorize. Today more than ever, the expectation is that therapists must focus treatment. Accordingly, therapists must also learn "selective attention" or be overwhelmed by the multiple therapeutic rabbits that can be chased. Treatment focus not only provides direction to treatment, it also "serves as a stabilizing force in

119

planning and practicing therapy in that it discourages a change of course with every shift in the wind" (Perry, Cooper, & Michels, 1987, p. 543).

How does a therapist specify a treatment focus? The treatment focus is identified in the process of developing a case conceptualization, and the basic theme of the case conceptualization further specifies the focus. Not surprisingly, because the case conceptualization is based on a conceptual map reflecting a theoretical orientation, the focus of treatment is also likely to be informed by the therapist's theoretical orientation. For example, in the interpersonally oriented dynamic therapies, the focus is usually the client's maladaptive interpersonal style or pattern. In the cognitive–behavioral therapies, the focus is typically maladaptive thinking and behaviors, and so on.

MAINTAINING THE TREATMENT FOCUS

Research is beginning to support the clinical observation that treatment outcomes are significantly improved when therapists maintain a treatment focus (Binder, 2004). However, maintaining that focus is not as easy as it may sound. After all, the lives of clients are complex and changing, and it is to be expected that they will want to discuss and process recent issues and concerns that arise between sessions. Oftentimes, these concerns are not directly related to the focus of treatment. The challenge is for therapists to "track" a treatment focus along "with flexibly modifying the content as new information arises and digressing from the initial focus as circumstances dictate" (Binder, 2004, p. 100). This section briefly discusses the value and challenge of maintaining a focus for treatment.

The primary reason for "staying on track" is that treatment is more likely to achieve the specified treatment goals than if the focus is lost. However, "staying on track" is a considerable challenge for therapists given that clients have a tendency to "shift," consciously or unconsciously, the focus of discussion to a less threatening or less demanding topic or concern. Accordingly, treatment can easily be slowed or derailed in ways that shift the therapeutic momentum away from the primary treatment focus. In such situations, therapists face a number of "decision points" in any session in which they can choose various ways of responding to their client. The choice they make directly affects whether the treatment focus is maintained or not.

Needless to say, staying on track can be a significant challenge, particularly for trainees and beginning therapists. Often because of inexperience and limited familiarity with refocusing strategies, beginning therapists tend to respond to client "shifts" with empathic statements or clarifying questions that may take the session in a direction different from that of the primary treatment focus. It is only as therapists become aware of such shifts or "decision points" that they can attempt to reestablish the primary focus of treatment.

The reality is that clients do chase "therapeutic rabbits" and that the therapist's role often involves discouraging "a change of course with every shift in the wind" (Perry et al., 1987). Typically, clients shift away from the focus because of being overwhelmed with a new life stressor, and they feel somewhat compelled to process that situation and reduce their distress. Other times, clients are hesitant to keep on track because resolving a problem or conflict means they would have to face difficult relationships or responsibilities in their lives for which symptoms or conflicts have safeguarded them from facing. Or, they may want to change but are ambivalent. With supervision and experience, therapists learn to discern the various reasons clients divert from the treatment focus.

TREATMENT FOCUS CONSIDERATIONS IN THERAPEUTIC APPROACHES

Treatment focus is determined primarily by the theoretical orientation that informs treatment. Not surprisingly, the treatment focus differs accordingly. This section briefly describes how each of the three major therapeutic approaches views treatment focus, the related considerations of basic treatment goals, and treatment strategy.

Dynamic Therapies

The primary goals of treatment are to foster insight, enhanced interpersonal problem solving skills, and corrective emotional and interpersonal experiences. The basic treatment focus is the client's current most important troublesome relationship pattern. The principal treatment strategy is to utilize therapeutic relationship to facilitate new relational experiences and understandings that replace the maladaptive pattern (Levenson, 1995). Besides the traditional dynamic interventions of clarification, confrontation, and interpretation, this approach utilizes incisive questioning, transference analysis, coaching, skill training, and practice (Binder, 2004). Chapter 8 will discuss these and other interventions in considerable detail.

Cognitive–Behavioral Therapies

The focus of treatment is the pattern of maladaptive thinking and behavior. The basic goal is to modify maladaptive thoughts and behaviors. Cognitive restructuring is a primary strategy to help clients recognize maladaptive beliefs and behaviors, teach them skills for changing these, and perform in-session and between-session (homework) exercises to generalize this new learning. Various intervention tactics such as Socratic questioning, role-playing, reattribution, exposure, systematic desensitization, eye movement desensitization, and rehearsal are employed with this strategy (Dobson, 2001; Goldfried & Davison, 1994; Leahy, 2003; F. Shapiro, 2001). Psychoeducation and replacement of thoughts and behaviors are basic intervention strategies in cognitive–behavioral analysis system of psychotherapy (CBASP; McCullough, 2000). Ongoing practice is usually necessary to change ingrained, maladaptive thoughts and behaviors. Chapter 9 will discuss these and other interventions in considerable detail.

Systemic Therapies

The basic goal, focus, and strategy of treatment in a particular systemic therapy are a reflection of its general case conceptualization. For example, in the solution-focused therapies, the basic goal of treatment is consistent with its general conceptualization: the smallest changes needed for clients to function better (de Shazer, 1985). The treatment focus is quite simply eliciting solutions, and the primary therapeutic strategies are goal clarification and solution amplification (de Shazer, 1985; de Shazer, Dolan, Korman, Trepper, McCullom, et al., 2007). Therapeutic interventions of this approach include exceptions, the miracle question, presuppositional questions, and scaling. Chapter 10 will discuss these and other interventions in considerable detail.

Tables 7.1 and 7.2 summarize these three approaches relative to treatment focus and related considerations.

Table 7.1 Treatment Focus and Goals of Common Therapeutic Approaches

Approach	Basic Treatment Goal	Treatment Focus
Cognitive–behavioral	Develop more adaptive beliefs and behaviors	Change maladaptive beliefs and behaviors
Dynamic	Achieve insight and new interpersonal experiences (TLDP)	Change maladaptive patterns of interpersonal relating through new experiences and insight
Systemic	Facilitate the smallest changes needed for better functioning (SFT)	Find exceptions and implement solutions

Note: SFT, solution-focused therapy; TLDP, time-limited dynamic psychotherapy.

Table 7.2 Basic Therapeutic Strategy of Common Therapeutic Approaches

Approach	Therapeutic Strategy
Dynamic	Clarify → confront → interpret → work through
TLDP	Identify the cyclic maladaptive pattern → modify pattern with various dynamic and other interventions
Cognitive–behavioral	Identify maladaptive beliefs and behaviors → modify beliefs and behaviors
Cognitive	Identify and clarify maladaptive beliefs → confront → restructure → practice
CBASP	Analyze situation → confront discrepancy of actual vs. desired outcomes → remediate
Systemic	Identify dysfunctional family pattern → modify pattern
Solution-focused	Clarify problem → amplify solution → assess → intervene: validate, compliment, provide suggestions

Note: CBASP, cognitive–behavioral analysis system of psychotherapy; TLDP, time-limited dynamic psychotherapy.

RECOGNIZING AND RESOLVING
THERAPY-INTERFERING FACTORS

The concept of "treatment-interfering behaviors" was developed by Linehan (1993) to describe behaviors that clients bring to bear within and between sessions which impede the progress of therapy. Common treatment-interfering behaviors include failure to attend sessions consistently, failure to keep to contracted agreements, arguing with the therapist, refusal to engage in conversation, and behavior that oversteps therapist limits. Although this designation gives a name to a class of behaviors that are problematic in therapy, Linehan's designation focuses entirely on the client. However, clinical observation suggests that besides clients, other factors can and do impede treatment progress. Accordingly, the broader designation *therapy-interfering factors* is used in this book. It includes client behaviors but also recognizes the influences of the therapist, client–therapist relationship, and intervention factors as impediments to treatment progress.

Effective treatment requires that therapists anticipate, recognize, and resolve these factors. Savvy therapists anticipate therapy-interfering factors from the first contact with the client, particularly while eliciting the developmental and social history. The potential of such therapy-interfering factors, as well as other potential treatment obstacles and challenges, should be included in the case conceptualization. Subsequently, appropriate resolution strategies can be contemplated before these factors emerge in the treatment process. This chapter provides a listing of the various interfering factors. Then, it illustrates various strategies for resolving specific interfering factors.

Types of Therapy-Interfering Factors

Four types of therapy-interfering factors are observable in clinical situations. They are client, therapist, client–therapist relationship, and treatment factors. A listing of specific factors is listed for each category. Judith Beck (1995, 2005) and Ledley and colleagues (2005) provide useful descriptions and strategies for dealing with several client factors that interfere with therapy. Chapter 4 of this book addresses client resistance and ambivalence. Chapters 5 and 6 of this book provide descriptions and strategies for dealing with client–therapist relationship problems, particularly alliance ruptures and transference enactments.

Client Factors

There are a number of client factors. These include Axis I and II pathology, particularly personality disorder dynamics, as well as high levels of reactance. Also included are refusal and outright resistance, ambivalence, treatment-interfering beliefs, and treatment-interfering behaviors exhibited both in session (e.g., missing appointments or arriving late, insisting they cannot change or that treatment won't make a difference) and between sessions (e.g. failing to do homework or engaging in self-harmful behaviors).

Therapist Factors

There are several such therapist factors. Most common are countertransference, therapist errors, inaccurate case conceptualization, and failure to use the case conceptualization to guide treatment. Also included are the inappropriate use of interventions, failure to provide adequate informed consent, and therapist conflict of interests, boundary violations, or breach of confidentiality.

Client–Therapist Relationship Factors

Factors related to the alliance between client and therapist that can impede treatment progress are few in number but have significant impact on the course of treatment and are major contributors to premature termination. These include strains and ruptures of the therapeutic alliance and transference–countertransference enactments which were described in Chapter 4.

Treatment and Intervention Factors

Various treatment factors can also seriously impede treatment progress. These include both internal and external factors. Examples of internal factors are infrequency of sessions, scheduling problems, session format, outside noise or distractions, poor lighting, difficulty finding parking, or temperature.

External factors include a client's comorbid medical conditions and/or limited finances, difficulties making referrals or use of adjunct resources, as well as a limited social support network or living in a toxic environment that fosters relapse with the use of drugs, for example.

TREATMENT FAILURE IN PSYCHOTHERAPY

The reality of clinical practice is that some, actually most, clients succeed in psychotherapy whereas others, a small number, fail. Such failure is known as treatment failure (TF). A reasonable question is how likely are competency-trained psychotherapist to experience TF? Adequately answering this question requires some discussion of the phenomenon of TF with regard to its recognition, its causality, research reducing and preventing it, and the therapist's level of expertise with regard to competencies.

Recognition of Treatment Failure

It is somewhat surprising that TF is not an entry in any of the common psychology and psychotherapy dictionaries. The closest these dictionaries come to addressing TF is under "Treatment Resistance" in the *APA Dictionary of Psychology*. The second usage of that term is "failure of a disease or disorder to respond positively or significantly to a particular treatment method" (VandenBos, 2007, p. 956). Under "Treatment Response" in a psychiatry dictionary, there is a short phrase: "failure to achieve a treatment response to the first treatment modality" (Ayd, 1995, p. 644). In contrast, medical practitioners seem to recognize that TF is a fact of life, and medical dictionaries are more likely to define TF. For example, TF is defined as "the inability of a medical therapy to achieve the desired result" (Google, 2010) and as "a measure of the quality of health care by assessing the unsuccessful results or consequences of management and procedures used in combating disease" (*Mondofacto Online Medical Dictionary*, 2010). It is noteworthy that these medical definitions emphasize that failure is attributed to a procedure or intervention.

In short, psychology dictionaries apparently do not consider TF in psychotherapy sufficiently worthwhile to define. Likewise, it is difficult to find psychotherapy texts that even address TF, suggesting that recognition of TF in psychology and psychotherapy is limited. Such limited recognition implies that TF does not occur or seldom occurs, that it is of little consequence to the field, and/or that it exists but therapists do not identify it early enough to make a difference.

Research on Treatment Failure

On the other hand, TF is a recognized research entity and, although the professional literature on TF in psychotherapy is small, it is increasing.

That research indicates that treatment failure is a significant problem in psychotherapy. Some 5% to 10% of clients worsen while in treatment, and another minority shows no response (Slade, Lambert, Harmon, Smart, & Bailey, 2008). A sobering finding of this research is that when treatment failure does occur, it is often a surprise to clinicians. The reality is that clients at high risk for TF can be predicted, prior to the first therapy session, with specific clinical outcome measures (Sperry, Brill, Howard, & Grissom, 1996). What is the cause of TF in psychotherapy? TF is multiply determined, meaning that it has many different causes, for example, low readiness or motivation, differing expectations between client and therapist, limited client resources, strains or ruptures in the therapeutic alliance, or inability of the therapist to focus treatment, to name a few. Unlike the medical definitions that TF is largely "caused" by a therapy intervention itself, TF in psychotherapy is just as likely to be due to a therapist being unaware of, or nonresponsive to, a client's preference for a different treatment modality or therapist style in delivering an intervention.

However, by responding to such high-risk clients in a timely fashion, TF can be avoided. Research demonstrates convincingly that monitoring client treatment response on a frequent basis reduces, and can even eliminate, TF (Lambert, 2010). Such monitoring is accomplished with comprehensive outcome measures, such as COMPASS, Polaris MH, or OQ-45, or with ultra-brief measures such as the Session Rating Scale and the Outcomes Rating Scale (Sperry, 2010).

Competency-Based Training and Treatment Failure

The basic premise of this book is that highly effective therapy is highly competent therapy. Accordingly, highly competent therapists are unlikely to experience TF because they have presumably assessed factors that promote and interfere with treatment and then continually monitor treatment response.

In fact, 10 of the 20 essential clinical competencies of psychotherapy have direct bearing on preventing or reducing early indications of treatment failure (Sperry, 2010). They are assess readiness and foster treatment-promoting factors; recognize and resolve resistance; recognize and resolve transference–countertransference; recognize and resolve therapeutic alliance ruptures; perform an integrative diagnostic assessment; plan treatment interventions and predict obstacles; recognize and resolve

127

treatment-interfering factors; modify maladaptive cognitions, behaviors, affects, and interpersonal relations; monitor progress and modify treatment accordingly; and evaluate progress and prepare clients for termination, which involves developing a relapse prevention plan.

It might be argued that a specific competency called something like "reverse treatment failure" should be added to the list of essential clinical competencies. There are two facts that are relevant: The first is that TF is multiply determined, and the second is that research finds that irrespective of its cause, TF can be prevented by ongoing assessment of clients' response to treatment. Accordingly, there is no need for an additional competency assuming that therapists, with a minimal level of competence in monitoring client response to treatment, do, in fact, monitor client response and upon recognizing the potential for TF, respond to it in a manner that reduces that risk.

Returning to the question posed at the beginning of this section, the answer is "not very likely." Highly effective therapists "anticipate" the client's response to treatment including the likelihood of treatment failure, and then tailor treatment and foster a therapeutic alliance that lessens its likelihood.

CASE ILLUSTRATION OF TREATMENT FOCUS, GOAL, AND STRATEGY

We return again to the case of Geri specifically to review the treatment focus, treatment goal, and treatment strategy. This case was informed by the cognitive–behavioral therapy orientation. Thus, the overall treatment goal was for Geri to develop more adaptive beliefs and behaviors. From this overall goal, three specific treatment targets were specified: reduce depressive symptoms, increase interpersonal relating and friendship skills while decreasing social isolation, and modify maladaptive beliefs regarding nontrust, defectiveness, and isolation. The treatment focus was established as changing maladaptive beliefs and behaviors. The therapeutic strategy was to utilize cognitive restructuring and behavior modification to achieve these treatment targets. Specific interventions employed were social skills training; behavioral activation strategies; cognitive restructuring of her interfering beliefs of self, others, and the world; and medication management targeting the biological basis of her depressive symptoms.

CONCLUDING NOTE

This chapter addressed the general clinical competencies associated with implementing a treatment plan. It described the clinical value of establishing and maintaining a treatment focus in achieving positive treatment outcomes. It also discussed the need for anticipating, recognizing, and resolving the inevitable treatment-interfering factors that impede the process of implementation and limit the attainment of the treatment goal and treatment targets. In Chapters 8 through 10, specific intervention implementation strategies are described for the dynamic, cognitive–behavioral, and systemic approaches.

8

Dynamic Strategies and Interventions

It is the rare trainee and practicing therapist who possesses both a solid understanding of psychodynamic theory and the capacity to effectively and appropriately apply common dynamic interventions. Obviously, this observation is not applicable to trainees enrolled in formal psychodynamic training programs. The point is that there is relatively limited education and training in psychodynamic theory and even less on dynamic intervention strategies in most graduate psychotherapy programs. Even books on psychodynamic psychotherapy offer little in the way of descriptions and illustrations of dynamic interventions (Gabbard, 2004; McWilliams, 2004). Nevertheless, the dynamic orientation has developed a number of potent therapeutic interventions that have considerable applicability in nondynamic psychotherapeutic situations. Trainees and practicing therapists with a therapeutic repertoire that includes knowledge, skills, and experience in using such strategies and interventions have a distinct advantage over those without. In this era of integrative therapies, as well as in the current culture of competency-based practice, those endeavoring to practice psychotherapy competently and effectively would do well to expand their therapeutic repertoires to include some dynamic interventions. It is interesting that the psychiatry profession, even though it is pharmacologically focused, mandates psychodynamic training for psychiatrists. Currently, psychiatry residency training programs require graduates to demonstrate basic competency in both cognitive–behavioral therapy (CBT) and psychodynamic therapy (Plakun et al., 2009).

This chapter is part of the section of the book on the core competency of intervention implementation, and it focuses on the clinical competency of dynamic strategies and interventions. The chapter has two main sections: The first is focused on insight-promoting strategies and interventions, and the second is focused on relationally oriented strategies and interventions. These strategies and interventions can be useful to therapists who are not enrolled in, or who have not completed, a certification program in a dynamic therapy approach.

INSIGHT-PROMOTING STRATEGY AND INTERVENTIONS

A basic strategy in many dynamic therapies is one involving the interventions of clarification, confrontation, interpretation, and working through. This strategy and related interventions are the basis of the therapeutic process in the older dynamic therapies, particularly those that emphasize insight (Bibring, 1954). As noted in Chapter 7, the basic therapeutic strategy for promoting insight is clarify → confront → interpret → clarify → confront → interpret, and so on. "Working through" is the process of repeating the sequence until the interpretation, or a variant of it, is accepted and internalized.

Clarification

Clarification means to see things in a clearer way, and it refers to matters that are conscious or subconscious, but not unconscious (Bibring, 1954). It is a response designed to enhance the therapist's and the client's understanding of the client's conscious and subconscious emotions and cognitions. Clarification can assist clients in becoming clearer about their feelings, attitudes, thoughts, behavior patterns, and perceptions, and therapists utilize it to highlight any contradictions among these.

Clarification is a process involving the use of empathic listening, empathic questioning, and empathic reflection. Empathic questions and reflections may pertain to immediate in-therapy thoughts and feelings or extra-therapy thoughts and feelings. In both situations, clarification aims to illuminate the nature of the client's subjective experience and establish a therapeutic alliance based on accurate empathy, concern, and unconditional regard. Some examples of clarifications are "I take it you were referring to your father's career expectations of you when you were an adolescent and not your own. Is that right?" "You are feeling very sad and helpless about the death of your friend's son."

Confrontation

Confrontation is a subcomponent of clarification (Meissner, 1980). It is a therapeutic response in which a therapist points out certain aspects of a client's cognitive, emotional, or behavioral reactions that are incomplete, contradictory, exaggerated, or unrealistic. Confrontation can come across as intrusive, whereas clarification appears as more neutral on the part of the therapist. Therefore, it is advisable to precede a confrontation response with a statement validating those aspects of the client's feelings, thoughts, and behaviors that are realistic responses to internal or external events.

Confrontations promote therapeutic change be challenging defensive distortions, and set the stage for interpretations. Here are some examples of therapeutic confrontations: "I agree with you that your daughter is sometimes irresponsible, but I do not agree that she is never responsible." "I can understand why you are angry with parents who can be very strict. But, it seems your anger can be excessive at times and makes it difficult for you to problem solve with them." "I hear your words saying 'yes' but I see you shaking your head 'no' as you say them. That seems to be a contradiction." "Your husband's attitude is a major factor in your marital problems. But, your attitude is an equally important factor."

Interpretation

Unlike clarifications and confrontations, interpretations deal strictly with unconscious material (Bibring, 1954). They are inferential hypotheses about the link between a client's behavior, conscious emotions, or conscious cognitions and his or her subconscious or unconscious emotions or cognitions. Interpretations are often preceded by one or more clarifications. There are three kinds of interpretations: dynamic, genetic, and transference. Data on which interpretations are based include overt verbal and nonverbal behavior, conscious thoughts and feelings, and dreams.

Dynamic Interpretations

Dynamic interpretations, also called clinical interpretations, are focused entirely on present reality. Some examples of this type of interpretation are "My sense is that beneath your anger is much hurt." "I suspect that you feel depressed because the self-critical side of you is telling you that you are worthless."

Genetic Interpretations

Genetic interpretations point to or suggest connections between the present and past. There are usually three elements to this type of interpretation: a confrontation or empathic reflection, a clarification of the pattern, and a guess as to its origins (Greenson, 1967).

For instance, when a client is silent, the therapist might offer this interpretation: "It seems difficult for you to speak about your feelings (empathic reflection). You have had similar problems with your wife as well as your work supervisor (pattern refection). Maybe you are afraid that others will take advantage of you if they knew how you were feeling (guess as to origin: silence because of a fear)". Other examples of this type of interpretation are "When your wife is emotionally distant, it could well touch off some very painful feelings in you about how emotionally distant your mother could be when you were growing up." "When your mother took sick recently perhaps it reminded you of when she was hospitalized when you were a child and how frightening that was for you."

Transference Interpretations

Transference interpretations are similar to genetic interpretations. Transference interpretations focus on the client's conscious and subconscious thoughts and feelings about important current relationships and the connection between these relationships and important, early life relationships in the client's family of origin, usually with parents. Common in therapy are client transferences involving the therapist, which the therapist may interpret when the timing is optimal. An example of this type of interpretation is "It seems like you feel quite hurt and angry about my going on vacation. Maybe a part of the reason you're feeling hurt and angry about me leaving is that your parents left you alone many times when you were a small child."

Insight

Insight is a process in which clients acquire conscious awareness of previously unconscious thoughts, feelings, or behaviors (Moore & Fine, 1968). Historically, insight has been viewed as the primary source of change in the dynamic therapies. Insight is now understood as either emotional or intellectual. Emotional insight, which is characterized by the new awareness containing both affective and cognitive components, is contrasted with intellectual insight, in which there is no affective component. Emotional insight is considered a significant factor in therapeutic change.

The new awareness resulting from affective insight may to be related to intrapsychic events such as thoughts and feelings or to interpersonal events such as relational behavior. Insight is mistakenly understood as applying to an awareness of past events. Actually, for insight to result in change, the awareness must be about the immediate present, even when a particular insight relates to events from the past as with experiences in the family or origin. Insight about the past can be helpful only if it promotes a new and heightened awareness of current emotional, cognitive, or behavioral reality (D. Shapiro, 1989).

Working Through

Therapists' interpretations are often not accepted and internalized by clients, at least initially. However, the technique of "working through" enables clients to move from rejection of an interpretation or mere intellectual acceptance of it to an emotionally meaningful insight that can lead to permanent change. In other words, working through is the process wherein repeated experiences of insight lead to lasting internal changes as resistance is overcome (Greenson, 1967). One major insight rarely results in lasting change; instead, clients face situation after situation in which they need to recognize, adapt, and apply the new awareness.

Like insight, effective working through consists of both an emotional and a cognitive component. The emotional component involves two related processes. The first is repeated exposure to anxiety-producing feelings, thoughts, images, memories, or sensations in a safe environment. Such repeated exposure results in anxiety reduction through the process of desensitization. The second is the repeated experience of emotional catharsis in which emotions such as sadness, guilt, shame, or rage are experienced and expressed in the context of an accepting and validating

135

therapeutic alliance. Awareness and nontraumatic expressions of these emotions help in reducing their intensity and promoting expression of the cognitive factors that trigger their arousal. The cognitive component of working through involves an increased understanding of the subconscious cognitive distortions, maladaptive schema, and irrational conflicts that are the basis of the emotional and behavioral dysfunction. Increased awareness, resulting in part from ongoing interpretations, fosters the development of more adaptive cognitive processes.

Corrective Emotional Experience

Franz Alexander and Thomas French (1946) described the corrective emotional experience as a central factor in therapeutic change. They contended that it is not sufficient for a client to understand, through insight, an early life traumatic experience. For true change to occur, the insight must be followed with a corrective experience. *Corrective emotional experience* means "to reexpose the patient, under more favorable circumstances, to emotional situations which he could not handle in the past. The patient, in order to be helped, must undergo a corrective emotional experience suitable to repair the traumatic influence of previous experiences" (Alexander & French, 1946, p. 66).

Historically, corrective emotional experience referred specifically to the positive effects of experiencing the discrepancy between how clients expected a therapist to react to them regarding an important life issue or event (e.g., in a critical manner) and how the therapist actually responded to them about the issue or event (e.g., in a supportive manner). Today, the term also has a more general meaning. It refers to all aspects of the therapeutic process that allow clients to experience an unexpected form of relational interaction that can help in healing a previously maladaptive pattern. Therapists can employ one or both of these understandings of the corrective emotional experience in therapy; that is, they can foster a corrective experience by actively processing clients' specific relational expectations, or, in a more general way, they can foster a caring, positive therapeutic alliance.

The value of this more general understanding should not be underestimated. Experiencing a therapist's caring, empathy, concern, and unconditional acceptance may be the first and most important corrective emotional experience in the lives of many clients. This experience can continue to occur throughout the therapeutic process as therapists respond to them in a manner that is respectful, accepting, and caring—often the opposite of their own parents or parental figures. Furthermore, corrective emotional experiences can occur outside therapy as clients begin discovering that, because of their corrective experiences with their therapists, others respond to them differently than in the past. In short, the genuine relationship between clients and therapists, and its constancy, often serves as an ongoing corrective emotional experience that can generalize to others.

RELATIONAL-ORIENTED STRATEGY AND INTERVENTIONS

This section describes some intervention strategies utilized in time-limited dynamic psychotherapy (TLDP) and other relationally oriented dynamic therapies. Note that some of these interventions are similar to ones discussed in the previous section.

Therapeutic Strategy

Implementation of TLDP interventions is not dependent on a specific set of techniques, but rather on a therapeutic strategy that fosters experiential interpersonal learning (Levenson, 2004). Because the treatment focus is on experiential interpersonal learning, conceivably interventions from any theoretical orientation (cognitive, behavioral, experiential, etc.) could be utilized. In other words, "any intervention (even psychodynamic standbys such as clarification and interpretation) must be assessed with regard to how much it might alter the interpersonal interchange in an undesirable direction or reenact the patient's cyclical maladaptive pattern" (Levenson, 2004, p. 169). In short, intentional pragmatism could be said to characterize the practice of TLDP.

New Experiences

In TLDP, therapists endeavor to achieve two basic therapeutic goals with clients: new experiences and new understandings. New experiences, akin to corrective emotional experiences, refer to a set of focused experiences throughout the course of therapy in which clients gain a different appreciation of self, of therapist, and of their interaction. These new experiences emphasize the affective–action component of change and are designed to undermine or interrupt the client's maladaptive interactive pattern. The therapist provides clients the opportunity to disconfirm their interpersonal schemas, promoting a corrective emotional–relational experience. This type of corrective experiential learning is a critical factor in lasting change, and such experiential endeavors can occur with the therapist or with others in the lives of clients. Such emotionally intense processes result in highly charged affective learning and allow progress to be made more quickly. How do therapists foster this experiential learning? "Specifically, a therapist can promote a new experience by selectively choosing from all of the helpful, mature, and respectful ways of being in a session those particular aspects that would most undermine a specific patient's dysfunctional style" (Levenson, 1995, p. 42). These experiences must be designed to help disrupt, revise, and improve the client's cyclical maladaptive pattern (Levenson, 2004).

For example, a female client's maladaptive relational pattern was to be shy and retiring, which was fostered by the criticism, humiliation, and ridicule of two alcoholic parents. During the sixth session, the client told a joke, while nervously wringing her hands. The therapist listened attentively, laughed politely, and did not interrupt her. For this client, the new experience was to be able to be the center of attention and not be criticized or humiliated by the therapist when the client was vulnerable. In this example, the therapist's response provided the client an opportunity to disconfirm the client's lifelong, maladaptive interpersonal schemas, specifically her expectations of others and the responses or actions of others toward her. Change was promoted by altering her basic relational schemas, which then reverberated to influence her self-view.

New Understandings

The second goal of TLDP is to provide new understandings—insight—by helping clients identify and comprehend their maladaptive pattern as it occurs. This goal focuses more specifically on cognitive changes in contrast to the emotional changes in new experiences. This new understanding may occur with the therapist or with others in their lives. To facilitate such a new understanding, the therapist points out repetitive patterns that have originated in experiences with past significant others, with present significant others, and in the here-and-now with the therapist (Binder, 2004). Therapists' judicious disclosing of their own reactions to clients' behaviors can also prove beneficial (Strupp & Binder, 1984). Clients begin to recognize how they have similar relational patterns with others in their lives, and this new perspective enables them to examine their own role in perpetuating these maladaptive interactions.

Although new experiences and new understanding have been presented as separate goals, they are actually two aspects of the same experience of change. In other words, new experiences are not fleeting events, because they contain cognitive elements of understanding of self and others. At the same time, new understandings are not mere intellectualizations, because they contain experiential and affective elements.

Working Through

In maladaptive relational patterns, "working through" involves unlearning old patterns and learning more adaptive ones until they become ingrained. Because a single insight is unlikely to bring lasting change, clients need to continually recognize, adapt, and apply new awareness and new responses until the adaptive pattern is fully incorporated. In neuroscience terms, clients endeavoring to develop new ways of responding need to relearn or strengthen activation of a higher number of adaptive neural circuits (Viamontes & Beitman, 2006). Working through begins when clients decrease the time between arguments and making up with their significant other. This process continues as they shorten their arguments and find more adaptive ways of discussing issues. Working through ends when couples both anticipate and recognize potentially problematic issues and find healthier ways of resolving differences before conflicts escalate. As clients practice maintaining these new relational patterns, more adaptive neural circuits are strengthened, further increasing the likelihood that the more adaptive relational pattern will take over.

Coaching and Practice

In the past, the primary intervention strategy in the dynamic therapies involved transference analysis and evaluation of transference–countertransference patterns (Binder, 2004). In time-limited forms of dynamic therapy, however, there is increasing emphasis on clients' relationships in the real world and in assisting clients in developing relational skills that permit them to continue their therapeutic work on their own. As a result, many have advocated for the incorporation of active strategies in dynamic therapy, including cognitive–behavioral interventions (Magnavita, 1997; Wachtel, 1993).

In brief interpersonally oriented dynamic therapies, therapists can function as a coach or mentor on relational issues. This often involves teaching and facilitating the use of interpersonal skills. Accordingly, effective dynamic therapists coach their clients in the acquisition of generic interpersonal skills by means of subtle questions and comments about the client's life experience that contain subtle structuring elements (Wachtel, 1993). Binder (2004) describes such a coaching strategy. It begins with identifying with the client a central theme of their maladaptive relational pattern. Then, the therapist explicitly encourages the client to look for evidence of this basic theme in a particular relationship. The next step is to "freeze the action," wherein the client identifies himself or herself in the maladaptive pattern. Then the client is helped to consider healthier alternative behavior and thinking. Finally, the client is encouraged to act differently.

Practice is a requisite for lasting change. "If therapeutic change is conceived as the development or enhancement of generic interpersonal skills, particularly around a central issue, then the primary means of achieving this change is through practice in using these skills" (Binder, 2004, p. 193). Relational experiences outside of the therapeutic relationship become the client's primacy focus for practicing relational skills acquired in therapy sessions. Practice leads to internalization, and "the cumulative impact of internalizing the corrective interpersonal experiences that occur in outside relationships hopefully serves to consolidate the new mental models and corresponding adaptive interpersonal patterns that the patient has been attempting to implement" (Binder, 2004, p. 196).

CONCLUDING NOTE

The effective and competent practice of psychotherapy requires the capacity to utilize conceptual maps, as well as therapeutic strategies and interventions, that match clients' needs and expectations. Presumably, this means that therapists will occasionally work with clients for whom dynamic interventions may be indicated as adjunct to the primary treatment. For this and other reasons, therapists would do well to develop some level of competence with dynamic interventions. At this time, only psychiatry training programs require graduates to demonstrate minimum competency in psychodynamic therapy. Although other mental health professional organizations do not yet, and may not, require specific competency in dynamic therapy for trainees, presumably these professional organizations will expect mental health workers to have some familiarity with dynamic interventions.

9

Cognitive–Behavioral Strategies and Interventions

Cognitive and behaviorally oriented interventions are probably the most commonly utilized ones in counseling and psychotherapy practice today. While surveys find that most psychotherapists identify eclecticism as their primary theoretical orientation, cognitive–behavioral therapy (CBT) is identified as the second most common (Norcross, 2005). Furthermore, therapists who identify with other therapeutic orientations also utilize cognitive and behavioral interventions. For example, a number of dynamically oriented theorists and therapists advocate the incorporation of cognitive–behavioral interventions in the course of dynamic therapy to accomplish specific therapeutic targets such as behavior change and interpersonal skill development (Binder, 2004; Frank, 1999; Magnavita, 1997; Wachtel, 1993).

This chapter describes many of the most commonly utilized cognitive and behavioral interventions. The first section focuses on a description common cognitive interventions including cognitive restructuring, which may be the key therapeutic strategy among the cognitive approaches. The second section focuses on a description of common behavioral interventions.

COGNITIVE INTERVENTIONS

This section describes a basic cognitive therapeutic strategy as well as a number of common cognitive interventions. These interventions can be useful in both CBT and non-CBT treatment contexts.

Cognitive Strategy of Cognitive Restructuring

Cognitive restructuring is one of the basic cognitive strategies for helping clients identify, challenge, and modify maladaptive and distorted beliefs so they become more adaptive (Meichenbaum, 1977). Cognitive restructuring is often considered the first step when using cognitive–behavioral strategies. It assists clients in becoming aware of both automatic thinking patterns and their influence on self and others; changing the way they process information and behavior; and learning to modify their beliefs about self, others, and the world. There are various techniques utilized in restructuring such beliefs; these techniques include Socratic questioning, examining the evidence (i.e., pro–con analysis), cognitive disputation, reattribution (i.e., modifying attributional style), and cognitive rehearsal (Wright et al., 2006).

Self-Monitoring

Clients can be taught to record their thoughts, feelings, and behaviors toward problem situations. This process not only provides useful information but also helps the client to take some control over their life situations by keeping a record (Kanfer, 1970). Whereas some clients easily engage in this record keeping, others need prompting and encouragement. It has been found useful to show clients that such personal record keeping is similar to the process of analysis that occurs in therapy. By doing the process on their own, they are taking one of the first steps toward becoming their own therapist. The intervention involves clients making a written notation of the situation, their thoughts, their feelings, and their resulting behavior.

Identifying the Strength of Beliefs

Using a scaling technique to determine the strength of a belief is a simple and valuable intervention (J. Beck, 1995). Therapists can ask clients to rate the strength of their old belief and then their new belief. For example, old belief: Because I didn't get the biggest raise, I'm not successful (55%); new belief: Money is only one way to measure success (75%). A belief can seldom be reduced completely, but scores below 30% are usually sufficient. Next, the focus shifts to creating self-enhancing thoughts that challenge, or are incompatible with, the self-defeating ones. These may involve situational coping statements or positive self-statements.

Dysfunctional Thought Record

The dysfunctional thought record, also known as the thought record, is a four-column chart used to identify and rate clients' dysfunctional thinking (A. T. Beck et al., 1979; J. Beck, 1995). In a way, the thought record combines elements of both self-monitoring and identifying the strength of beliefs interventions. Clients are taught in session to use a four-column chart to identify the situation, negative feelings, automatic negative thoughts, and more adaptive thoughts. Between sessions, clients are encouraged to record and track these same data on a daily basis. The thought record can be a potent intervention for inducing cognitive change.

1. *Identify the upsetting situation.* In the first column, clients describe the event or problem that is upsetting them. For example, "studying for advanced statistics test."
2. *Identify negative feelings.* In the second column, clients specify their negative feeling, for example, sad, angry, frustrated, anxious, guilty, or hopeless. Then, they rate the negative emotion on a scale from 1% (least) to 100% (most). For example, "I'll never master this stuff. It's totally beyond my comprehension" (95%).
3. *Identify negative thoughts.* In the third column, clients specify the negative thought or thoughts associated with their negative feelings. They identify what they are saying to themselves about the problem and write these thoughts in the third column and record how much they believe each one between 0 (not at all) and 100% (completely). For example, "80%."
4. *Identify adaptive thoughts.* In the fourth column, clients specify an adaptive or more rational response to the situation. Then they rate how much they believe between 0 (not at all) and 100% (completely). For example, "I just need to pass the test, I don't need to get an A. I'll just learn the key points and won't sweat the fine details" (70%).

145

Cognitive Disputation

A key intervention in cognitive restructuring is cognitive disputation, which is disputation of irrational or maladaptive beliefs. This intervention involves the challenging of such beliefs with a series of logical and empirical refutations (Ellis, 1962). In utilizing this intervention, therapists actively challenge clients' irrational beliefs and teach them to challenge their irrational thinking between sessions. Such challenges are of two types: logical debate and testing by comparing beliefs with external evidence. For example, in logical debate, challenging begins with a question such as "What does it matter if life is not precisely the way you want it to be?" In testing with external evidence, the challenge of irrational beliefs begins with a question like "What specific evidence is there for this belief?" Through a series of such challenging questions and refuting statements, the therapist helps clients develop more adaptive beliefs and rational thinking. This intervention can be effective when two conditions are met. First, a positive and strong therapeutic alliance is already established, and second, the client has the cognitive capacity for postformal thinking, or consequential thinking.

Examining the Evidence

Examining the evidence is a cognitive therapy intervention to help clients to question and to challenge their automatic thinking (A. T. Beck et al., 1979; J. Beck, 1995; Leahy, 2003). This intervention typically is framed with Socratic questioning. For example, a client who has been experiencing debilitating anxiety and depression may say, "Things will never get better for me." Instead of trying to persuade the client that things will get better or offer a dynamic interpretation, the therapist might ask the question "Is there any evidence that things might change in the future?" or "Is there another way in which you might think about your future?" The client may be given an examining the evidence form for use between sessions. The form has two columns to examine a particular belief: evidence for and evidence against (Leahy, 2003). This intervention can be quite effective, particularly if utilized in the context of collaborative empiricism. Collaborative empiricism is a general therapeutic stance in which the therapist views the client as an equal partner in addressing issues and fostering change from the perspective of the scientific method (A. T. Beck et al., 1979). Finally, while examining the evidence appears to be the same as cognitive disputation, it is different. In cognitive therapy, the therapist does not directly challenge an automatic thought because it would violate collaborative empiricism. Instead, the "therapist and patient together examine the automatic thought, tests its validity and/or utility, and develop a more adaptive response" (J. Beck, 1995, p. 108).

Cognitive–Behavioral Replacement

An alternative to restructuring maladaptive beliefs (and modifying maladaptive behaviors) is to replace maladaptive or unhelpful thoughts or interpretations and behaviors with more adaptive and helpful ones, that is, thoughts or interpretations and behaviors that are more likely to achieve the client's desired outcomes. For many clients who are not responsive to cognitive restructuring interventions such as cognitive disputation, cognitive–behavioral replacement can be an effective intervention. It is adapted from cognitive–behavioral analysis system of psychotherapy (CBASP) and is applicable to a wide range of clients and presentations (McCullough, 2000; Sperry, 2010).

Thought Stopping

Dysfunctional thoughts are particularly problematic when they become recurrent and cannot be easily turned off (Wolpe, 1990). Called ruminative thinking, these thoughts reverberate, snowball, or are a running commentary that endlessly recycle and seem unstoppable. This repetitive pattern not only increases clients' distress but further erodes their sense of personal control, which results in more distress, helplessness, and hopelessness. Thought stopping is an effective cognitive intervention to inhibit this progression. Clients can be taught various tactics that reduce distress and reestablish a sense of self-efficacy. Therapists guide clients in developing and practicing one or more therapeutic tactics in session that can be employed between sessions when they become aware of this ruminative pattern (Cautela & Wisocki, 1977). Several tactics have been found to be effective. These include visualizing a stop sign, saying or thinking "stop," "hearing" a bell ring or siren blare, or snapping a rubber band around their wrist. Presumably, these tactics weaken the ruminative pattern by disrupting the dysfunctional, reverberating neural circuit that is constantly activated. Helping the client find a thought stopping tactic that is effective increases both the client's sense of self-efficacy and his or her confidence in the therapist and the therapeutic process.

BEHAVIORAL INTERVENTIONS

This section describes some of the more common behavioral interventions. These interventions can be useful in both CBT and non-CBT treatment contexts.

Exposure

Exposure is an intervention that involves intentional and prolonged contact with a feared object, combined with actively blocking undesirable avoidance behaviors (i.e., response prevention). It confronts the client with a stimulus that has previously elicited an unwanted behavior or emotional response. Although the client will experience increased anxiety in the short term, in the long term, repeated and incremental exposure to that feared stimulus in vivo (live), or in the client's imagination, will result in a reduction of anxiety and the extinguishing of the avoidance response. There are a variety of exposure techniques that can be employed, including systematic desensitization, guided imagery, flooding, and implosion (Goldfried & Davison, 1994).

Systematic Desensitization

Systematic desensitization is a common and effective intervention used to help clients deal with anxiety-provoking situations (Wolpe, 1990). It is similar to the medical treatment used to help patients deal with allergies. In behavioral terms, the client has become allergic to a specific situation and is anxious and attempts to avoid the situation. The desensitization process inoculates the individual by having them experience the anxiety-provoking situation while in a relaxed state. This process builds a tolerance or immunity to the anxiety-provoking situation. By exposing themselves to their fears and anxieties, they become flooded with uncomfortable symptoms. However, the symptoms soon reach their crest and fade away. As they fade, clients often experience exhilaration instead of the shame and humiliation associated with the anxiety. Two forms of systematic desensitization are imaginal desensitization and in vivo desensitization.

Learning to relax is the first step in the systematic desensitization process. Relaxation is based on the observation that in relaxing one's muscles, it is possible to reduce anxiety. A common relaxation procedure is deep muscle relaxation wherein the therapist asks clients to get comfortable and to close their eyes. Then, the therapist teaches the clients to systematically relax each muscle group by tensing and relaxing muscles so that muscle tension is released. The therapist uses a calming voice to create a safe context. Once clients recognize the difference between tensed and relaxed muscles, they can learn to create a relaxed state very quickly. Clients can also learn to use their breathing and imagination to relax. For example, by breathing in a slow deep fashion, clients can close their eyes and imagine that they are at a special imaginary or real place where they are relaxed, such as a beach, meadow, or mountain top, for example.

The desensitization continues with clients being helped to develop a fear hierarchy, that is, a list of a series of increasingly stressful situations. For instance, for clients with fear of flying, hearing they must take a trip may be the lowest item on the list, whereas an item in the middle of the list might involve driving to the airport, and higher on the list is waiting at the gate for the flight to board. Once the list is developed, the therapist has the client become relaxed. Clients are then asked to visualize the scene that is lowest on their hierarchy. While visualizing the situation completely, clients are asked to continue to focus on being relaxed. When the scene can be imagined for 20 to 25 seconds without conscious anxiety, the process moves on to the next higher scene on the fear hierarchy. This process continues by pairing relaxation with situations at increasing levels of the hierarchy. The pace of the desensitization process is determined by clients' ability to relax completely while imagining the anxiety-provoking situation. The final step of the process is helping clients to relax in the actual anxiety-provoking situation.

In vivo desensitization involves the same principles and process as imaginal desensitization, but instead of imaging the scenes, the clients experience them directly. For example, a child with a school phobia would be helped to develop a fear hierarchy. Then, the child would be asked to actually experience each of the scenes, starting with the least fear-producing one and proceeding to the most feared one. Typically, the therapist, a family member, or both would accompany the child to provide support and direction.

Sometimes clients find it too distressing to quickly deal with scenes, especially those near the top of their fear hierarchy. Accordingly, the exposure and desensitization process needs to be more flexible and gradual. This allows them to stop and back off whenever their anxiety becomes too intense. Nevertheless, continuously challenge their fears leads to desensitization. Research indicates that systematic desensitization is a highly effective intervention for reducing fear responses (Paul, 1969).

Eye Movement Desensitization and Reprocessing

Eye movement desensitization and reprocessing (EMDR) is an intervention designed to help clients deal with traumatic memories (F. Shapiro, 2001). It is an information processing procedure that attends to the past traumatic experience; the current situations that trigger dysfunctional emotions, beliefs, and sensations; and the positive experience needed to enhance future adaptive behaviors and mental health. During treatment, various techniques and protocols are utilized. A key technique is dual stimulation using bilateral eye movements, tones, or taps. During the reprocessing phases, the client attends momentarily to past memories, present triggers, or anticipated future experiences while simultaneously focusing on a set of external stimuli. It is in this phase that clients generally experience the emergence of insight, changes in memories, or new associations. The therapist helps the client to focus on appropriate material before initiation of each subsequent set. After EMDR processing, clients often report a decrease in emotional distress and an increase in cognitive insight.

Behavioral Rehearsal

Behavioral rehearsal is an intervention that helps clients to learn new response patterns to specific situations. This intervention allows clients to try out a set of behaviors that they would like to carry out in their real life, and the therapy setting provides a safe atmosphere for the practice of new behaviors. Role-playing is used to simulate the problematic situation in the session; new behavioral patterns are initiated, and the client rehearses or practices them until they can be effectively carried out in real-life situations. Role reversal is a indispensable component wherein the therapist assumes the role of the client and models the desired behaviors while the client assumes the role of the individual(s) with whom he or she has a problem (Lazarus, 1966). Through practice or simulation, the client can develop the courage to achieve the behaviors called for in the particular situation.

For example, a shy and avoidant client needs to increase her social support system and wishes to make a couple of new friends. In therapy, the client is engaged in behavioral rehearsal. In sessions, she will practice making eye contact, initiate a conversation, make small talk, and invite another to join her in a given activity. The therapist's role is to provide direction, modeling, encouragement, support, and feedback that allow the client to develop the needed skills.

150

Social Skills Training

Frequently, clients need direct help in developing or learning the skills required to solve their presenting problems. Skill deficits may be noted in areas such as assertiveness, problem solving, communication, friendship skills, feeling identification and expression, empathy, negotiation, and conflict resolution (Goldfried & Davison, 1994). Skill training is based on three assumptions. The first is that interpersonal behavior is based on a set of skills that are primarily learned behaviors. The second is that social skills are situation-specific. It is important to know that cultural and situational factors determine social norms, or what is expected of an individual in a specific situation. The third assumption is that the effective use of social skills requires reinforcement. In other words, they need to work effectively within the social context. There are various means by which clients can be helped to learn new and more adaptive interpersonal skills patterns such as assertive communication. Skill training can occur in both individual and group therapeutic contexts and typically employs a mix of interventions, including instruction, role-playing, modeling, feedback, and social reinforcement and practice (Alberti, 1977; Goldfried & Davison, 1994).

Assertiveness Training

Training in assertiveness usually involves assertive communication and assertive behavior. Goal clarity is an important component of assertiveness training and an essential prerequisite of assertive behavior. Once the goals or intentions are clear, the client needs to learn how to ask for feedback, how to give feedback, and how to express acceptance of other individuals' points of view. Assertiveness involves an individual asserting his or her own rights without infringing on the rights of others. The first step is to assess the client's actual behavior. The therapist and client then need to identify the hoped-for response or goal. The therapist then creates a simulation where they can model the new behavior for the client. This is followed by having the client practice the new behavior with the therapist before taking the new learning into real life (Alberti, 1977).

Problem-Solving Training

This training is intended to help individual clients, couples, and families to develop more constructive methods for defining and solving their problems (Goldfried & Davison, 1994). It involves three necessary skills: receiving skills, which include attending to and accurately perceiving cues and contextual elements of interpersonal situations; processing skills, which include generating response alternatives, weighing the consequences of each alternative, and selecting optimal options; and sending skills, or using the chosen option for an effective social response that integrates both verbal and nonverbal behaviors (Urbain & Kendall, 1980). The therapist's role is to help clients to identify the problem area and to develop a preferred way to respond. The new response is often practiced in the therapy session, and potential problems or roadblocks are identified and discussed. Clients are urged to practice and report the effect in a subsequent session.

Communication Skills Training

Effective communication involves three basic components (Myers & Smith, 1995): giving an understanding statement, taking partial responsibility, and offering to help. An understanding statement introduces feelings into the discussion, particularly empathy. A partial responsibility statement indicates that the client is willing to accept a role in creating or solving a specific problem. A final way to enhance communication is through an offer to help. Taken together, these components deliver a message of wanting a change, but with a willingness on the part of the requester to be actively supportive in the process. Various methods are utilized to teach effective communication skills to individual clients, couples, and families. These include direct instruction, coaching, blocking specific types of communication, task setting, avoiding counterattacking and defensive talking, and keeping a diary of the client's communication patterns (Sherman, Oresky, & Rountress, 1991). The expected outcome of communication training is a decrease in defensiveness and more open lines of communication.

CONCLUDING NOTE

This chapter has provided an overview of some of the most common cognitive and behavioral interventions. These interventions are widely utilized by therapists from many theoretical orientations.

10

Systemic Strategies and Interventions

Why does a book that is ostensibly oriented to the practice of individual psychotherapy have a chapter on systemic strategies and interventions? There are at least three reasons. First, solution-focused therapy (SFT) is the most commonly practiced form of systemic therapy both in family therapy and in individual therapy contexts. In fact, some therapists utilize SFT exclusively with individual clients. Second, many therapists who were trained primarily for the practice of individual therapy will occasionally consult with family members or spouses of their individual clients. Typically, this is a single meeting to gather collateral information, enlist the spouse or member's support in the client's treatment, or make a focused intervention. To the extent to which therapists have some degree of competence with a few systemic interventions, they are more likely to be effective and confident in such consultative sessions. Third, and most importantly, there are a number of systemic interventions that can be effective adjunctive treatments with individual clients. One of these, called the interventive query strategy, is equally effective in both individual therapy and systemic therapy contexts. Although originally developed and utilized in the systemic therapies, it can be incorporated as an effective adjunct with any therapeutic approach. For example, the scaling question—one form of this query strategy—is commonly utilized by many individual therapists of most theoretical orientations often without the awareness that it is a systemic intervention.

The chapter begins with a discussion of six relatively common systemic strategies for changing maladaptive relational patterns. Besides being utilized with couples and families, these strategies can be used with individuals. The chapter also describes the clinical use and value of interventive query strategy and provides clinical descriptions and clinical illustrations of the use of eight kinds of interventive queries in both individual therapy settings and in couples and family consultation contexts.

INTERVENTIONS FOR CHANGING
RELATIONAL PATTERNS

The well-being of individuals, couples, and families can be significantly compromised by maladaptive relational patterns. Sometimes these habitual patterns of relating can be changed relatively easily with an appropriate strategy, whereas other times the pattern is more resistant to change (Gehart, 2009). Following are some systemic-oriented strategies for changing relational patterns. These strategies have a place in individual therapy contexts, couple and family consultation contexts, as well as in couples and family therapy contexts.

Reframing. Reframing is a strategy that puts the presenting problem in a different perspective. The facts of an event do not change, but the meaning of the situation is viewed from a fresh perspective. The original meaning of an event or situation is placed in this new context in which an equally plausible explanation is possible (Minuchin, 1974). Families often perceive problems in ways that appear to have no workable solution. The new perspective allows the family to work effectively with a problem when they use a different formula or to see it from a new viewpoint. This often involves giving a positive connotation to a negative behavior. Reframing is an important relational skill because there are advantages and disadvantages to every behavior. It is thought that by accepting the behavior, the person will often decrease it (Madanes, 1981).

Reframing does not change a situation, but the alteration of the meaning invites the possibility of change (Piercy & Sprenkle, 1986). For example, when a partner appears to be tuned out, it may actually be that he or she is being thoughtful about what was just said. The mother who is accused of nagging is reframed by the therapist as one who is intensely interested and caring. The therapist feeds back the pattern of behavior in a different, positive frame of reference so that the clients will see it differently. Viewing the present situation from another perspective allows the clients to think and feel differently about it. This may create the motivation necessary to approach the problem differently.

Relabeling. Relabeling involves substituting a positive adjective for the negative ones used in the blaming stances of many dysfunctional families. For example, the wife says the husband is controlling and the therapist relabels, saying that the husband is overburdened. This relabels the husband's behavior as a part of the family structure. The therapist can then help the family to divide up the responsibilities of the family in a more equitable fashion. This strategy is very similar to reframing (Sherman et al., 1991).

Unbalancing. Unbalancing is a strategy to create disequilibrium in a relationship. In therapeutic terms, unbalancing occurs when therapists use their authority and power to break a stalemate by supporting one of the individuals in a conflict. It is not done randomly and must be used with precision to challenge the rules, interaction patterns, or other unbalancing factors that keep families stuck. The challenge of unbalancing is with the system and not the individuals. The goal of this strategy is to change the relationship of members within a subsystem (Hanna & Brown, 1999). Some therapists can have difficulty with this concept because it represents taking sides and is counter to therapist neutrality. However, it is important to note that the therapist is not judging who is right or wrong but rather unbalancing the unhealthy stalemate.

Boundary Restructuring. Boundary restructuring is a strategy used to realign boundaries by either increasing closeness or distance. Dysfunctional relationships are characterized by overly rigid or diffuse boundaries (Minuchin, 1974). In very close or highly enmeshed families, the therapist strengthens the boundaries between subsystems and attempts to increase the independence of the family members. For example, family members are urged to speak for themselves; anyone who tries to interrupt will be blocked. This occurs when therapists have to help parents to stop children from interrupting their dialogue. Families that are detached or disengaged avoid conflict to minimize interaction with one another. The therapist must prevent escape or avoidance and help the family members to learn to face one another. This involves learning first to express feelings directly and then to resolve problems with positive interaction (Minuchin & Fishman, 1981).

Paradox. Paradox is a strategy that if followed results in the opposite of what is intended. It is a cognitive construction that frustrates or confuses family members to the extent that they search for alternatives to their present situation, or it gives them permission to do something they are already doing and is intended to eliminate or reduce resistance (Haley, 1976). For instance, a very conflicted couple may be asked to schedule specific times for fighting during the week, or a highly conflict-avoidant couple may be asked to actively resist talking to each other about negative feelings for a week. As with individuals, when couples follow these suggestions, they can gain a sense of mastery and control over a specific problem; when they resist, positive individual or relational changes may result. So, to the extent to which the conflictual couple resists scheduling conflicts, they may become less conflictual, and by actively avoiding talking about negative feelings, the conflict-avoidant couple may start talking about those very feelings. Needless to say, caution must be exercised in the use of paradox. Experienced therapists limit the use of this strategy to those individuals, couples, or families they believe will benefit from its use (Boscolo, Cecchin, Hoffman, & Penn, 1987; Sherman et al., 1991).

INTERVENTIVE QUERY STRATEGY

Traditionally, therapy was thought of as having two phases: a diagnostic phase and a therapeutic phase. The purpose of the diagnostic phase was to elicit information, while the purpose of the therapeutic phase was to utilize that information in facilitating insight and changing beliefs and behaviors. Furthermore, the therapeutic phase would not begin until the diagnostic phase had been completed. Today, therapy is more likely to be viewed as a process that facilitates change during both phases, in fact, during all phases of treatment. The interventive query strategy, originally called interventive interviewing (Tomm, 1987a, 1987b), is a diagnostic and therapeutic strategy that facilitates therapeutic change by framing questions that not only elicit useful information but, at the same time, provoke change within the client as he or she processes and responds to these questions. In the process of answering the clinician's question, various changes begin occurring within the client, such as expansion or change of one's frame of reference as with circular questions, getting in touch with one's sense of self-efficacy as with empowering questions, or mobilizing one's problem-solving skills as with reflexive questions.

Rather than spending the one or two sessions asking several diagnostic, information-seeking questions as a basis for establishing a formulation and a treatment plan, and then following up with therapeutic questions and interventions in subsequent sessions, the interview process is short-circuited. After asking a diagnostic question or two, the therapist follows up with an appropriate interventive question or two. Accordingly, within the very first session, therapeutic change and movement can occur and should be expected (Sperry, 1997).

Although this intervention strategy was originally developed and utilized in the systemic therapies, it also has considerable value in individual therapy contexts. Accordingly, therapists trained in individually oriented therapies can utilize this interventive questioning strategy to enhance their therapeutic outcomes with individual clients as well as to increase their effectiveness in consulting with a couples or families.

Diagnostic-Linear Questions

Before providing a detailed description of the use of this interventive strategy, it is essential that clinicians distinguish it from the traditional diagnostic strategy, which relies on diagnostic-linear questions. As noted earlier, diagnostic-linear questions are information-seeking rather than change-provoking, whereas interventive questions are primarily change-provoking questions (Tomm, 1987a). Typical examples of diagnostic-linear questions are "How would you describe your depression?" and "How would rate your depression on a 1 to 10 scale?" Both of these questions have diagnostic value but little or no therapeutic value. On the other hand, when these diagnostic-linear questions are combined with interventive questions, the clinical and therapeutic value is significantly increased.

Interventive Query Strategy Questions

In contrast to such diagnostic-linear questions, this section describes and illustrates eight different types of interventive questions or queries useful in working therapeutically with individuals as well as in consulting with couples and families. These questions are briefly described along with their functions. Then, illustrations of their use in individual therapy and in couples and family consultation are provided.

1. Circular Questions

Description. Circular questions can be quite useful in understanding and mapping the individual's relational world. This type of question is based on a circular rather than linear view of reality or causality. For instance, in linear causality, it can be said that event A effects event B, but not vice versa. However, in a circular view of causality, event A can be said to effect event B, but at the same time event B also effects event A.

Function. These questions are most helpful in eliciting the type and extent of relational patterns that connect individuals (Tomm, 1987a). They are questions about comparisons or differences, and they form the basis for reframing specific life circumstances and affects. Presumably, while processing the therapist's circular question, the client expands his or her perspective on a situation that previously was framed negatively. The therapist's role is to prompt the client to reframe a troubling relationship or symptom in a new way.

Clinical Illustration. *Individual therapy context.* "Besides you, who else worries about your daughter's depression? Who worries more, you or your husband? When your daughter is depressed, how do you respond? How do you respond to her response? How does your husband react to this?"

Couples-family consultation context. "When you start talking in that tone, how does your partner respond? How do you respond to her response?" [To partner] "Is that the way you experience it? When you become quiet, does your partner draw closer to you or move further away? Do you see this in a similar or different way?"

2. Reflexive Questions

Description. Like circular questions, reflexive questions are based on circular assumptions of reality. They ask the listener to shift to a different point of reference in terms of person, place, or time. As a result, reflexive questions help individuals generate new perspectives and contexts.

Function. These questions are useful in influencing a client, couple, or family in an indirect or general manner (Tomm, 1987b, 1988). Their intent is to mobilize the listener's own problem-solving processes. They prompt the listener to reconstruct meaning or shift contexts. This type of question encourages listeners to think about the implications of their current perceptions or behaviors and consider alternatives. The therapist's role is to guide clients to mobilize their own intellectual or emotional resources to solve previously unsolvable problems.

Clinical Illustration. *Individual therapy context.* "Suppose this therapy is successful and someday in the future you reflect on it; what will you consider to have been the turning point?" "Suppose you were to imagine yourself free of depression. What would that be like?"

Couples-family consultation context. "Suppose you were to share with him how worried you are about him and his depression; what do you suppose he might think and do?" "Just suppose he was resentful about your family, but feared bringing it to your attention; how could you convince him it was safe to talk about it?"

3. Strategic Questions

Description. While strategic questions are the mainstay of strategic therapy approaches (Haley, 1976), they are also an essential component of interventive interviewing. Strategic questions are directive in nature and are intended to provide a corrective influence on a client, couple, or family. The directiveness of the clinician is usually masked because the corrective statement is packaged in the form of a question (Tomm, 1988). Whereas some clients may bristle at being asked this question type, others find it quite compatible with their typical pattern of interaction. Unlike the other interventive questions, strategic questions are essentially linear questions.

Function. These questions are useful in altering the individual's behavior in a therapeutic direction. Although based on linear assumptions of causality, this type of question assumes that when the clinician discovers dysfunctionality, he or she can proceed to work with the client to correct or change it. Strategic questions are a powerful mode of influencing individuals, couples, or families either overtly or covertly. The clinician's role is to confront, in an indirect fashion, the client's resistance to change.

Clinical Illustration. *Individual therapy context.* "When are you going to stop talking so pessimistically about your future?" "Is this habit of making excuses something new for you?"

Couples-family consultation context. "Why don't you talk to your husband about your worries instead of talking to your daughter about them?" "What would happen if for the next week you would suggest that she make breakfast every morning instead of staying in bed until noon?" "Would you prefer making sure she gets up every morning or confronting her with your fears that she might overdose?"

4. Empowering Questions

Description. Empowering questions are particularly useful in drawing out a client's strengths and building on whatever past successes they have had inside or outside of psychotherapy. Talmon (1990) and White and Epston (1990) have illustrated several question types that are framed to empower and reconstruct selfhood once a client or family has

framed their problems and concerns as somehow separate from themselves. In this regard, empowering questions are similar to externalizing
questions.

Function.   These questions are useful in eliciting the patient's sense
of self-efficacy by drawing on their previous knowledge, experience, and
previous successes in other areas of life and bringing them to bear on the
therapeutic task at hand. The therapist's role is to draw out the clients'
strengths and sense of self-efficacy so that they come to believe, perhaps
against great odds, that life can be different.

Clinical Illustration.   *Individual therapy context.* "In those occasional
instances when you were not depressed, what were you thinking then?"
"When you see yourself refusing to accept a lifestyle of depression, what
does that then say about you as a person?"

Couples-family consultation context. "Imagine, for a moment, having
total control over the situation with your daughter's acting out behavior.
What would you do differently?" "If you were to think of a very small but
significant step in the right direction that would give you just one ray of
hope that your relationship would get back on track, what would it be?"

5. Scaling Questions

Description.   Scaling questions ask for metaphoric descriptions to
be quantified. Clinical experience suggests that individuals benefit from
looking at their problems as continuous rather than as dichotomous.

Function.   These questions help the individual and the clinician map
the strength of various aspects of the problems or the solutions (de Shazer,
1988). The general form of the question is, "On a 1 to 10 scale, with 10 equal
to the worst problem you could have and 1 equal to the least, what would
you rate the current problem?" Through the use of this type of questioning, the therapist is able to more accurately assess the client's perception
of symptomatic distress, impairment, and progress to change than he or
she would get by asking less focused questions.

Clinical Illustration.   *Individual therapy context.* "On a 1 to 10 scale, with
10 meaning 'I'll do whatever it takes' and 1 meaning 'There's nothing I can
do about it,' how would you rate your readiness today to solve this problem?"
"What could make your readiness go up one point? Go down one point?"

Couples-family consultation context. "If I (clinician) were to ask your
wife how she would rate your readiness for change, what would she have
guessed your rating would be on a 1 to 10 scale? How do you account for
the difference?" "On a scale of 1 to 10, with 10 meaning you have totally

achieved the goals you came to couples therapy for, and 1 meaning that you haven't started yet, where would you rate yourself today? (The couple says 5.) What do you need to do to move from 5 to 6?"

Scaling questions can also facilitate the therapy process in approaching the time-honored ideal of being truly "client-centered" or "client-driven" (Berg, Sperry, & Carlson, 1999). That is because scaling questions assess the client's ideal—not the clinician's ideal—of what constitutes an adequate resolution to the client's presenting problem or concern. Because the client rates on his or her own scale, not on the clinician's expert scale, the clinician can say, "Are you content to live with your mood at a 6 level?" If the client says, "Yes, it's as good as things can be for now," the clinician does not have to be disappointed because the client did not set his end point at a 7 or 8, which may have been the clinician's ideal for this client. Besides being a very effective method of intervention, this kind of questioning is respectful of the client. It says to the client, "I know you know what you want for yourself. I know you know what's good for you. So you just tell me." As a result, clinicians do not have to take all the responsibility for coming up with the right solutions or answers for the client, as much of the responsibility is given back to the client. It is very different from saying, "I know what's good for you, to get your mood up to 7 or 8."

6. Exception Questions

Description.   This type of question assumes that there are times and circumstances when the client's problem or symptoms do not occur and is used to attempt to learn whether those times and circumstances can be a foundation for further change. This question type emphasizes any unrecognized, successful client action(s) that could serve to leverage therapeutic progress in some way or another.

Function.   These questions are useful in spotlighting successful efforts on the client's part that have been unrecognized (Berg & Miller, 1992). Exception questions assume that clients can and do change on their own, but that clients may ignore those changes unless they are attended to by the clinician. It also assumes that important changes can occur, even prior to the first session. The therapist's role in utilizing such questioning highlights successful efforts, no matter how small, that are critical in encouraging the client to continue the difficult and painful process of therapy.

Clinical Illustration.   *Individual therapy context.* "What is different about those occasions when your symptoms are not so strong or noticeable?

What might be causing those exceptions? How do they occur?" "During the past week, were there any occasions when the problem did not occur?" "Have there been times when the problem almost occurred, but you were successful at neutralizing it?"

Couples-family consultation context. "Sometimes a couple will notice a change between the time they call for an appointment and their first session. What kinds of changes might you have noticed?" "You say there's been no change in arguing and fighting since we met last. Well, what might you have done to keep things from getting any worse?"

7. Outcome (Including Miracle) Questions

Description. One of the reasons why clients terminate therapy prematurely is that they are dissatisfied with their treatment. Often, this means that the clinician and client had different goals for the therapy. When treatment goals are not discussed and specified, and there is little or no goal alignment between clinician and client, therapy cannot be successful and satisfying. The "miracle question" (de Shazer, 1988) is a type of outcome question.

Function. These questions are helpful in eliciting and specifying the client's goal or end point for change (Berg & Miller, 1992). The therapist's role in using this form of questioning is to assist the client to clarify and specify their specific expectations for the outcomes of psychotherapy.

Clinical Illustration. *Individual therapy context.* "Who will notice, without being told by you, that you made progress in therapy? What will they notice?" "Suppose in the middle of the night tonight, a miracle happens, and the problem that brought you into therapy is solved. But, because it happens while you are asleep, you don't realize it. Tomorrow when you wake up, what will tell you the problem has been solved? What will be the first sign that this is happening?"

Couples-family consultation context. "How will you know when you are both getting what you want from couples therapy?" "If we had a video camera that would tape you whenever your relationship was going well, what would we see you both doing on that tape?"

8. Coping Questions

Description. During the course of some therapies, it becomes evident that there are few, if any, useful exceptions, or that the client feels so hopeless that he or she cannot even imagine a positive outcome from therapy and so is unable to respond to outcome questions. Instead, the client may report suicidal thoughts or plans. When circumstances seem ominous or the client becomes increasingly hopeless about change, that is the time to explore the client's coping strategies. In the process of exploring coping strategies, the client's life is indirectly reframed in terms of the capacity to heroically cope with difficult external influences (Berg & Miller, 1992).

Function. These questions explore the client's coping strategies as well as his or her past successes in making personal changes. The therapist's role in using this form of questioning is to assist the client to explore times in which they have been successful in making and sticking with changes, and the self-management, problem-solving, and relationship skills that the client brought to bear in those circumstances.

Clinical Illustration. *Individual therapy context.* "What are you doing to keep your depression from really getting you down? "What kind of things have you been doing to fight the urge to hurt yourself?" "How have you managed to keep things from getting worse?"

Couples-family consultation context. "Given how worried you are about your son's cancer, how do you both manage to keep going every day?" "With all these financial burdens and problems with your children, how have you been able to keep your marriage together?"

STRATEGY FOR UTILIZING INTERVENTIVE QUERIES

Some interventive questions, such as outcomes and scaling questions, are particularly useful in making the therapy process more focused and less vague. Scaling questions may be the most commonly used intervention to clarify clinician–client interactions. Asking a scaling question or two can reduce the sense of vagueness and indefiniteness that both clients and clinicians experience when they appear to be talking about the same reality, but neither is sure. And, neither feels particularly hopeful or empowered about changing the situation. For example, back-to-back scaling questions such as "Where has your mood been for the last week or so on a 1 to 10 scale where 1 is the worst and 10 is the best?" (Client: 4) "What could you do to raise it to a 5 or 6?" This kind of questioning can lead to a very specific and different kind of discussion than if the clinician predictably asks, "How have your moods been lately?" (Client: "Pretty bad.") "Why do you suppose that is?" (Client: "I'm not sure.")

The therapist's choice of a question type usually follows from situational demand. For example:

1. When the client is feeling overly discouraged and helpless, consider using coping, empowering, and positive description questions.
2. When the client appears to be frightened or ambivalent about making changes, consider using externalizing and exception questions.
3. When the client appears stuck and resistant to moving toward his or her outcome goals, consider using strategic questions, particularly when therapeutic confrontation and clinical interpretations have not been particularly effective.
4. When gaining insight or another frame of reference is needed, consider using circular and reflexive questions.
5. Finally, consider using scaling questions anywhere in the course of treatment to assess the client's perceptions of distress, impairment, motivations, readiness for change, or progress toward treatment goals. (Sperry, Carlson, et al., 2003)

A fuller treatment of interventive interviewing is provided in Tomm (1987a, 1987b, 1988).

CONCLUDING NOTE

Systemic strategies are effective ways to disrupt and change ineffective relational patterns. Some of these strategies are also effective in changing individual patterns. This chapter has described and illustrated a number of such strategies that can be used as adjunctive interventions in individual therapy settings as well as in consultation with couples and families.

Section VI

Core Competency 5: Intervention Evaluation and Treatment

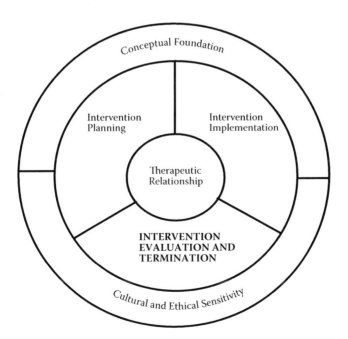

11

Outcome Assessment

In this era of accountability, therapists are expected to both provide effective treatment and demonstrate its effectiveness. How many therapists and trainees can meet this expectation? Apparently not many, as most therapists—and trainees—have relatively little training and experience in monitoring and evaluating the quality and effectiveness of their work. In fact, many training programs consistently ignore and avoid addressing this core competency even though it is integrally related to the other core competencies. On the other hand, highly competent and effective therapists often ask themselves during each therapy session, "Is this intervention I'm doing right now benefitting the client?" (J. Persons, 2007).

In addition, research findings increasingly support the importance and necessity of treatment monitoring and evaluation, particularly ongoing treatment monitoring. Although several studies will be reviewed in subsequent sections of this chapter, one study pretty much says it all. Based on a meta-analysis, it was concluded that when clinicians collect and review a measure of outcome at every therapy session, clients have better outcomes than when clinicians do not monitor these outcomes (Lambert, Whipple, Hawkins, Vermeersch, Nielsen, et al., 2003). What this and other studies are saying is that the effective and competent practice of psychotherapy requires ongoing monitoring of treatment outcomes.

This chapter focuses on two competencies that address this matter of monitoring and evaluating treatment effectiveness. It begins with situating ongoing assessment (treatment monitoring) and final outcome assessment (treatment evaluation) in the larger context of the various forms of assessment in psychotherapy practice. Then, it briefly reviews premature termination and the role of outcomes monitoring and client feedback in eliminating treatment dropout. Next, it describes various treatment outcome measures and client feedback that can be incorporated into everyday clinical practice. It also discusses how treatment outcome measures can be employed in the context of clinical supervision to enhance supervisor feedback. Finally, it reviews treatment monitoring and evaluation considerations in three of the most commonly practiced therapeutic approaches. A case example illustrates these points.

OUTCOME ASSESSMENT COMPETENCIES

This chapter addresses two essential clinical competencies involving outcome assessment which are associated with the core competency of intervention evaluation and termination.

Monitoring Progress and Modifying Treatment Accordingly

This competency involves the capacity to use various methods to assess client progress in treatment and then appropriately modify treatment focus and direction based on that feedback.

Utilizing Supervision to Monitor and Evaluate Treatment Progress

This competency involves the capacity to effectively use clinical supervision to share and receive feedback on client progress in treatment and then appropriately modify treatment focus and direction based on that feedback.

ANOTHER TYPE OF ASSESSMENT: TREATMENT MONITORING

In Chapter 5, three types of assessment were described: diagnostic assessment, theory-based assessment, and pattern-based assessment. These represent what can be called the initial assessment. There are actually two other types of assessment: ongoing assessment and final outcome assessment. Ongoing assessment (also referred to as formative evaluation) involves the monitoring of specific treatment indicators over the course of treatment, usually at each session or at other specified intervals, such as every other or every third session. The purpose of this type of assessment is to provide the therapist with information that provides a real-time assessment of given indicators such as data on the therapeutic alliance, specific symptoms and levels of functioning, or other indicators of progress or lack of progress, which allow the therapist to make an appropriate course correction with regard to treatment targets, treatment focus, or interventions (Sperry, Carlson, et al., 2003). The fifth type of assessment, final outcome assessment, is the overall evaluation (also referred to as summative evaluation) of what was achieved or not achieved in the treatment process. This evaluation may involve standardized measures utilized in a pre–post test manner. For example, in a case where depression was the presenting problem, Beck Depression Inventory scores at or near the end of treatment are compared with scores on that inventory at the start of treatment. Or, it might involve a review of treatment outcomes in terms of the original treatment goals and objectives. Chapter 12 extends the discussion of final outcome assessment. The remainder of this chapter focuses primarily on various types of ongoing assessment.

FROM PREMATURE TERMINATION TO POSITIVE THERAPEUTIC ALLIANCES AND TREATMENT OUTCOMES

It is a surprise to many trainees that clients leave treatment early and that often their departure is precipitous, unplanned (at least as far as the therapist is concerned), and against the therapist's advice. Published estimates of dropout rates range from 30% to 60% of clients (Reis & Brown, 1999). A meta-analysis of several studies on premature termination from psychotherapy shows it to be a significant problem, with dropout rates averaging about 47% (Wierzbicki & Pekarik, 1993). Another review of several studies found that upward of 65% to 80% of clients end treatment before the 10th session; the percentage is higher for adolescents and minority clients (Garfield, 1994). Besides potentially deleterious effects on clients in distress, premature termination also limits opportunities for trainees to develop psychotherapy competencies involved in middle- and late-stage treatment. So why do clients leave therapy prematurely? Recent studies on treatment dropout identified several reasons, including abuse history, interpersonal difficulty, comorbid Axis I and II psychiatric diagnoses, cognitive dysfunction, legal issues, and problems with therapists or the treatment itself (Aubuchon-Endsley & Callahan, 2009).

Of these various reasons, therapists have some control and influence over the last one: issues with the therapist or the treatment itself. For all practical purposes, clients drop out of therapy either because the treatment is not helping them or because they are not sufficiently engaged in the treatment process because of an alliance problem (S. Miller, Duncan, Sorrell, & Brown, 2005). Therefore, it is essential to identify if the clients' expectations of treatment are being met and to engage them in the treatment process. Monitoring the treatment process and outcomes is a strategy for accomplishing both of these.

Some therapists informally monitor treatment progress and may make treatment adjustments based on their impressions of the client's response to treatment. Yet, therapists' ability to make accurate assessments and clinical judgments, even late in therapy, has been questioned, especially with clients who show signs of deterioration (Lambert & Ogles, 2004). Monitoring of treatment remains largely intuition and based on clinical experience, even though research indicates that clinical experience makes little or no difference in therapists' clinical judgment. Nevertheless, "mental health experts often justify predictive judgments on the basis of their years of experience. This situation is particularly troubling when coupled with the research evidence that therapists are reluctant to recognize deterioration, tend to overestimate improvement rates ... and are inclined to devalue actuarial/ statistical data" (Hannan, Lambert, Harmon, Nielsen, Smart, et al., 2005, p. 156). In short, therapists who monitor treatment but do not use standardized outcomes measures are likely to underestimate negative outcomes and overestimate treatment progress, usually to the detriment of clients.

The alternative is to utilize standardized outcome and process measures. The basic premise of highly effective therapy is that therapists need feedback. Research rather consistently shows that when therapists receive feedback on their work with clients, their therapeutic relationships and treatment effectiveness increases significantly. One study showed that when therapists had access to outcome and therapeutic alliance information, their clients were less likely to drop out of treatment, were less likely to deteriorate, and were more likely to achieve clinically significant changes (Whipple, Lambert, Vermeersch, Smart, Nielsen, et al., 2003). Another study evaluated client–therapist relationships that were at risk of a negative outcome. It found that therapists who received formal feedback were 65% more likely to achieve positive treatment outcomes than therapists who did not receive such feedback (Lambert et al., 2001). A third study of more than 6,000 clients found that therapists who utilized ongoing, formal feedback measures had markedly higher retention rates and a doubling of overall positive effects compared to therapists without such feedback (S. Miller, Duncan, Brown, Sorrell, & Chalk, 2006). In short, when both therapist and client know how the client rates the therapeutic relationship and treatment outcomes, three things can be predicted: (1) An effective therapeutic relationship is more likely to be developed and maintained, (2) the client will stay in treatment, and (3) positive treatment outcomes will result. Thus, ongoing monitoring of the treatment process and outcome appears to be essential to effective and highly effective therapy.

TRAINING AND USE OF OUTCOMES MEASURES

The obvious question is why don't more clinicians use formal outcome measures in daily clinical practice? Were they not trained in the use of such measures? If they were trained to use such measures, do they use them after completing training? Research addressing such questions is quite sobering. Recent survey results shows that only about 47% of American Psychological Association–accredited APPIC (Association of Psychology Postdoctoral and Internship Centers) internship sites use outcome measures to inform their treatment decisions and clinical practices. Even more puzzling is that there is considerable discrepancy between the percentage of interns who are trained in outcome assessment measures and those that utilize outcome assessment measures afterward in independent practice. Data indicate that only 29% to 37% of these clinicians report using outcome assessment measures in practice (Mours, Campbell, Gathercoal, & Peterson, 2009).

In the era of accountability, it is distressing that less than half of accredited internship sites seem to be serious about issues such as high rates of premature termination and providing effective treatment to clients. It is even more distressing that so few clinicians who were trained in outcomes assessment fail to utilize this essential competency. At this point in time, researchers and commentators have yet to provide reasonable explanations for these troubling findings.

171

TREATMENT OUTCOMES AND
PROCESS ASSESSMENT SCALES

A number of commercially available outcome and process measures are available. Following is a brief description of some of the best known and highly regarded measures.

Polaris-MH

Polaris-MH is a comprehensive outcomes and diagnostic system. Like its predecessor, COMPASS-OP (Howard, Kopta, Krause, & Orlinsky, 1986; Howard, Lueger, Maling, & Martinovich, 1993; Sperry et al., 1996), Polaris-MH is a psychometrically sophisticated, computer-based assessment system. Polaris-MH provides both treatment process and outcome feedback in addition to a number of diagnostic and critical indicators. Like other comprehensive treatment outcome measures, Polaris-MH provides the following outcome information and indicators: suggested treatment focus, treatment progress, client satisfaction with treatment, and therapeutic alliance. Polaris-MH also provides the following information and indicators: severity and nature of the patient's symptoms, impact of the patient's problems upon his or her life functioning, presence of comorbid conditions (chemical dependency, psychosis, and bipolar disorder), and presence of critical conditions (e.g., suicidality, psychosis, violence).

The Polaris-MH measures three domains: Subjective Well-Being, Symptoms, and Functional Impairment. The Symptoms scale is a composite of subscale scores: depression, anxiety, post-traumatic stress disorder, obsessive-compulsive disorder, somatization, panic disorder, phobia, and an overall scale of symptomatic distress. The three subscales of Functional Impairment are personal, social, vocational, as well as a scale of overall functioning. Polaris-MH also assesses for general health problems, substance abuse, psychosis, and bipolar disorder. In addition, it measures resilience, meaning, treatment motivation, satisfaction with treatment, and the therapeutic alliance or bond.

Polaris-MH consists of three measures or questionnaires. The Patient Intake form provides detailed information for treatment planning. The Patient Update form provides information concurrently with treatment about the client's condition, progress, and satisfaction with treatment. The Brief Patient Update form provides a global mental health status indicator and the severity of symptoms of depression. Polaris-MH also provides reports that

172

provide information for clinical decision support (individual patient reports) and for outcomes assessment (program-level aggregate data).

OQ-45

The OQ-45 (Lambert, Morton, Hatfield, Harmon, Hamilton, et al., 2004) is probably the most commonly used commercial treatment outcome measure today. It is a brief 45-item self-report outcome and tracking instrument that is designed for repeated measurement of client progress through the course of therapy and following termination. It measures client functioning in three domains: symptom distress, interpersonal functioning, and social role. Functional level and change over time can be assessed, which allows treatment to be modified based on changes noted. The OQ-45 also contains risk assessment items for suicide potential, substance abuse, and potential violence at work. It has been translated into more than 10 languages and is based on normative data and has adequate validity and reliability. It can be administered and scored in either electronic or paper format.

Session Rating Scale

The Session Rating Scale (SRS; Duncan, Miller, Parks, Claud, Reynolds, et al., 2003) is a short and easy-to-administer measure of therapeutic alliance. The instructions are simple and straightforward. The client is given a sheet of paper on which four horizontal lines 10 centimeters long are printed. On the first line, the client rates how well understood and respected he or she felt in the just completed therapy session. On the second line, the client rates how much the client and therapist worked on what he or she wanted to talk about. On the third line, the client rates how good a "fit" the therapy approach was for him or her. On the fourth line, the client rates how satisfied he or she felt about the session. The scale is completed by the client immediately after the session has ended. Use of the SRS is free of charge to individual mental health practitioners by license agreement found at www.talkingcure.com.

Outcomes Rating Scale

The Outcomes Rating Scale (ORS; S. Miller & Duncan, 2000) is a short and easy-to-administer outcome measure consisting of four items. The instructions are simple and straightforward. The client is given a sheet of paper on which four horizontal lines 10 centimeters long are printed. The client is asked to mark with a pen stroke, somewhere along each horizontal line, how things went in the past week. On the first line, the client rates his or her personal well-being. On the second line, the client rates his or her relationships. On the third, the client rates his or her social and work life. On the fourth, the client rates his or her general, overall sense of well-being. The scale is typically completed by the client immediately before the session begins, although it may be administered after the first meeting. Use of the ORS is free of charge to individual mental health practitioners by license agreement found at www.talkingcure.com.

UTILIZING SUPERVISION TO EVALUATE TREATMENT PROGRESS

At first glance, this competency may seem out of place in this chapter or even this book. It might seem that this competency would be better included in a book or training manual on supervisory competencies. Actually, because supervision is a primary means of developing and evaluating psychotherapy competencies, many consider the effective use of supervision by trainees to be an essential intervention competency (Haynes, Corey, & Moulton, 2003). For this reason, this competency is addressed in this chapter.

The primary purpose of clinical supervision is to help trainees become more effective therapists. Although it agreed that specific feedback is a key ingredient in effective supervision, there is relatively little research on feedback and its effect on client outcomes (Freitas, 2002). Fortunately, a new model of feedback-based supervision has been described that has promising research support. The model is based on tracking client outcomes and using these data to guide supervision.

Because tracking client outcomes and the therapeutic relationship across treatment is now a recommended practice for therapists (Lambert & Ogles, 2004), a clinical research project investigated whether this practice would extend to trainees if the data gained from clients were provided to their supervisor for use within supervision (Reese, Usher, Bowman, Norsworthy, Halsted, et al., 2009). Trainees were assigned to a continuous feedback condition (received and reviewed ORS and SRS with clients) or no-feedback condition (received but did not review) for one academic year.

Results indicated that trainees in both conditions demonstrated better client outcomes at the end of their practicum training than at the beginning, but those in the feedback condition showed *twice* as much improvement. It is noteworthy that this finding is consistent with research on experienced therapists who utilize both measures with client feedback (Anker et al., 2009; Reese, Norsworthy, & Rowlands, 2009). What accounted for this doubled level of improvement among trainees? In the feedback group, supervisors used the client feedback data to organize supervisory sessions such that clients who were making less progress were given more attention in supervision. Both trainees and supervisors agreed that client feedback was useful, with supervisors agreeing that it assisted them in providing trainees with challenging feedback and helped to identify clients who needed more attention in supervision (Reese, Usher, et al., 2009).

It may well be that using outcome data consistently in supervision can provide trainees with a more accurate perception of their abilities and may encourage them to share information about clients, particularly when things are not going well. Presumably, trainees who have access to here-and-now evidence that their clients are improving will experience increased self-confidence and self-efficacy in their competence as therapists. Furthermore, because recent research found that supervisors are significantly related to client outcome, training programs should routinely track client outcomes as an objective indicator of quality supervision (Callahan, Almstrom, Swift, Borja, & Heath 2009). In short, the use of client outcome data in supervision holds the promise of facilitating these training outcomes.

TREATMENT MONITORING IN THREE THERAPEUTIC APPROACHES

Cognitive–Behavioral Therapies

Of all the therapeutic approaches, cognitive–behavioral therapy (CBT) seems most cognizant of the value of formal monitoring of treatment outcomes. Besides contributing to improved outcomes and quality of care, a second reason for cognitive–behavioral therapists to use ongoing assessment with objective measures is that it can increase understanding of the mechanisms of therapeutic change (Persons, 2007). It may well be that this scientific perspective on clinical work more easily translates to formally monitoring clinical outcomes for those practicing CBT than for other approaches. In addition, there are a number of formal, theory-based measures in CBT that are sensitive to session-to-session change. Among others, these include the Beck Depression Inventory, the Beck Hopelessness Scale, and the Beck Anxiety Inventory (J. Beck, 1995). Another common measure, SUDS (Subjective Units of Distress Scale), is a client self-rating measure of their anxiety and distress on a 1 to 100 scale that clinicians can monitor from session to session (Wolpe, 1969). It is not uncommon for those practicing cognitive therapy to routinely monitor session-to-session scores on one or more of the Beck scales.

When it comes to research applications of treatment monitoring in CBT, several studies have been reported on the use of formal theory–based measures. For example, Kuyken (2004) monitored Beck Hopelessness Scale scores from session to session on depressed clients. He found that if hopelessness symptoms did not improve within the first four sessions, the Beck Hopelessness Scale predicted poor treatment outcomes as measured by scores on the Beck Depression Inventory. Persons (2007) reports on a number of similar studies.

Dynamic Psychotherapies

Except for research purposes, standardized outcome measures do not appear to be employed in the clinical practice among the various dynamic psychotherapies. When it comes to research, several measures, including the Symptom Check List (SCL-90; Derogatis & Cleary, 1977) and various measures of therapeutic alliance such as the Working Alliance Inventory (WAI; Horvath & Greenberg, 1989), are commonly employed. Because the therapeutic alliance is central to many of the dynamic therapies, it is not surprising that pre–post assessment with the WAI is a commonly used outcome measure in dynamic therapy research.

In actual clinical practice, there do not appear to be much in the way of nonstandardized outcome measures either. Nonetheless, a time-limited dynamic therapist could monitor treatment progress in terms of therapeutic focus. Because research indicates that tracking a therapeutic focus, such as salient maladaptive interpersonal themes, contributes to positive treatment outcomes, Binder (2004) proposes "a strategy of tracking a structured content focus combined with flexibly modifying the content as new information arises and digressing from the initial focus as circumstances dictate" (Binder, 2004, p. 100). Another such nonstandardized outcome measure is the resolution of transference enactments demonstrated by a client's corrective emotional experience.

Systemic Therapies

Generally speaking, specific systemic therapies (e.g., structural family therapy, strategic therapy, narrative therapy, etc.) do not advocate the use of formal, standardized measures for evaluating progress in therapy. However, at least one family therapy textbook suggests the use of the OQ-45, the SRS and ORS, or the SCL-90, or similar measures to monitor ongoing change or overall change (Gehart, 2010).

On the other hand, a nonstandardized outcome measure is commonly used in some systemic therapies, most notably in solution-focused therapy: It is scaling or the scaling question (de Shazer, 1994). Scaling is a client-rated scale (from 1 to 10, wherein 1 is the worst or lowest and 10 is the best or highest rating). Clinicians strategically ask clients to scale how they rate a situation, their reaction or a symptom, or their progress. As a measure of progress, scaling questions invite clients to identify small steps toward goal attainment. For instance, if a client rated his or her progress as a 4, the clinician might ask, "What things might need to happen for you to tell me at our next session that your rating is a 5?" "Ongoing scaling in sessions presupposes change and provides feedback on differences among family members" (Carlson, Sperry, & Lewis, 2005, p. 38).

In sum, these theory-based approaches place little or no emphasis on monitoring and evaluating treatment outcomes, at least with standardized measures. The exception is CBT, which probably reflects its scientific perspective on clinical practice. Table 11.1 summarizes the use of treatment monitoring in clinical practice. Note that the table does not include research efforts involving treatment monitoring and evaluation.

CASE EXAMPLE

We return to the case of Geri to illustrate the treatment monitoring with the use of the SRS and the ORS in the first session. Geri rated the social scale of the ORS as a 1, a 5 on the individual scale, 2 on the interpersonal scale, and a 3.5 as her overall rating. The very low social scale rating probably reflected her exquisite sensitivity to criticism and the expectation that it would be almost impossible to work for a new boss in an office setting where she did not know or trust the other support staff. The therapist reflected Geri's concerns and suggested that addressing the promotion/job transfer with both Geri and her supervisor would be a priority of the therapy. On the SRS, a measure of therapeutic alliance, Geri had rated the

Table 11.1   Monitoring Treatment in Clinical Practice in Three Therapeutic Approaches

Approaches	Focal Considerations
Dynamic	Observation and interview assessment of the therapeutic focus or of resolution of transference enactments with resultant corrective emotional experiences
Cognitive–Behavioral	Use of specific measures such as SUDS, the Beck Depression Inventory, and the Beck Anxiety Inventory to monitor client progress from session to session
Systemic	Observation and interview assessment with the use of scaling questions to monitor client progress both within sessions and from session to session

relationship scale as a 3 and the others as a 6. A brief discussion ensued about what Geri was thinking when she rated the relationship scale. She said it was very, very difficult to be around new people. She also added that at first she was going to rate the relationship scale as a 1 or 2 but changed her mind, thinking that she did not feel as awkward and anxious as she thought she would. Anticipating that being too warm and too positive too quickly might activate Geri's avoidant pattern (just as if she had been surprised and perhaps a bit disappointed at Geri's low ratings), the therapist nodded, smiled slightly, and said she understood.

Case Commentary. The SRS and ORS ratings were useful to the therapist in getting feedback from Geri while at the same time not reacting in an evaluative manner, which would have meant that the therapist failed the first "trust" test of their relationship. Because the therapist anticipated Geri's "testing" attitude and behavior, she expected that it might take three, four, or more sessions before sufficient trust was established and the ratings would rise considerably.

CONCLUDING NOTE

In this current era of accountability when psychotherapists are expected to demonstrate the effectiveness of their treatment, the clinical competency of treatment monitoring continues to be woefully neglected in that less than one half of American Psychological Association–accredited internships provide training in outcomes assessment. The consequences of this neglect are multiple and far reaching. The first such consequence is the deleterious effect of premature termination, which has been attributed to failure to identify clients' expectations for treatment (Callahan, Aubuchon-Endsley, Borja, & Swift, 2009). Another consequence is that trainees have less experience in developing the necessary competencies involved in the middle and end phases of treatment because of premature termination. A less obvious, but very real, consequence is the public's crisis of confidence about psychotherapy. In a national survey commissioned by the American Psychological Association about reasons for not seeking help from mental professionals, 77% of respondents said they would not seek psychotherapy because they lacked confidence in the outcomes of this form of treatment (Penn, Scheon, & Berland Associates, 2004).

Besides being neglected in too many training programs, there is little apparent awareness of the interdependency of this core competency with the other core competencies. For example, why teach trainees how to develop a therapeutic alliance and a case conceptualization and treatment plan, or to implement interventions, if the trainees are not also taught how to monitor and seek feedback from clients on the therapeutic alliance, the case conceptualization, and the implemented interventions? For this reason, this chapter advocated for training in and use of ongoing assessment in everyday clinical practice. Emphasized were the use of formal and standardized measures of therapy process (assessment of the therapeutic alliance) and outcomes (assessment of clinical outcomes). Finally, this chapter also advocated for the incorporation of ongoing assessment in the context of clinical supervision.

12

Termination

Termination is the last phase of treatment and represents both an event and process. As an event, termination means client–therapist contact ends, and as a process it means that the client's level of responsibility increases as the nature of the client–therapist relationship changes. Facilitating the process of terminating and preparing the client for termination is the therapist's primary focus in the last phase of treatment. Preparing for termination is a time for clients to express their thoughts and feelings about what the therapeutic process and the therapist has meant to them, as well as an opportunity to review their progress in achieving treatment goals. It is also a time to plan for maintaining treatment gains and to anticipate the inevitable lapses and setbacks that may ensue. Finally, preparing for termination is a time to reflect about what remaining therapeutic tasks clients might work on in the future and what additional therapeutic contact with the therapist or other treatment might be indicated.

Too often the clinical competency of preparing for termination has been neglected or downplayed in training programs and in textbooks. The situation has not improved appreciably in the past 30 years since training programs were criticized: "Not only are criteria and techniques for termination not taught and discussed, but termination as a valuable therapeutic opportunity is undoubtedly neglected" (Weddington & Cavenar, 1979, p. 1303). An indicator of this neglect is high dropout rates from psychotherapy. As noted in Chapter 11, premature termination rates are approximately 50% (Clarkin & Levy, 2003; Wierzbicki & Pekarik, 1993) and appear to be much higher in training programs. A recent study found that the rate of premature termination observed in one training clinic was 77% (Callahan, Aubuchon-Endsley, et al., 2009).

Nevertheless, effective and competent psychotherapy practice assumes the capacity to deal effectively with termination issues. Accordingly, this competency is addressed in this chapter as well as a related competency: maintaining treatment gains. This chapter begins with a discussion of maintaining treatment gains and preventing relapse before discussing the competency of termination. Then it describes considerations about termination in three psychotherapeutic approaches. Finally, it illustrates preparing for termination with a case example.

TERMINATION COMPETENCIES

This chapter addresses two essential clinical competencies involving termination which are associated with the core competency of intervention evaluation and termination.

Maintaining Treatment Gains

This competency involves the capacity to assist clients in maintaining the therapeutic gains they have achieved in treatment. It also involves the capacity to assist clients in developing and implementing a relapse prevention plan that further ensures their gains will be maintained.

Preparing for Termination

This competency involves the capacity to prepare the client for planned termination from formal treatment. This preparation is a process that begins with the first session and continues through the last session.

MAINTAINING TREATMENT GAINS

Making progress in therapy usually consists of some combination of the client gaining insights, being less symptomatic, feeling better, thinking more positive, or acting in more adaptive ways. There is no guarantee that such progress or treatment gains will be maintained. Progress in therapy can be additive, but just as often regressions occur. The client's challenge is to stay the course and continue to practice and apply the skills and strategies learned in the course of therapy. Such ongoing efforts are essential for maintaining gains (therapeutic change). This section briefly reviews some research on treatment gains and describes relapse prevention and self-therapy. Relapse prevention and self-therapy are important components of the early and middle phases of therapy and are also critical components of the final phase of therapy when preparing the client for termination.

Research on Maintenance of Treatment Gains

Therapists typically expect that their clients will continue to improve after termination. However, a meta-analysis of research studies suggests that there is commonly a reduction of the therapeutic effect over time (Smith, Glass, & Miller, 1980). Therapists may also expect that their clients will maintain their treatment gain or effect. However, research reveals that clients do not routinely maintain their treatment gains. Several studies suggest that long-term treatment gain is a function of various factors, which include treatment modality (individual therapy, mediation, group, etc.), the therapeutic approach (cognitive–behavioral, dynamic, systemic, etc.), length of treatment (brief or long term), presenting problem (anxiety, depression, post-traumatic stress disorder [PTSD], etc.), and whether provision for preventing relapse or setbacks were employed. Cognitive–behavioral therapy (CBT) is a psychotherapeutic approach that is an effective and sustaining treatment given its emphasis on maintaining treatment gains and relapse prevention. Research has rather consistently supported this contention. For example, in a review of several meta-analyses, it was concluded that CBT is indeed an effective treatment for the following presenting problems: adult depression, adolescent depression, generalized anxiety disorder, panic disorder, social phobia, as well as childhood depressive and anxiety disorders (Butler & Beck, 2000). In another meta-analysis of eight studies in which treatment consisted of either CBT or medication, differential treatment gains were noted 1 year after treatment was discontinued. Among those receiving medication, only some 60% relapsed, whereas only 30% receiving CBT relapsed (Gloaguen, Cottraus, Cucharet, & Blackburn, 1998). It seems that CBT helped clients to make lasting changes, whereas the changes initially produced by the medication diminished after discontinuing it. In short, when clients have a plan and the skills to prevent relapse, are motivated, and have a plan for continued growth, the treatment effect is likely to be maintained and even increased. Clearly, relapse prevention is a key factor in maintaining treatment gains.

Planning and Preventing Relapse

Relapse prevention is a self-control strategy for helping clients to anticipate and cope with the problem of relapse or recurrence of symptoms or problematic behaviors (Daley, 1989). Although it was initially developed as a treatment adjunct with addictive behaviors (Marlatt & Gordon, 1985), it has been applied to smoking cessation, pain control, weight management, sleep disorders, and most psychiatric disorders (Sperry, Lewis, Carlson, & Englar-Carlson, 2003). In short, relapse prevention is a strategy for anticipating and reducing the likelihood of relapse.

Relapse prevention planning (Marlatt & Gordon, 1985) begins with the assessment of a client's likely interpersonal, intrapersonal, environmental, and physiological risks for relapse and specific stressors and situations that may precipitate it. Once these potential triggers and high-risk situations are identified, cognitive and behavioral techniques are implemented that incorporate specific interventions to prevent them or manage them if they do occur. It also involves a discussion of more global strategies to address lifestyle balance, cravings, and cognitive distortions that could expose the client to high-risk situations where relapse is most likely. Such a relapse plan is likely to increase the client's sense of self-efficacy and effectiveness in maintaining treatment gains (Carroll, 1996).

Self-Therapy

It is commonly said that the ultimate goal of treatment is to assist clients in becoming their own therapists. But, how do clients become their own therapists? J. Beck (1995) addresses this question and suggests how clients can develop what she calls a "self-therapy" program. In self-therapy, clients take responsibility for conducting their own therapy much like their sessions with a cognitive–behavioral therapist. That is, they set an agenda, review past homework, address a particular problem and process it, decide on new homework, and schedule their next self-therapy session. Becoming one's own therapist begins during the last phase of therapy. Here clients are urged to apply self-therapy as problems or issues arise and then discuss their efforts with their therapist in the next scheduled session. Thus, after termination, a client will already have the experience of doing self-therapy and be able to handle most problems, relapses, or setbacks. "If she is unsuccessful, at least she has had an opportunity to use her skills once more. If she does need another appointment, the therapist can help the patient discover what got in the way of her handling the setback or problem independently, and they can plan what the patient can do differently in the future" (J. Beck, 1995, p. 278).

PREPARING FOR TERMINATION

Although preparing a client for termination is usually considered a key task of the final phase of therapy, some approaches such as cognitive therapy consider it a task that begins much earlier (J. Beck, 1995). As noted previously, the treatment formulation component of the case conceptualization serves as a guide to both specifying treatment outcomes and anticipating obstacles and challenges to achieving those outcomes. More specifically, it assists the therapist in anticipating particular difficulties a specific client may experience with termination. Thus, the therapist will not be surprised when a particular client experiences difficulty with termination because of a history of losses or a pattern of clinging or dependency on others (Cucciare & O'Donohue, 2008).

Indicators of Readiness for Termination

Different therapeutic approaches describe theory-specific criteria for determining when termination is indicated. However, there are also some general indicators common to these various approaches that are useful in assessing a client's readiness for termination from treatment. These include the following:

1. The client's presenting problem is essentially resolved, or symptoms are reduced or alleviated.
2. The client has developed sufficient insight to understand the problem and patterns that led to treatment.
3. The client's coping skills are sufficiently improved for dealing with life circumstances.
4. The client has more capacity to plan and work productively on post-termination issues (based on Heaton, 1998).

Typical Scenario in Discussing Termination

During the course of a planned termination, several activities and processes are commonly observed. These include "a retrospective look at how therapy has proceeded, sharpening of client's future plans for life without the therapist, discussion of possible return appointments, and a statement of appreciation by both client and therapist" (Good & Beitman, 2006, p. 211).

The therapist does well to begin the process by asking the client to recount the most important changes the client has made in the course of treatment. "Reviewing progress with patients may enable them to more clearly see the significance of their treatment gains, potentially motivating them to continue maintaining gains and building on the progress that they have made during treatment" (Dobson & Haubert, 2008, p. 314). A corollary is to discuss the skills they have learned in therapy.

TERMINATION CONSIDERATIONS IN THREE THERAPEUTIC APPROACHES

Dynamic Therapies

The issues involving termination are somewhat different among the various dynamic approaches, often as a function of the length of therapy. For example, the incidence of premature termination from intensive (long-term) psychoanalytic psychotherapy and psychoanalysis is high, particularly among trainees who "have the highest dropout rate, with more than one-third of their first cases leaving prematurely and often precipitously" (Frayn, 2008, p. 50). This researcher found that during the initial assessment, these trainees consistently underestimated the degree of psychopathology among analysands (clients). In contrast with long-term dynamic therapy, termination in brief dynamic therapy can be particularly difficult for both client and therapist. If not handled well, termination can undermine previous treatment gains (Levenson, 1995). Issues of loss are especially problematic. Fortunately, for the brief forms of interpersonally oriented dynamic therapies such as time-limited dynamic psychotherapy (TLDP), issues of loss are dealt with throughout the course of treatment and not just at termination. "As termination approaches, one can expect to see the patient's anxiety handled in ways characteristic for that particular patient's CMP [cyclical maladaptive pattern]. The best advice to the TLDP therapist is to stay with the dynamic focus and the goals for treatment, while examining how these patterns are evidenced when loss and separations issues are most salient" (Levenson, 1995, p. 204).

In preparing for termination where ending the therapeutic relations is likely to be problematic for a client, the therapist's own preparation for termination should include the following considerations: Begin by reviewing the central therapeutic themes and issues that have been the focus of treatment. Next, identify how the client construes and imagines what ending the therapeutic relationship will be like. Then, consider how the client's characterological style will influence his or her reaction to termination (Binder, 2004). For example, take the client who has been working on dependency, rejection sensitivity, impulse control, and trust issues; who views termination as a form of rejection that she had come to expect from significant others; and who is emotionally dependent on the therapist. It should be no surprise that such a client is likely to react in a characteristically defensive fashion, possibly by acting out with threats of self-harm.

Accordingly, the therapist would anticipate discussing the client's termination, rejection expectations, and fears, possibly in the context of a transference enactment, hopefully resulting in a corrective emotional experience and greater confidence that the client can not only tolerate termination but also grow as a result of the experience. Therapists need to explicitly describe the time-limited nature of TLDP and "if a termination date is set early in treatment, the therapist does so only after the patient's psychological resources and interpersonal support network have been evaluated and a focus for the therapeutic work has been formulated and accepted by the patient" (Binder, 2004, p. 239).

Five criteria are given for determining timing of termination from TLDP: (1) Client shows positive changes in interactions with significant others (most important criterion), (2) client has one or more corrective emotional experiences, (3) there is a change in the level of client–therapist relating, (4) there is a shift in therapist's countertransference to client, and (5) client evidences some insight into his or her relational dynamics and role in maintaining them. Meeting most of these criteria, particularly the first, likely indicates termination is feasible (Levenson, 1995).

Cognitive–Behavioral Therapies

Because CBT is a time-limited approach, therapists and clients must think about termination from the very beginning of therapy (J. Beck, 1995). This means that therapists must establish a clear end point for the treatment process and make the client aware of it in the context of time limits. Having such an end point prompts the client to make changes by a specific time. Instead of viewing therapy as an indefinite process with the expectation of slow, steady progress, the client realizes that there are only three or four sessions left to make needed changes. Bearing the end point in mind prompts the therapist to continually reevaluate the treatment formulation and whether the intervention plan is working. Each session is structured and goal-oriented, and "each session must inform the subsequent session, in effect creating a path to termination. After each session, a clinician should ask him- or herself, 'What do I need to do next to accomplish the goals of the therapy?'" (Ledley et al., 2005, p. 196).

The ultimate end point of CBT is for clients to become their own therapists, such that clients can use their newly acquired understandings and skills to deal with their problems and concerns. As termination approaches, the therapist should elicit the client's automatic thoughts about termination and then help the client to process them (J. Beck, 1995). "When both clinician and client feel confident that the client knows how to be his or her own therapist, the time has probably come to terminate therapy" (Ledley et al., 2005, p. 201). This may mean that treatment can end when the time limit has been reached (e.g., 12 sessions), or it may mean that the therapeutic contract is revised, with needed additional sessions to reach the ultimate end point.

Once the client has experienced symptom reduction and learned basic CBT tools, "therapy is gradually tapered, on a trial basis to once every 2 weeks and then to once every 3 to 4 weeks" (J. Beck, 1995, p. 269). In addition, booster sessions are scheduled at 3, 6, and 12 months after termination, primarily to foster maintenance of treatment gains. Prior to termination, preparing for setbacks and a self-therapy plan may be discussed (J. Beck, 1995). In CBT, this process of preparing for setbacks is often called a relapse prevention plan.

Of the three therapeutic approaches, CBT has continued to research and refine its recommendations for relapse prevention and termination based on clinical practice and research (Antony, Ledley, & Heimberg, 2005; O'Donohue & Cucciare, 2008; Cucciare & O'Donohue, 2008). Research has led to specific relapse prevention recommendations for the various Axis I disorders (e.g., panic disorder, PTSD, depression, bipolar disorder, etc.). For instance, in high-risk clients with depression, post-termination maintenance therapy, that is, spaced out sessions resembling regular therapy sessions, has been shown to reduce relapse better than booster sessions (Rowa, Bieling, & Segal, 2005).

Systemic Therapies

Unlike individual therapy, termination is not considered a major therapeutic issue or special event in the course of treatment. This is particularly the case in the briefer systemic approaches, which view therapy to be "intermittent" (occurring when needed) rather than "ongoing" (regularly scheduled weekly sessions). In the intermittent view, therapy sessions occur based on immediate need, and the therapist functions like a family physician who sees patients only when medical need arises (Cummings & VandenBos, 1979). Viewed from this perspective, "it follows that 'termination' is not viewed as a special event" (Quick, 2008, p. 135).

In strategic therapy, talk of termination is usually replaced with some general therapist comments near the end of a session. For example, the therapist may recommend that the client "go slow" and hold back on making further improvement for the time being, may predict a "relapse" and offer a suggestion for dealing with that relapse, or may suggest a return for a "booster session" (Fisch, Weakland, & Segal, 1982).

In solution-focused therapy, termination is similarly underplayed. Instead, two treatment options may be offered when the client's presenting problem is resolved to the client's satisfaction. The first is not to schedule a follow-up session, and the second is the option of resuming treatment if the same problem or another problem surfaces (de Shazer, 1991).

Clients are asked to consider their current situation and to make a judgment: "If things stay like they are, is that good enough for you?" Coping "sufficiently" or "well enough" with a difficult situation may be sufficient. Acceptance of one's situation is considered an important part of the solution. Some who practice solution-focused therapy consider each session to be either a first or last session (Walter & Peller, 1992). "Either the therapist is essentially saying, 'Keep doing what works, go slow on additional change, and you know where I am if you need me' (a 'last session message') or the therapist is clarifying the problem, exploring desired solutions, and inquiring about attempted solutions ('first session behavior')" (Quick, 2008, pp. 138–139).

Table 12.1 summarizes termination considerations in these three approaches.

Table 12.1 Termination Considerations in Three Therapeutic Approaches

Approach	Considerations
Dynamic	Termination process differs depending on approach and time frame (brief or long term). In TLDP, the challenge is usually with clients who have difficulty with ending relationships with significant others. Strategy is to review the themes and central issues related to therapeutic focus, consider their personality style, and explore the clients' perceptions of termination. Key criteria for termination is whether client evidences positive changes in interactions with significant others.
Cognitive–Behavioral	Planning for treatment begins in the first session, and the time-limited nature of CBT prompts both client and therapist to collaborate on change. End point of termination is the clients' readiness to be their own therapist so they can apply what they have learned to resolve issues as they emerge. Developing a relapse prevention plan is essential in preparing for termination.
Systemic	A less formal and structured view of termination than most individual therapy approaches. To the extent treatment is viewed as intermittent rather than continuous, each session can be viewed as either a first or last session. In solution-focused therapy, the criteria for stopping sessions is the client's determination that he or she is coping "well enough" or that "acceptance" is a sufficient solution to a difficult situation.

A CASE ILLUSTRATION OF TERMINATION

We return a final time to the case of Geri. She collaborated in a combined treatment involving medication, individual therapy, and group psycho-education. Her medications were to be monitored by her primary care physician, and a contract for 16 individual CBT sessions and 6 group sessions was mutually established. Given her shy and avoidant style, Geri participated in 4 individual sessions, which prepared her for transition into the psychoeducation group. She continued in individual sessions while also participating in 6 group sessions, after which she was to continue in 6 additional individual sessions. The individual sessions focused on symptom reduction, cognitive restructuring of maladaptive schemas, and returning to work, while group sessions focused on increasing social relatedness and friendship skills training. Because the therapy was cognitive-behaviorally oriented, a brief discussion and preparation for termination began in their first therapy session. The case conceptualization anticipated that Geri would likely have difficulty with termination given her limited social network and tendency to be overly reliant on the few individuals whom she could trust, of which the therapist would be one. To reduce the likelihood of difficulty with termination, treatment very early focused on increasing her social network and friendship skills. During their 12th individual session, discussion focused on planning for termination as only 4 scheduled sessions remained. By then Geri had been back to work for 5 weeks. Because of the therapist's advocacy efforts with Geri's supervisor, Geri remained in the same office as the senior administrative assistant to the vice president she already knew and whom she considered reasonably safe. The previous senior administrative assistant was agreeable to moving to the office of the newly hired vice president.

In that session, the therapist reviewed Geri's progress in individual and group sessions as well as in homework efforts. Geri agreed that she had increased her social network by renewing her relationship with her aunt and making another "close" friend. There was also some improvement in assertive communication. Nevertheless, Geri was anxious, as noted when the therapist elicited her automatic thoughts about termination: "It's really scary, I don't think I can stand it," "I want to just keep coming to these sessions." After processing these thoughts and associated feelings, a relapse prevention plan was established, and Geri agreed to tapering sessions to 2 weeks for the 13th and 14th sessions, and then 4 weeks for the 15th and 16th sessions. During the 16th session, Geri was feeling more confident and more ready for a phased termination plan in which maintenance sessions would be scheduled at 2-month intervals over the next 12 months. The decision to utilize maintenance rather than booster sessions was informed by recommendations based on research of follow-up care with clients highly prone to relapse—depressed, unmarried females (Rowa et al., 2005).

Given Geri's avoidant personality, the recommendation for maintenance rather than booster sessions seemed most reasonable. Bimonthly maintenance sessions continued for a year, during which time Geri's antidepressant medication was discontinued. Booster sessions were scheduled at 4-month intervals for another year after which it was mutually agreed that only as-needed sessions would be scheduled. At 24 months after the initial termination, Geri reported "doing well" without formal therapy.

CONCLUDING NOTE

This chapter focused on maintaining the gains achieved in therapy, preventing relapse, and terminating treatment. As already noted, these strategies are often overlooked in clinical training. Nevertheless, the effective practice of psychotherapy requires that trainees and experienced clinicians exhibit these competencies.

Section VII

Core Competency 6: Cultural and Ethical Sensitivity

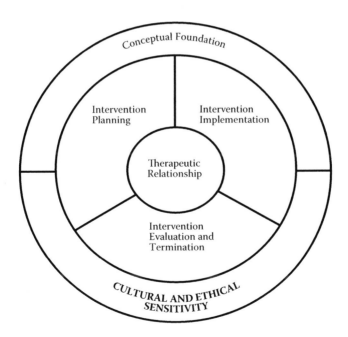

13

Cultural Sensitivity

Diversity and cultural awareness have been increasingly embraced within mental health training programs in the past decade. This is particularly evident in required course work in which cultural awareness is the primary focus. Although cultural awareness is a necessary condition, it is by no means the sufficient condition for effective treatment. Sufficient conditions include cultural sensitivity and cultural competence. Cultural competence is demonstrated by the capacity to achieve culturally sensitive therapeutic alliances, cultural formulations, and culturally sensitive interventions, as well as positive treatment outcomes. So, how culturally sensitive and competent are trainees and clinicians? Available data that address this question are somewhat sobering. A study of practicing psychotherapists found that the overwhelming majority believed that it was most important to develop cultural formulations and also important to use these culturally sensitive case conceptualizations to guide their clinical practice. In other words, there is a high level of cultural awareness. However, very few clinicians—only about 14%—reported that they actually developed or used these formulations to guide their clinical practice (Hansen, Randazzo, Schwartz, Marshall, Kalis, et al., 2006) suggesting that cultural sensitivity and competence are low. Trainees seem to share a similar fate (Neufield, Pinterits, Moleiro, Lee, Yang, et al., 2006). Because cultural sensitivity and cultural competence increasingly will be expected of mental health professionals, the need for training in this core competency is becoming more pressing. This chapter addresses this need.

Cultural sensitivity plays a key role in the core competency of intervention planning, particularly with regard to case conceptualization and treatment planning. Accordingly, this chapter focuses on the clinical competencies of cultural formulation and culturally sensitive interventions. This chapter begins by briefly defining basic constructs related to cultural sensitivity and cultural competence. It then describes these two culturally sensitive, essential clinical competencies and their application in psychotherapy practice. Clinical examples illustrate both of these competencies.

CULTURAL SENSITIVITY COMPETENCIES

This chapter addresses two culturally sensitive essential clinical competencies that are associated with the core competency of cultural and ethical sensitivity.

Develop Effective Cultural Formulations

This competency involves the capacity to develop a compelling explanation for the client's presenting problem and maladaptive pattern when cultural factors are operative.

Plan Culturally Sensitive Interventions

This competency involves the capacity to develop a treatment plan and incorporate culturally sensitive treatment when cultural factors are operative and indicated.

DEFINITIONS

Often terms like *cultural knowledge, cultural awareness, cultural sensitivity,* and *cultural competency* are used synonymously. Although there is some similarity among these constructs, they also differ and these differences can be significant. For instance, it is possible to possess cultural knowledge without possessing either cultural awareness or cultural sensitivity. It is possible to be culturally sensitive without being culturally competent. Thus, it is important to know the specific denotations and meanings of them. There is a progression of meaning from cultural knowledge to cultural competence, and bearing this progression in mind permits an accurate use of these terms. Let's begin with cultural knowledge, which is a familiarization with selected cultural characteristics, like the history, values, beliefs, and behaviors of another cultural heritage. Next in the progression is cultural awareness, which is an understanding of, and some degree of openness to, another cultural heritage. Next in the progression is cultural sensitivity, and in a sense, cultural awareness is a prerequisite for it. Cultural sensitivity is the capacity to appropriately respond to the attitudes, feelings, circumstances of clients and others of a different ethnic, racial, religious, or cultural heritage. The operative phrase is "capacity to appropriately respond." Finally, cultural competence is the capacity to translate cultural sensitivity into prosocial behaviors or actions that have positive influence on an individual or individuals from another cultural heritage. In a clinical context, cultural competence is the capacity to translate clinicians' cultural sensitivity into behavior that results in an effective therapeutic relationship and treatment process as well as positive treatment outcomes (Paniagua, 2005).

It should also be noted that cultural competence typically results in what has been called achieved credibility (Okazaki, 2000; Sue & Zane, 1987), or clinician credibility as it is referred to in this book. Clinician credibility refers to a culturally diverse client's perception that his or her clinician is effective and trustworthy based on how that clinician instills faith, trust, and confidence in the client regarding the treatment process and outcomes. Table 13.1 summarizes these and other definitions that appear throughout the chapter.

CULTURAL ASSESSMENT

Becoming culturally competent requires the capacity to perform an accurate and comprehensive cultural assessment. Such an assessment will include the following: cultural identity, age, ethnicity and race, gender and sexual orientation, religion, migration and country of origin, socioeconomic status, level of acculturation, language, explanatory model and illness perceptions, dietary influences, and education (GAP Committee on Cultural Psychiatry, 2002, pp. 20–47). Typically, clinicians elicit and report only 3 of these 12 factors: age, gender, and ethnicity. For example, the first sentence in the "Identifying Information and Chief Complaint" section of a clinical

Table 13.1 Culturally Sensitive and Competent Treatment: Some Key Terms

Cultural sensitivity	Clinicians' awareness of cultural variables in themselves and in their client that may affect the therapeutic relationship and treatment process.
Cultural competency	The capacity to translate clinicians' cultural sensitivity into behavior that results in an effective therapeutic relationship and treatment process as well as positive treatment outcomes. It also involves achieving clinician credibility.
Clinician credibility	The culturally diverse client's perception that the clinician is effective and trustworthy based on how the clinician instills faith, trust, and confidence in the client for the treatment process and outcomes.
Cultural identity	An individual's self-identification and perceived sense of belonging to a particular culture or place of origin.
Acculturation	The degree to which individuals integrate new cultural patterns into their original cultural patterns.
Brief Acculturation Scale	A measure of three levels of acculturation (low, medium, high) based on the client's language (native vs. English), generation (first to fifth), and social activities (preference for friends—same racial group vs. different racial group).
Explanatory model	The client's own personal explanation for what is causing his or her problems, symptoms, and impaired functioning. It is akin to the counselor's case conceptualization.
Illness Perception Inventory	An instrument that assesses a client's beliefs about his or her illness in terms of its identity or diagnostic label, its causes, its effects, its timeline, and the control of symptoms and recovery from it. It is an excellent measure of a client's specific cultural beliefs and cultural intervention practices regarding the presenting problem.

report usually begins with a statement of ethnicity, age, and gender: "This is a 34-year-old African American female." Although gender may be specified, sexual orientation is seldom indicated. Three others are either assumed or specified somewhere else in a clinical report. These are language, education, and socioeconomic status. This means that the remaining 5 of the 12 dimensions of culture are not elicited or addressed at all by most clinicians. Eliciting information regarding these cultural factors can be accomplished in approximately 7 to 8 minutes. This information can be valuable in understanding clients' coping and social resources as well as in planning and implementing interventions (Ridley & Kelly, 2007).

This section will focus on these often forgotten factors: cultural identity, level of acculturation, illness perceptions and explanatory model, as well as treatment expectations. It also includes personality dynamics and relevant psychosocial factors, as they interact with the aforementioned cultural factors to influence the client's presenting problem. Each of these factors is briefly described relative to clinical practice.

Cultural Identity

Cultural identity is an individual's self-identification and perceived sense of belonging to a particular culture or place of origin (Paniagua, 2005). This identity can reflect the individual's ethnicity or place of origin, or it can reflect the individual's current cultural context. The cultural identification of the members of the same nuclear family may differ, often reflecting individual family members' level of acculturation.

Acculturation

Acculturation is the process by which immigrants adapt to a new culture, and it reflects the level or degree to which individuals integrate new cultural patterns into their original cultural patterns (Dana, 1993). There are several ways of assessing acculturation. A short and clinically useful method is the Brief Acculturation Scale. This scale is a measure of three levels of acculturation (low, medium, high) based on the client's language (native vs. English), generation (first to fifth), and social activities (prefers for friends—native vs. mainline; Burnam, Hough, Karno, Escobar, & Telles, 1987). The scale and its scoring system for three levels (low = 1.0–1.75; medium = 1.76–3.25; and high = 3.26–5.0) are available in Paniagua's book (Paniagua, 2005, pp. 11–12).

Explanatory Models

Clients' perception of cause (i.e., explanation of why they have their illness or situation) is referred to as an explanatory model (Kleinman, 1988; Sperry, 2009). This construct emerged from cultural and medical anthropology about 50 years ago to assist research on individuals' beliefs about causality of personal matters, particularly illness, whether it was physical or psychological. An explanatory model is elicited through interview questions such as, "What do you suppose is causing your situation? How do you explain your illness? Why is it that you are experiencing these symptoms (conflict, etc.) now?" Responses such as stress, "nerves," a chemical brain imbalance, or early childhood trauma are consistent with the scientific mind-set of mainstream culture. On the other hand, responses such as demonic influence, spirits, hexes or spells, being tested by God, or punishment from God are more likely to be made by clients with nonmainstream cultural beliefs and values and who likely demonstrate lower levels of acculturation. Follow-up questions allow the clinician to further explore the influences of cultural beliefs in the client's life, often as expressed in their clinical presentation.

Illness Perceptions

Illness representations or perceptions are an extension or iteration of explanatory models (Leventhal, Diefenbach, & Leventhal, 1992). In addition to beliefs about causality, illness perceptions include clients' beliefs and perceptions about the identity, timeline, consequences, and cure and control of their presenting problem or condition (Weinman, Petrie, Moss-Morris, & Horne, 1996). They are clinically useful in understanding clients' cultural beliefs about the kinds of treatment methods and practices that they expect will heal or cure them. Illness perceptions can be elicited by interview or by an instrument such as the 80-item Illness Perception Questionnaire (Weinman et al., 1996). A shorter version, called the Brief Illness Perception Questionnaire (Broadbent, Petrie, Main, & Weinman, 2006) can rapidly assess illness perceptions as well as monitor treatment progress. It consists of 9 items and can be completed in 2 to 3 minutes or less. It has been translated into more than 30 languages.

Treatment Expectations

Expectations about what clients want from treatment and their level of involvement in the process is called treatment expectations (Sperry, 2009). These expectations are often influenced by cultural factors and norms. For example, among some Hispanics, it is common for family members to accompany the designated client to sessions, and an unspoken expectation is that family members will be included in the treatment process. Similarly, there may be silent expectations about the type of intervention utilized. Clients from some cultures may expect action-oriented approaches or more education-like therapies (such as cognitive–behavioral therapy [CBT]) over talk-oriented therapies. In other cultures, the expectation may be that healing requires some measure of touch or contact (Sperry, 2006). Clients can have high, low, or ambivalent expectations for change, and these expectations may be realistic or unrealistic. Generally speaking, patients with moderate to high realistic expectations of change experience more change than patients with unrealistic or minimal expectations or patients who assume little responsibility for change (Sotsky, Galss, & Shea, 1991). Accordingly, the competent clinicians will elicit such expectations for treatment.

Personality Dynamics and Psychosocial Factors

Personality dynamics refer to the client's personality style and personal dispositions. A central consideration in developing a cultural formulation is identifying the influence of cultural factors in contrast to personality dynamics that influence the client. Psychosocial factors refer to all situational and community factors—except cultural factors—that also influence the client.

DEVELOPING EFFECTIVE CULTURAL FORMULATIONS

An effective cultural formulation is based on an accurate and complete cultural assessment. As noted in Chapter 5, the cultural formulation is the third of the four components of a case conceptualization. This section describes the purpose and structure of a cultural formulation and briefly discusses two cultural formulation models. It then describes the five dimensions in cultural formulation and provides an example of such

201

a formulation. Because a cultural formulation is based on an integrative cultural assessment, we begin with a discussion of the essential aspects of that assessment.

Cultural Formulation

A cultural formulation supports the clinical formulation and can inform treatment focus and the type of interventions chosen. The cultural formulation is a systematic review of cultural factors and dynamics that have been described in the "Social History and Cultural Factors" section of a clinical case report. It answers the "what role does culture play" question. More specifically, the cultural formulation statement describes the client's cultural identity and level of acculturation. It provides a cultural explanation of the client's condition as well as the impact of cultural factors on the client's personality and level of functioning. Furthermore, it addresses cultural elements that may impact the relationship between the individual and the therapist and whether cultural or culturally sensitive interventions are indicated (GAP Committee on Cultural Psychiatry, 2002). The decision about whether cultural interventions, culturally sensitive therapy, or culturally sensitive interventions should be implemented is complex and beyond the scope of this chapter.

Models of Cultural Formulation

There are two models for developing cultural formulations. The first model conceptualizes cases in terms of two dimensions: the degree to which cultural elements "cause" the client's presenting problem, and the extent to which cultural elements are integrated in treatment; that is, culturally sensitive interventions are indicated for effective treatment (Constantine & Ladany, 2000). The second model views cultural formulations in terms of five dimensions that are assessed and integrated into a formulation statement that guides treatment. The five dimensions are the client's cultural identity, the client's cultural explanation of illness, the client's psychosocial environment, the cultural elements likely to influence the relationship between client and therapist, and the cultural elements likely to be operative in the treatment process (GAP Committee on Cultural Psychiatry, 2002). Because the five-dimension model is easier and more straightforward, particularly for trainees, it is described and illustrated here.

Developing a Cultural Formulation

Here is a strategy for developing a cultural formulation utilizing the five dimensions as a structure for such a formulation. Three examples of cultural formulation statements are provided near the end of the chapter.

1. Client's Cultural Identity and Level of Acculturation

The cultural formulation begins to take shape during the diagnostic assessment. As part of the "Social and Cultural History" of that assessment, the therapist presumably elicited sufficient information to specify the client's cultural identity and level of acculturation.

2. Client's Cultural Explanations of Illness and Expectations

A client's explanation of the reason he or she believes he or she is experiencing the problem or concern is very revealing, as are the words and idioms he or she uses to express distress (Bhui & Bhugra, 2004). Therapists should routinely elicit the client's explanatory model and illness perceptions because they inevitably reflect key cultural beliefs of the client. In addition, the client's expectations and preferences for treatment, and, if indicated, past experiences of healing in his or her culture should also be elicited.

3. Cultural Elements in the Client's Psychosocial Environment

The client's psychosocial environment includes both stressors and supports related to the client's cultural background. It also includes cultural beliefs and practices that help the individual cope with such psychosocial stressors.

4. Cultural Elements Likely to Be Operative in the Therapeutic Relationship

Awareness of the client's cultural beliefs and practices allows the therapist to accommodate such beliefs in the case conceptualization. These include the way the client relates to others, ease or difficulty in communicating, the potential for transference enactment, gender and age of the therapist, and the need for referral when cultural questions extend beyond the therapist's expertise.

5. Identify Cultural Elements Likely to Be Operative in the Treatment Process

The treatment process includes assessment, diagnosis, interventions, and termination. The culturally sensitive therapist will identify the extent to

203

which cultural elements are operative and will tailor treatment accordingly. By assessing the interaction of cultural elements with the influence of biological factors, personality dynamics, and situational factors, the therapist can more effectively plan and implement cultural interventions or culturally sensitive interventions.

PLANNING CULTURALLY SENSITIVE TREATMENT

The expectation is that effective clinicians have the capability to plan culturally sensitive treatments when indicated. The question is how does a clinician decide if, when, and how to utilize a cultural intervention, a culturally sensitive therapy, or a culturally sensitive intervention instead of a conventional western intervention? Unfortunately, graduate training and the professional literature provide little guidance and few specific guidelines for answering this question. This section provides a clinically useful strategy for selecting such treatments. It begins by briefly distinguishing cultural intervention, culturally sensitive therapy, and culturally sensitive intervention. Then it provides general guidelines for making such decisions.

Types of Culturally Sensitive Treatments

1. Cultural Intervention

A cultural intervention is an intervention or healing method or activity that is consistent with the client's belief system regarding healing and is potentially useful in effecting a specified change. Some examples are healing circles, prayer or exorcism, and involvement of traditional healers from that client's culture. Sometimes, the use of cultural interventions necessitates collaboration with, or referral to, such a healer or other expert (Paniagua, 2005). Still, a clinician can begin the treatment process by focusing on core cultural value, such as *respito* and *personalismo*, in an effort to increase the "clinician's achieved credibility," that is, the cultural client's perception that the clinician is trustworthy and effective.

2. Culturally Sensitive Therapy

Culturally sensitive therapy is a psychotherapeutic intervention that directly addresses the cultural characteristics of diverse clients, that is,

204

beliefs, customs, attitudes, and socioeconomic and historical context (La Roche & Christopher, 2008). Because they utilize traditional healing methods and pathways, such approaches are appealing to certain clients. For example, cuento therapy addresses culturally relevant variables such as *familismo* and *personalismo* through the use of folk tales (*cuentos*) and is used with Puerto Rican children (Costantino, Malgady, & Rogler, 1986). Likewise, Morita therapy, which originated in Japan, is now used throughout the world for a wide range of disorders ranging from shyness to schizophrenia (Li & He, 2008). These kinds of therapy appear to be particularly effective in clients with lower levels of acculturation.

3. Culturally Sensitive Intervention

A Western psychotherapeutic intervention that has been adapted or modified to be responsive to the cultural characteristics of a particular client. Because of their structured and educational focus, CBT interventions are acceptable to many cultures and are the most often modified to be culturally sensitive (Hays & Iwanasa, 2006). For example, particularly in culturally diverse clients with lower levels of acculturation, disputation and cognitive restructuring of a maladaptive belief are seldom the CBT interventions of choice, whereas problem solving, skills training, or cognitive replacement interventions (Sperry, 2010) may be more appropriate.

Strategy for Selecting Culturally Sensitive Treatments

Here is a six-part strategy useful in deciding when and if to plan and implement culturally sensitive treatments. The strategy assumes that both client and therapist are willing to discuss treatment options. If a culturally sensitive assessment and cultural formulation have already been completed, the clinician can begin with part 3.

1. Elicit or identify the client's cultural identity, level of acculturation, explanatory model (i.e., his belief about the cause of his illness, e.g., bad luck, spirits, virus or germ, heredity, early traumatic experiences, chemical imbalance in brain, etc.), and treatment expectations.
2. Develop a cultural formulation framing the client's presenting problems within the context of her cultural identity, acculturation level, explanatory model, treatment expectations, and interplay of culture and personality dynamics.

3. If a client identifies (cultural identity) primarily with the mainstream culture and has a high level of acculturation and there is **no** obvious indication of prejudice, racism, or related bias, consider conventional interventions as the primary treatment method. However, the clinician should be aware that a culturally sensitive treatment may (also) be indicated as the treatment process develops.

4. If a client identifies largely with the mainstream culture and has a high level of acculturation and there **is** an indication of prejudice, racism, or related bias, consider culturally sensitive interventions or cultural interventions for the cultural aspect of the client's concern. In addition, it may be useful to utilize conventional interventions for related noncultural concerns (i.e., personality dynamics).

5. If a client identifies largely with his ethnic background and level of acculturation is low, consider cultural interventions or culturally sensitive therapy. This may necessitate collaboration with, or referral to, an expert and/or an initial discussion of core cultural values.

6. If a client's cultural identity is mainstream and acculturation level is high, but that of their family is low, such that the presenting concern is largely a matter of cultural discrepancy, consider a cultural intervention with the client and the family. However, if there is an imminent crisis situation, consider conventional interventions to reduce the crisis. After the crisis is reduced or eliminated, consider introducing cultural interventions or culturally sensitive therapy.

CASE EXAMPLES OF CULTURAL FORMULATIONS AND TREATMENT SELECTION

Case 1: Geri

Here is the cultural formulation for the ongoing case of Geri. It highlights the five dimensions.

Geri identifies herself as a middle-class African American but with few ties to her ethnic roots, and it appears that Geri and her parents are highly acculturated. She believes that her depression is the result of stresses at work and a "chemical imbalance" in her brain. There are no obvious indications of prejudice or conflicting cultural expectations or other cultural factors. Instead, it appears Geri's personality dynamics are significantly operative in her current clinical presentation. Gender dynamics could impact the therapeutic relationship between Geri and her African American male therapist, given her strained relationship with her father and limited involvement with men ever since she was a child. However, it is not anticipated that other cultural dynamics will negatively impact the therapeutic relationship. Given her shyness and avoidant style, it may take awhile for her to become comfortable and engaged in group therapy, but it is less likely that cultural factors will be operative in a Caucasian female-led group of middle-aged women of different ethnic backgrounds. Overall, it appears that Geri's avoidant personality dynamics are more operative than cultural factors in her current clinical presentation, and it does not appear that cultural factors will negatively impact or interfere with the therapy process or outcomes. Furthermore, treatment progress does not seem dependent on cultural or even culturally sensitive interventions.

Case Commentary. This cultural formulation statement addresses all five dimensions on which key intervention decisions were made. The primacy of personality dynamics over cultural dynamics is obvious. Therefore, culturally sensitive treatment did not appear to be indicated, at least at the time the treatment plan was developed. However, if there is little or no treatment progress, the matter of culturally sensitive treatment would need to be revisited.

Case 2: Carlos

Here is a case example that illustrates a cultural formulation based on the five dimensions. The cultural formulation follows some background information on the case.

Carlos is a 32-year-old, unmarried male of Mexican American heritage who presents with depressed mood, insomnia, and grief following the recent death of his fiancée in a car accident. He had dated this Caucasian female, whom he met at his job, for over 2 years, and they had been engaged for about 4 months before the accident. Carlos is the second of four children; he has an older brother, older sister, and younger brother. His parents are both alive, and his father is recently retired. He arrived with his family in the United States nearly 35 years ago and completed elementary and high school here. Carlos is a skilled machinist at

207

a company that manufactures inboard and outboard boat motors; he has been employed at this company for the past 9 years. He had enlisted in the army immediately after completing high school and was honorably discharged after completing a 3-year tour of duty in Germany. He denies having any arrests or legal difficulty. Although he was reared as a Catholic, he reports that he doesn't "practice it like my parents." He indicates that his sexual preference is heterosexual. Carlos identifies himself with the dominant middle-class culture, in contrast to his siblings and parents, "who pretty much stick to the old Mexican ways." Although those family members are bilingual, they continue to reside in a neighborhood that speaks primarily Spanish and "holds on to the old values." Although bilingual, Carlos prefers to speak English and he is not active in the Mexican community like his parents or his older sister and brother. Even though there are two other Hispanic machinists at his factory, he socializes primarily with Caucasian workers. He believes that his depression is directly related to the loss of his fiancée and believes that he will likely respond well to antidepressants. He has not engaged in therapy before but is willing to combine a brief course of therapy with medication management by the clinic's psychiatrist.

Here is the cultural formulation statement: Carlos identifies with the dominant Caucasian culture and appears to be highly acculturated. His explanatory model and illness perceptions regarding his grief and depressive symptoms are realistic. There appears to be little, if any, cultural influence to his explanatory model, and cultural factors do not appear to be affecting his symptoms or level of functioning. Rather, personality dynamics and situational factors are operative. Although there is a notable discrepancy in levels of acculturation between Carlos and his family, it will not influence the intervention plan because the family has had little or no influence on him since he left home to enlist in the military and because he has maintained relatively little contact with them since then. Cultural dynamics are not anticipated to negatively impact the relationship between Carlos and his female Caucasian therapist; in fact, it may facilitate the therapeutic process.

Case Commentary. Much like the case of Geri, personality dynamics are prominent, whereas cultural dynamics do not appear operative. Unlike the case of Geri, there is a discrepancy in acculturation levels between Carlos and other family members. But because the family's influence on him is presumably negligible, the point is moot. In contrast, when family influence is strong, acculturation discrepancies usually require some form of culturally sensitive treatment. In short, conventional therapeutic interventions rather than cultural ones will be employed.

Case 3: Ivette

Ivette is a 23-year-old single, first-generation Haitian American female. She presented at the mental health clinic with complaints of sadness. Her mood was depressed, and she admitted experiencing increased social isolation and hypersomnia. Ivette also noted that she was also having difficulty dealing with a "tough situation." She presented as shy and passive, and her mood was sad with constricted affect. She is the oldest of three siblings and lives with her mother and younger sister in a predominantly Haitian community since having migrated from Haiti.

She believed that her depression (explanatory model) is due to distress and grief about leaving law school because of being emotionally isolated from the largely Caucasian student body and being unable to stand up for herself. Specifically, no first-year study group would invite her to participate, and student comments that she was admitted on the basis of quotas rather than merit upset her deeply. The reality is that she had a 4.0 undergraduate average and scored in the top 10% on the LSAT. She also believes she cannot return to school for fear of reexperiencing racism. Ivette disclosed that at age 11 she had just begun the school year in a new school that was primarily European American. On her first day, other students teased her so mercilessly about her dark skin and kinky hair that she cried and sobbed until her mother came and took her home. This apparent show of racism was short-lived, as the principal and her mother quickly arranged a transfer to a charter school for the arts that had an integrated student body. From then, it appeared that Ivette avoided all confrontations, and so it was not surprising that she refused to confront the law school situation. Instead, she quietly withdrew. Her treatment expectations are to be less troubled by criticism and to be more assertive in "tough situations." Ivette identifies herself as a "middle-class American and Haitian by birth" and demonstrates a high level of acculturation. After securing her consent, the clinician interviewed Ivette's mother and her younger sister. They also believe that Ivette's depression stems from her withdrawal from law school.

Here is the cultural formulation statement, including a treatment plan: Ivette identifies closely with the dominant culture and is highly acculturated, as are her mother and siblings. She explains her depression as a result of being forced to withdraw from law school and her inability to stand up for herself in the situation. Consequently, her increased depressive symptoms and social isolation appear to be triggered and exacerbated by her experience with racism leading to her withdrawal from school. In addition, it appears that Ivette's dependent and avoidant personality dynamics are also operative in her clinical presentation. In short, her depression and social isolation seem to be driven equally by both personality and cultural factors. Establishing and maintaining a therapeutic alliance will likely require considerable sensitivity on the part of the Caucasian female therapist. The challenge will be to foster a trustful, caring, and nonevaluative climate in the sessions and in between sessions during phone calls, and so forth. Neither gender nor age dynamics are likely to be operative. Accordingly, the resulting intervention plan contains both conventional and culturally sensitive interventions.

This mutually agreed on plan involved four treatment targets. The first was to alleviate depressive symptoms, which would be addressed with CBT. A medication evaluation for consideration of an antidepressant was arranged. The second target was her avoidant behavior that was culturally influenced, for which culturally sensitive interventions would be directed at dealing more effectively with "tough situations" such as prejudice and racism. The clinic's Haitian female therapist would be involved with this treatment target as well as the third target in which she would serve as cotherapist with Ivette's Caucasian therapist in group therapy. This third target involved the personality component of Ivette's avoidant style for which conflict resolution and assertive communication skills training would be a central part of the group work. The fourth target involved career exploration, including the possibility of reinstatement in law school. Her therapist would consult with and involve the school's minority affairs director, who is an African American male.

Case Commentary. Unlike the first two cases, clear cultural dynamics are operative and thus culturally sensitive treatments are a part of the treatment and intervention plan, in this case culturally sensitive interventions. However, had Ivette's explanatory model of depression and her treatment expectations been more culture-based, consideration would have been given to cultural interventions or perhaps culturally sensitive therapy. Similarly, if there was a discrepancy on acculturation levels between Ivette and her mother and younger sister, cultural interventions might have played a more prominent role in the treatment plan. As it was, culturally sensitive therapeutic interventions were employed (target 2) as well as the advocacy consultation (target 4), which could be considered cultural sensitivity organizational intervention. Here the therapist's advocacy efforts would likely be successful given that Ivette meets the Americans for Disability Act (ADA) criteria for disability. Under ADA, Ivette would inevitably be entitled to "reasonable accommodation" which, in addition to readmission, could include involvement in an accommodating, receptive, and nonabusive study group.

CONCLUDING NOTE

Those with a modicum of supervisory experience with psychotherapy trainees and/or recent graduates are not likely to be surprised by the research finding that relatively few develop cultural formulations and use them to guide their therapy. Most trainees and even experienced clinicians have had little or no training in developing an effective cultural formulation and probably no formal training in making decisions about the appropriate use of culturally sensitive treatments. The reality is that competent and effective therapists need to demonstrate cultural sensitivity with clients, including developing and utilizing cultural formulations, particularly with the planning and implementation of culturally sensitive treatments.

14

Ethical Sensitivity

Competent and effective psychotherapy practice is ethically sensitive practice. This means, first and foremost, that competent psychotherapy practice is not possible without ethical sensitivity. It also means that competent therapists are not only knowledgeable about ethical and legal guidelines, but they are also sensitive to situations and circumstances that can affect the welfare and well-being of their clients. These include personal, cultural, community, and institutional factors and dynamics. Although it might seem that ethical sensitivity would be consistently high among trainees and clinicians, it is not. A review of research studies found that between 25% and 33% among trainees and clinicians in psychology, counseling, and social work routinely failed to recognize ethical issues in clinical settings (Fleck-Hendersen, 1995). Two reasons are given to explain this finding. One is that trainees and practicing therapists get caught up in the technical and clinical aspects of their work and "miss" even obvious ethical issues, and the other is that these trainees and practitioners fail to be ethically sensitive due of lack of empathy (Duckett & Ryden, 1994; Rest, 1994). Accordingly, Rest (1994) recommends both extended empathy training and extended ethics education. Whereas trainees and clinicians are likely to have been exposed to some type of professional ethics training, it is unlikely that the training specifically emphasized ethical sensitivity in the context of psychotherapeutic practice. This chapter embodies that emphasis.

The chapter begins with a definition of ethical sensitivity and a description of three ethical perspectives. This serves as background for discussing the two essential clinical competencies of ethically sensitive practice: making ethically sound decisions and providing professional

213

services in an ethically sensitive manner. Presented are an integrative model of decision making and a discussion of four basic ethical skills and considerations in psychotherapy practice: confidentiality, informed consent, conflicts of interest, and competency. A case example illustrates key points of the chapter. First, the two competencies are briefly introduced.

ETHICAL SENSITIVITY COMPETENCIES

This chapter addresses two ethically sensitive essential clinical competencies that are associated with the core competency of cultural and ethical sensitivity.

Make Ethically Sound Decisions

This competency involves the capacity to engage in an intentional decision-making process when anticipating or encountering clinical concerns and issues and base clinical decisions on sound professional, ethical, and legal criteria. Making ethically sound decisions involves ongoing ethical sensitivity as well as the skills of ethical sensitivity, problem identification, information gathering, analysis, decision making, and implementation of the ethical decision.

Practice in an Ethically Sensitive Manner

This competency involves the capacity to provide professional services to clients and others, including psychotherapy, in an ethically sensitive manner. Ethically sensitive practice involves the ability to perform competently, to ensure confidentiality, to ensure informed consent, and to minimize conflicts of interest.

BACKGROUND CONSIDERATIONS: ETHICAL SENSITIVITY AND ETHICAL PERSPECTIVES

Ethical Sensitivity

Ethical sensitivity, also referred to as moral sensitivity, has been defined as "the awareness of how our actions affect other people. It involves being aware of different possible lines of action and how each line of action could affect the parties concerned. It involves imaginatively constructing possible scenarios, and knowing cause-consequences chains of events in the real world; it involves empathy and role-taking skills" (Rest, 1994, p. 23). Furthermore, it has been said that "persons who have empathy and can take the perspective of others, and who care for others," even people who are quite different from themselves, "are likely to exhibit high levels of moral sensitivity" (Duckett & Ryden, 1994, p. 60). It appears then that being empathically competent (as described in Chapter 1)—that is, having empathic understanding and empathy skills (including perspective taking and empathic stance, i.e., concern for others)—is a component of the competency of ethical sensitivity. As already noted, a sizeable percentage of trainees and clinicians in the various mental health disciplines do not exhibit ethical sensitivity, much less high levels of it (Fleck-Hendersen, 1995). However, high levels of ethical sensitivity are associated with highly effective and competent practice, and so therapists who aspire to practice competently must increase their ethical sensitivity.

Three Ethical Perspectives

Besides, or in addition to, a lack of empathy or getting caught up in the technical aspects of their clinical work, trainees and clinicians may exhibit limited ethical sensitivity for another reason. That is their basic ethical perspective or outlook on clinical practice. Three perspectives characterize the current practice of psychotherapy (Sperry, 2007a). The three are designated as Perspectives I, II, and III. Perspectives I and III are polar opposites, whereas Perspective II is basically an intermediate position.

Perspective I
In this perspective, the focus of ethical thinking is limited to ethical codes, ethical standards, and legal statutes. The emphasis is on enforceable rules and standards. The focus is on misconduct problems and ethical dilemmas. There is a preoccupation with avoiding malpractice, and risk management is typically viewed as the basic strategy for achieving ethical practice. It is grounded in the belief that there must be sanctions for misconduct. There is usually limited discussion of ethical issues, and health professionals view rules, codes, policies, and laws as independent of one another; for the most part, one's personal and professional ethics are separated.

Perspective II
This perspective represents a midway position between Perspectives I and III. For many, it is a transition to Perspective III. It represents an

effort to comply with ethical standards and rules, while at the same time expressing some willingness to consider self-reflection, contextual considerations, and self-care. The extent to which individuals holding this perspective experience cognitive and emotional dissonance is a function of how much allegiance they have to Perspective I: the more allegiance, the less dissonance and vice versa. Although these individuals may express some interest in integrating their personal and professional values, there is little commitment to such an effort.

Perspective III
This perspective provides a comprehensive focus wherein it is possible to integrate professional codes, as well as other ethical traditions, with one's personal ethics. Here, virtues and values are considered as important as ethical codes, standards, and rules. The main focus in this perspective is on positive behavior and virtues, ethical ideals, character development, and integrating one's personal philosophy of life with one's professional goals and career aspirations. Self-care is valued and considered essential in this perspective because it is believed that as professionals take care of themselves, they are better able to care for others. In this perspective, which values prevention, risk management is integrated with personal and professional development. Ethical decision making involves the professional, the contextual, and the ethical domains as well as personal, relational, and organizational considerations. Ethical sensitivity is essential in this perspective as is an integration of the therapist's personal and professional ethical values. It is also the requisite attitude and value of the highly effective and competent therapist.

Table 14.1 summarizes some key distinctive features of Perspectives I and III.

MAKING ETHICALLY SOUND DECISIONS

The capability to make informed and ethically sound professional decisions involves a specific set of skills (Jonsen et al., 1986; Roberts & Dyer, 2004). This skill set includes ethical sensitivity, identification, information gathering and analysis, decision making, and decision implementation. These skills are essential for effective ethical decision making, and they are sequenced as steps in the decision-making process. Ethical competency requires requisite knowledge, these skill sets, and the core attitude and value that the therapist's primary responsibility is to ensure the client's well-being.

Table 14.1 Distinctive Characteristics of Differing Perspectives on Ethical Practice

Perspective I	Perspective III
Ethics and professional practice are tangentially connected.	Ethics and professional practice are integrally connected.
Attention is primarily to rule-based ethics, i.e., standards and statutes.	Attention is primarily to virtue and relational or care ethics, while mindful of standards and statutes.
Ethics is an add-on, limited to specific ethical issues and dilemmas.	Ethics is integral to all aspects of professional practice as well as personal well-being.
There is legal sensitivity and proactive focus on risk management.	Ethical sensitivity has a relational and developmental focus, yet mindful of the need to minimize risk.
Professional ethics is separate from personal ethics.	Professional ethics is best integrated with organizational and personal ethics.
This perspective is more characteristic of trainees and beginning therapists and counselors.	This perspective is more characteristic of highly effective and competent therapists and counselors.
This perspective characterizes the traditional practice of counseling and psychotherapy.	This perspective is the emerging trend in the practice of counseling and psychotherapy.

1. Ethical Sensitivity

Ethical sensitivity is the *sine qua non* of making sound ethical decisions. It is a perspective on both clinical practice and the capacity to anticipate ethical challenges or to interpret their ethical and moral implications irrespective of whether or not an ethical dilemma is present. It is a general, ongoing capability as well as a situation-specific capability. As this skill is mastered, clinicians tend to more readily anticipate and respond proactively to various professional and ethical challenges, often before they emerge as problems or dilemmas.

2. Problem Identification

This skill involves the capability of identifying ethically important, value-laden, and potentially problematic aspects of a clinical situation. It involves sensitivity to, and recognition of, a potential or actual conflict or dilemma as well as possible untoward outcomes. It also includes the capability to adequately conceptualize and define the problem. It is essential to clarify whether the problem is primarily ethical, legal, professional, or some combination. Sometimes the problem is primarily professional and involves ethical or legal considerations. Other times, the problem is first and foremost an ethical dilemma, with legal and professional considerations. Clearly, this skill requires and builds on ethical sensitivity.

3. Information Gathering and Analysis

This skill involves the capability of gathering and analyzing professional, contextual, ethical, legal information that can clarify and illuminate the problematic situation. *Professional information* includes relevant findings from the theoretical, scholarly, and research literatures and evidence-based studies and best practices that have direct bearing on the situation. *Contextual information* includes relevant cultural, community, institutional, and personal dynamics that are operative in the situation (Sperry, 2007b). Such information includes input on family, subcultural, and community norms and values, as well as institutional (i.e., agency or clinic) norms, written policies, and procedures. *Ethical and legal information* includes input on agency or clinic values, results of ethics audits, professional codes of ethics and legal statutes, opinions of peers and supervisors, as well as consultation with experts who can clarify specific ethical, legal, religious, and personal dynamics, that is, how the clinician's own personal values and ethics as well as needs and countertransferences might influence the decision-making process.

The purpose of such information gathering is to achieve a fuller understanding of the identified problem and alternative solutions. In addition to collecting relevant information, this skill also involves the capability to analyze and integrate the information in a useful and meaningful way.

4. Decision Making

This skill involves the capability of considering and weighing the options and alternative courses of action via a systematics decision-making model. There are various ethical decision-making models (Cottone & Tarvydas, 2003; Kitchner, 1992; Sperry, 2007b), all of which emphasize the value and importance of articulating a clear rationale for the decision. This skill also

218

involves documenting the decision, the decision-making process, and the rationale for the course of action chosen.

5. Decision Implementation

This skill involves the capability of implementing the decided course of action. This involves working collaboratively to achieve the commitment to the course of action by the client and relevant stakeholders. It also involves evaluation of the entire decision-making process, including the impact of the decision, in the short and long term, on the client. Because the decisional process has developmental ramifications for the clinician, it can be useful to review the decision and the decision-making process with various "ethical tests," such as publicity, universality, moral traces, and justice, which considers whether the clinician would respond the same way in a similar situation (Sperry, 2007b).

PRACTICING IN AN ETHICALLY SENSITIVE MANNER

The second competency involves providing professional services, particularly psychotherapy, in an ethically sensitive manner. Probably the majority of professional ethical concerns a clinician faces in everyday clinical practice involve matters of confidentiality, informed consent, conflicts of interest, and competence, particularly scope of practice. Thus, this competency involves knowledge and various skills sets in these four areas. It also involves the requisite attitude of ethical sensitivity and emphasizing the client's well-being.

1. Professional Competence

Professional competence refers to a clinician's capacity to provide a minimum quality of services within the clinician's and the profession's scope of practice (Sperry, 2007a). Scope of practice refers to a recognized area of proficiency in professional practice, involving specific competence, proficiency, or skills acquired through appropriate education and experience. Clients expect that the clinicians with whom they consult will be competent. Clinical competence can be defined as sufficiency in reference to external standards, where sufficiency refers to the capability to provide counseling and clinical services responsibly and proficiently within one's scope of practice, and external standards include legal statutes, regulations, and professional codes of conduct (Falender & Shafranske, 2004).

Competence is much more than completing graduate training and achieving professional certification or licensure. Rather, competence is an ongoing developmental process in which an initial level of competence is achieved and maintained and then updated and enhanced as new developments arise and the profession and the professional grow and change. Failure of competence may involve incompetence or impairment, which can be reflected in negligence.

The competency of providing competent clinical services involves the following knowledge and skill set: (1) capability to limit the scope of one's professional practice within the boundaries of one's competence, based on education, training, supervised and professional experience, and state and national professional credentials; (2) capability to seek and accept employment only for positions for which one is qualified by education, training, supervised and professional experience, and state and national professional credentials; (3) capability to continuously monitor one's professional effectiveness and to take steps to improve when necessary; (4) capability to maintain level of professional competence, to be open to new interventions and methods, and to keep current with the diverse and/or special populations with whom the clinician works; (5) capability to refrain from offering or providing professional services when one's physical, mental, or emotional problems are likely to harm a client or others; (6) capacity to be alert to the signs of impairment, seek assistance for one's problems, and, if necessary, limit, suspend, or terminate professional responsibilities; (7) capability to expand the scope of one's practice only after appropriate education, training, and supervised experience; and (8) capability to foster and enhance competence by practicing professional and personal self-care strategies.

2. Confidentiality

Confidentiality is the duty of clinicians to respect the privacy of clients by not revealing to others information communicated to them by clients during clinical sessions (Sperry, 2007a). In other words, it is an obligation of nondisclosure in a relationship that is based on trust. Trust is essential in counseling and psychotherapy, as breaching confidentiality can and often does diminish or even break the therapeutic relationship. There are certain limits to confidentiality, that is, conditions or circumstances such

as abuse, neglect, or exploitation for which state statute requires mandatory reporting, or for which there is a duty to warn or protect relative to
threats of harm to self (i.e., suicide) and others (i.e., violence). These situations may require breaching confidentiality to ensure client safety or the
safety of others. In those circumstances in which confidentiality must be
breached, the clinical challenge is to explain the need for reporting or
warning, involve the client in the process, and attempt to safeguard and
maintain the therapeutic relationship.

This competency involves the following knowledge and skill set: (1)
knowledge and understanding of a given state's statutes regarding mandatory reporting and duty to warn and protect statutes; (2) knowledge
and understanding of suicide risks and threats of harm to self or others;
(3) recognition of the exceptions for breaching privacy and confidentiality; (4) the capacity to establish and maintain privacy and confidentiality
in a therapeutic relationship; (5) the capability for mandatory reporting
of abuse, neglect, or exploitation; (6) the capability to warn and protect
intended victims; and (7) the capability to continue working with a client
and to maintain a therapeutic relationship when mandatory reporting or
warning is indicated.

3. Informed Consent

Informed consent is the client's right to decide whether to participate in
treatment after the clinician has fully described the services to be ren-
dered in a manner that is understandable to the client (Sperry, 2007a).
Informed consent is more than a signed and witnessed document; it is a
relational process between a clinician and client that typically unfolds in
a five-part process. The first part of the process involves the client reading the informed consent form. In the second part, the clinician offers
a description of the meaning and purpose of informed consent. Then
the clinician asks and then answers any questions the client may have
about anything covered in the informed consent document. The third
part involves the clinician discussing the specifics of the planned treatment process. Unlike the discussion of the clinic's informed consent form,
which details the overall nature of clinic operations and *general* information on the treatment process, this discussion involves *specific* information on the treatment options, risks and benefits, and outcomes the client
can expect. The fourth part of the process involves the client attesting to
his or her understanding of the general and specific aspects of informed

221

consent by signing the informed consent document for which a description of *specific* treatment considerations is appended or is added to a chart note. The fifth part of the process is the ongoing manner in which the clinician informs the client of developments or options as treatment progresses. This five-part process is key to effective clinician practice because it highlights the ongoing collaborative relationship between clinician and client, particularly collaborative decision making.

For a client to consent to treatment in an informed manner, the client must be apprised of specific aspects of planned interventions, such as potential risks and benefits of the treatment, alternative treatment options, the clinician's competence in these interventions, privacy of health information, and so on. Clients must be made aware that they have the right to refuse or discontinue treatment without penalty, and that they are not being coerced to accept the proposed treatment. Obviously, the client must be cognitively competent to adequately understand and voluntarily provide such informed consent. Thus, the clinician is required to assess and document such competency.

The competency of providing informed consent involves the following knowledge and skill set: (1) the capacity to assess the client's decisional competence; (2) the capacity to assess the client's capacity for voluntariness (i.e., making an autonomous decision); (3) the capacity to share, answer questions about, and discuss relevant information, including risks and benefits, that the client needs to make an informed decision and consent to treatment; (4) the capacity to develop, modify, or append an informed consent document that adequately addresses the general and specific treatment considerations; and (5) the capacity to provide ongoing information and feedback about course corrections and changes in the treatment planning and implementation as treatment proceeds.

4. Conflict of Interest

A conflict of interest occurs when clinicians have competing interests that may interfere with the duty to faithfully exercise their professional judgment and competence in working with a client (Sperry, 2007a). Because of the unique relationship between clinician and client, potential competing interests can be particularly problematic. Psychotherapy typically involves unidirectional sharing of a client's innermost thoughts and feelings to the clinician, who is also ascribed as an expert in personal well-being and human relationships. As such, there is an inherent imbalance in power, a power differential, between client and clinician with regard to expertise.

The ethical principles of beneficence, which requires that the clinician act in the best interest of the client, and nonmaleficence, which requires the clinician to do no harm, are jeopardized when a conflict of interest arises. For example, such a conflict of interest arises where a clinician provides counseling for a clinic administrator's family member. The clinician's desire to have her administrator view her positively can compete with effectively assessing and treating the administrator's family member, and consequently, the clinician's professional judgment may be impaired. If the clinician allows his or her own needs or interests (e.g., to be viewed by her boss in a positive light) to take precedence over the client's needs or interests, a conflict of interest exists which could harm the client.

Conflicts of interest are involved when dual or multiple relationships exist, that is, when the clinician plays both the professional role and one or more additional roles, such as friend, employer, or landlord. These various roles can create a conflict of interest because these additional roles increase and complicate relationship and boundary issues that may interfere with the clinician's professional judgment. Boundary crossings are deviations, typically benign, of clinician behavior from traditional clinical practice, such as the clinician accepting or giving a small gift to a client who is a child. Boundary violations are exploitive or harmful clinical practices, such as having a sexual relationship with a client, that represent an ultimate conflict of interest. Accordingly, clinicians need to be mindful of the power differential and boundaries to avoid conflicts of interest and boundary violations. Maintaining a high level of well-being and balance between one's personal and professional life presumably can reduce the risk of boundary violations and other conflicts of interest.

Becoming competent in dealing with issues of conflict of interest involves the following knowledge and skill set: (1) knowledge and understanding of the code of professional ethics and state and federal statutes regarding conflicts of interest and multiple relationships; (2) the capability to objectively assess particular circumstances of the power differential between clinician and client; (3) the capability to recognize and minimize boundary crossings and violations; (4) the capability to seek supervision or consultation when a potential conflict of interest exists or could arise; (5) the capability to evaluate additional influences, such as emotional need and financial concerns when making clinical decisions involving the client; and (6) the capability to practice self-care strategies to ensure the clinician's health and well-being, and presumably reduce the risk of boundary violations and other conflicts of interest.

ETHICAL CONSIDERATIONS AND PERSPECTIVES

Thus far, the description of these four basic ethical considerations appears to be objective and categorical, that is, one either safeguards confidentiality or does not. The reality is a bit more complex in that there are various views or perspectives on what constitutes confidentiality and the others. Table 14.2 describes each of the basic considerations from Perspectives I and III.

CASE EXAMPLE: PROVIDING ETHICALLY SENSITIVE TREATMENT

The following case describes how a competent and effective clinician deals with the challenges of providing ethically and culturally sensitive clinical treatment, including psychotherapy, to a client. The case illustrates the competency of making ethically sound clinical decisions. It also illustrates the competency of providing competent professional services, ensuring confidentiality and informed consent, and minimizing conflicts of interest.

Kara is a 24-year-old, unmarried, female graduate student who presents with 3 weeks of increasingly scary dreams and nightmares. She says she has never had any counseling previously, but while reading a *Time* magazine article on child sexual abuse was surprised to learn that disturbing dreams, like the kind she was having, probably indicated early sexual abuse. She wants counseling to help her process what she believes are early childhood sexual abuse issues. Jillian is a licensed mental health counselor and one of four therapists in a small community mental health clinic in a rural community about 40 miles from a medium-size city. She has been on staff for 2 years and is particularly interested in working with women's issues, couples issues, and family issues. Being a conscientious clinician, she listens to Kara's treatment expectations, and then she performs a comprehensive initial evaluation that includes a family, cultural, health, and developmental history, as well as mental status exam. After completing the evaluation, Jillian set a follow-up appointment with Kara to discuss treatment goals and recommendations. In the ensuing week,

Table 14.2 Comparison of Key Ethical Issues in Terms of Two Ethical Perspectives

Ethical Issue	Perspective I	Perspective III
Conflicts of interest, power, and boundaries	Views boundaries as rigid and inflexible; boundary crossings lead to boundary violations, which foster exploitive, harmful, and sexual dual relationships, all of which are unethical, below the standard of care, and/or illegal and thus should be avoided. Conflicts of interest should also be avoided at all costs (this reflects both risk management view and analytic therapy practice.)	Views boundaries more flexibly; boundary crossings differ from harmful boundary violations; if appropriately employed can increase therapeutic alliance and outcomes. Dual relationships are unavoidable in some locales and not unethical or below the standard of care, unless harm or exploitation arises, i.e., conflicts of interest; sexual dual relationships are always avoided.
Competence	Viewed as achieving at least a minimum level of competence and maintaining it by completing minimum continuing education requirements. Views impairment as a legal liability. Goal is to avoid liability and censure.	Viewed as an ongoing, developmental process seeking to achieve expertise; life-long learners, who continually monitor their level of competence and seek out needed supervision, consultation, and continuing education. Goal is to broaden and enhance their clinical abilities.
Confidentiality	Viewed in the narrow, legal sense of the duties to warn or protect, mandatory reporting, HIPAA regulations, i.e., safeguarding records, and therapeutic privilege. Goal is to avoid legal liability and/or professional censure.	Viewed as the cornerstone of counseling relationship in which corrective secure attachments and positive therapeutic change can and likely will result. Arises from beneficence, nonmaleficence, respect for privacy, and an ethic of care.

(continued)

Table 14.2 Comparison of Key Ethical Issues in Terms of Two Ethical Perspectives (Continued)

Ethical Issue	Perspective I	Perspective III
Informed consent	Viewed primarily as involving written documents signed by the client. Because the goal is to reduce risk and liability, the contents of the signed document are discussed with the client and that discussion is documented in the client's record. Full disclosure may be withheld.	Viewed in terms of written documentation as well as ongoing discussion with client about optimal treatment considerations that aim at full disclosure to the extent the client is competent. Goal is primarily to foster the therapeutic relationship, client well-being, and treatment outcomes.

Jillian came to realize that complicating clinical, cultural, and ethical concerns would make it difficult for her to accede to the client's treatment expectation to work on trauma issues, at least initially.

Jillian's conclusion is based on the decision-making process described earlier. In terms of problem identification, it appeared that the client wanted a form of therapy that might be too regressive and risky given her clinical presentation and history. In terms of the step of information gathering and analysis, Jillian reviewed the following professional, contextual, and ethical considerations.

Professional Considerations

Jillian had done some research and found an article that reviewed the literature on treatment involving sexual abuse and trauma issues, which concluded that client readiness and psychological resiliency were important considerations in choosing interventions. Specifically, it noted that even clients with relatively high readiness and resiliency—that is, reasonably high levels of psychological functioning—often found processing of traumatic memories and feelings painful, distressing, and somewhat regressive. In speaking with her graduate school mentor who had considerable experience with clients such as these, she learned that many best practice guidelines suggest that therapists deny or postpone such work with "brittle" clients who do not possess sufficient psychological resiliency and have a high likelihood of significant regression during efforts to process extremely painful memories, particularly those involving early sexual abuse. For individuals with borderline personality disorder with low to moderate levels of functioning, focusing directly on trauma issues is discouraged until later in the course of therapy, after the client has become more psychologically resilient.

Contextual Considerations

Here, contextual refers to any cultural, institutional, community, interpersonal, or personal dynamics that are operative. Kara's developmental history and personal level of coping and functioning were assessed. It appeared that she was involved with ongoing sexual abuse by a paternal uncle from age 6 to 11, and had limited psychological resilience, meaning that her capacity for dealing with the stress of processing trauma and abuse issues was low. She met criteria for Borderline Personality Disorder with a GAF of 52, indicative of low moderate functioning. Other key contextual considerations included the cultural dynamic that Kara is a second-generation Muslim and that discussion of sex is a taboo subject in her family. Talking about it to outsiders, such as a therapist, is also forbidden. In this culture, as well as other family-oriented cultures, individual needs and wishes are subordinated to family and community needs and customs. In terms of institutional dynamics, it is interesting to note that a new therapist at Jillian's clinic is recruiting clients for a group of female victims of sexual and domestic violence. Although her colleague has some experience as a cotherapist in such a program while she was an intern, this would be her first experience as the primary group therapist with Jillian as the cotherapist. Referring Kara to this group would be convenient for Jillian and would win her points with the clinic administrator who really wanted to offer this kind of group locally rather than losing revenue by having to refer such clients to a private speciality clinic in the city. Thus, the administrator expected that all staff would routinely refer all such clients to their newest group program.

Ethical Considerations

Jillian thought about the basic ethical principle that acting in the best interests of the client is the main criterion for determining the goodness and effectiveness of counseling. It seemed that the ethical values of autonomy, beneficence, and nonmaleficence were involved in this case and that there appeared to be a conflict among them. Autonomy involves respecting the client's wishes and right to self-determination, and in this case it would mean acceding to Kara's expectation for counseling. Beneficence involves doing good, helping, and benefitting clients, while nonmaleficence involves the responsibility of a professional to do no harm to clients. Based on the professional consideration that there is a reasonable possibility that focusing therapy initially and primarily on abuse issues could be harmful to Kara, the conflict among the three values is reasonably resolved by focusing on beneficence and nonmaleficence and supporting Kara's family orientation over autonomy. Furthermore, it would be critical to address at the outset the cultural taboo against discussing sexual abuse issues.

In the next steps, Jillian made a decision and then implemented it. As much as she would have liked to work with Kara as a cotherapist in the newly forming female group therapy in their clinic, she decided she could not. Rather, providing ethically sensitive and effective care would mean preparing Kara for referral to a therapist in the city, Dr. Wentworth, who specialized in working with "brittle" clients with early sexual abuse histories in individual rather than group therapy. In two subsequent sessions, Jillian discussed a number of matters with Kara, beginning with the cultural issue, the risks involved with acceding to Kara's request, and the referral to a specialist. Jillian emphasized the necessity and advisability of increasing Kara's psychological resilience before beginning trauma work with a specialist like Dr. Wentworth. Jillian offered to provide that kind of counseling and make the referral. The result of this processing was that Kara agreed with and committed herself to working on increasing resilience with Jillian and the subsequent referral to Dr. Wentworth.

Afterward, Jillian reflected that this case had challenged her to grow professionally and increase her ethical and cultural sensitivity. She also recognized that a core tenet of clinical lore that she had learned in graduate school and meant much to her—"follow the client's lead," that is, accede to the client's treatment expectations—was really not applicable in all cases and was probably professionally unsound in Kara's case.

Following 12 sessions of resiliency-focused therapy, Kara began intensive individual treatment with Dr. Wentworth. During that time, she kept in contact with Jillian. About 2 years later, Kara indicated that she had successfully completed therapy with Dr. Wentworth and was totally asymptomatic and was engaged to be married.

Jillian also demonstrated the competency of providing competent clinical services, ensuring confidentiality and informed consent, and minimizing conflicts of interest. Whereas not all clinical cases and situations involve all four of these basic ethical and legal domains, this case did.

In terms of the competency of providing competent clinical services, Jillian demonstrated the capability of performing a comprehensive evaluation and developing a case conceptualization and treatment plan that integrated various critical professional, contextual, and ethical considerations. In the process, she engaged in professional and ethical decision making, based, in part, on effectively consulting with expert resources, and concluded that Kara's treatment expectation was problematic. Accordingly, she decided that working with Kara's trauma issues either as an individual therapist or as a cotherapist was beyond her scope of practice and that referral to a specialist was indicated. Instead, she would work to increase Kara's resiliency with social skill training, an intervention strategy that was within her scope of practice.

With regard to the competency of providing clinical services that ensure informed consent, Jillian thoroughly discussed the risks and benefits of the various treatment options and facilitated Kara's consent to a treatment approach that subsequently helped her recover from her trauma. Had she not, and merely acceded to Kara's expectation for immediately engaging in trauma-focused therapy, Kara might have been harmed. Instead, together they achieved the positive outcome with the two-phased treatment, involving Jillian's resiliency work followed by Dr. Wentworth's specialized trauma work.

With regard to the competency of providing service that minimized conflicts of interest, Jillian withstood the expectations of her clinic administrator, and presumably the primary clinical therapist, for referring Kara to the newly forming group therapy for female victims of sexual and domestic abuse. Because Jillian was the cotherapist for that group, it would have been in her best interest rather than in Kara's best interest to have one of her own clients in that group, thereby pleasing the clinic administrator at the same time. In this case, as in other cases, clinicians may have to exercise courage in standing firm against administrative expectations or even demands, for all practical purposes, to put the needs of the clinic before those of clients.

Finally, with regard to the competency of providing clinical services that ensure confidentiality, Jillian safeguarded Kara's privacy by responding to the clinic's administrator in general, rather than specific, terms about why she had not referred Kara to the newly forming group therapy.

The administrator had a master's in business administration but no clinical training or licensure. He had seen the receptionist's appointment log with the indication that Kara was seeking an appointment with a therapist "to discuss childhood sexual abuse." When he asked Jillian to review her referral letter and initial evaluation report on Kara to Dr. Wentworth, Jillian indicated that the information was highly sensitive, and it would not be appropriate for him to have access to it.

CONCLUDING NOTE

After reading this chapter, one might be inclined to conclude that providing competent psychotherapy that is ethically sensitive is not particularly easy. This is not an unreasonable conclusion to reach given the statistics that one fourth to one third of all trainees and experienced mental health clinicians lack sufficient ethical sensitivity to function competently.

Unfortunately, providing highly competent psychotherapy involves much more than developing an expanded knowledge base and highly developed technical skills. Again, therapists are confronted with the attitudinal dimension of a competency when dealing with any ethical considerations. Not only is the attitudinal dimension involved with ethical sensitivity in the guise of the empathic stance, but so also is the attitudinal dimension central to moving, developmentally, from Perspective I to Perspective III. Chapter 15 continues this focus on the attitudinal component and the developmental process of becoming a highly competent psychotherapist.

Section VIII

Conclusion

15

Becoming a Highly Competent and Effective Therapist

This final chapter shifts the focus from the core psychotherapy competencies to some of the processes involved in becoming a highly competent therapist. You may recall that competency was defined in Chapter 1 as the capacity to integrate knowledge, skills, and attitudes reflected in the quality of clinical practice that benefits others, which can be evaluated by professional standards and is developed and enhanced through professional training and reflection. Competencies were also noted to consist of three components: knowledge, skill, and attitude. This chapter will highlight two features of competencies: (1) their development and enhancement through professional training and reflection and (2) their attitudinal component, that is, therapists' basic attitudes toward clients and the therapy process, as well as their motivation for becoming a therapist.

The chapter begins by describing three factors that are related to highly competent therapy: work orientation, the developmental stages of expertise, and mode of practice. It will be noted that the work orientations of calling and vocation, the expert stage of development, and the practice mode of reflectivity tend to characterize the attitudes, values, and aspirations of those practicing highly effective and competent psychotherapy. Throughout this chapter, the developmental process and attitudinal component of becoming a highly effective and competent therapist will be emphasized. Two case examples are provided to illustrate these key points.

WORK ORIENTATION

A heated but revealing discussion about differing attitudes toward work occurs in the movie *Across the Universe*. In it, Max, the main character, asserts that "you do what you are," meaning one's identity determines what type of work one chooses, to which his uncle quickly retorts, "No Max, you are what you do," meaning just the opposite, that one's identity is determined by one's work. Max quickly seeks to neutralize the uncle's comment by asking his friend Jude for his opinion. Not wanting to get embroiled in the matter, Jude adroitly responds, "Well, isn't it really how [and why] you do what you do that counts?" Basically, each of these viewpoints reflects three differing work orientations.

Work orientation refers to one's view and attitude toward work as determined by intrinsic values and aspirations and the experience of working (Bellah, Madsen, Sullivan, Swidler, & Tipton, 1985). Three work orientations of North American professionals have been studied: job, career, and calling (Wrzesniewski, McCaukley, Rozin, & Schwartz, 1997). Each reflects different values and behaviors.

Job Orientation

In the job orientation, individuals relate to their professional work as simply a job. Their main value in working is the material benefits of work to the relative exclusion of other kinds of meaning and fulfillment. In other words, for these individuals, work is simply a means to a financial end allowing them to enjoy their time away from work. Inevitably, the interest and ambitions of those with job orientations are expressed outside the domain of work (Wrzesniewski et al., 1997) and involve hobbies and other interests.

Career Orientation

In contrast to those with a job orientation, those with a career orientation value the rewards that come from work advancement within their school, clinic, or agency or through a professional organization. For those with this self-oriented work orientation, the increased pay, prestige, and status that come with promotion and advancement are the main focus of their work. Advancement brings higher self-esteem, increased power, and higher social standing (Bellah et al., 1985).

Calling Orientation

Those with a calling orientation work neither for financial reward nor for advancement but rather for the sense of purpose or meaningfulness that their work provides. Unlike the job and career orientations, which are primarily self-focused, the calling orientation is more other-focused, wherein work is performed primarily in the service of others or society. In the past, the term *calling* often was used specifically to mean a "call" from God to engage in morally or social significant work (Weber, 1958). Today the term is used more generally to mean doing work that contributes to the well-being of others or making the world a better place, whether it is based on spiritual or other aspects (Davidson & Caddell, 1994). The determination of whether the work actually contributes to making a difference is largely determined by the professional. For example, a surgeon who views his or her work as a source of a comfortable six-figure income does not have a calling, whereas a street cleaner who sees his work as making the world a cleaner and healthier place probably has a calling.

Vocation Orientation

Career and calling orientations are clearly differentiated by whether values are self-oriented (career) or other-oriented (calling). However, the distinction between *calling* and the more commonly used term *vocation* is not so clear. In fact, many use these terms synonymously. Others, however, find it useful to distinguish between calling and vocation. Researchers have recently proposed a useful working definition of both constructs. They distinguish between "people who connect their work to an overall sense of meaning toward other-oriented ends, but who do so for purely internal reasons (vocation), from those who attribute this motivation for working to an external source such as God, a family legacy, or a pressing societal need (calling)" (Dik, Duffy, & Eldridge, 2009, p. 625). Thus, although individuals with both vocation and a calling experience work as serving others and bringing meaning to their lives, the reasons differ: internal reasons versus a "transcendent summons" (Dik et al., 2009). Whether the vocation orientation is actually a fourth work orientation or just a variant of the calling orientation has yet to be determined. At the very least, the difference is noteworthy and presumably has clinical as well as research implications.

Research links work orientation to life satisfaction, fulfillment, and personal well-being and finds that those with a calling orientation report higher job satisfaction and higher life satisfaction than those with either job or career orientations (Wrzesniewski et al., 1997). Interestingly, these professionals also derive more satisfaction from their work than from leisure, whereas those with job and career orientations rank satisfaction from leisure (e.g., hobbies and friends) higher than work satisfaction. What is increasingly clear is that for professionals with a calling orientation, work is their passion, whereas for other professionals, their deeper satisfaction is found in leisure or in relationships outside of work. Research on what could be called the vocation orientation reveals similar findings: Those with other-oriented work values demonstrate higher levels of helping behaviors, cooperation, and increased work performance (Bing & Burroughs, 2001), and those who find a sense of meaningfulness in their work beyond financial gain or career advancement have greater work satisfaction and performance, lower levels of work-related stress, and longer tenure (Claes & Ruiz-Quintanilla, 1994).

Large-scale survey research data show that more than 40% of undergraduates believe they have a calling to a particular line of work (Duffy & Sedlacek, 2010), and between one third and one half of employees in a wide variety of occupational endeavors indicate that they have a calling to their work (Wrzesniewski et al., 1997). Presumably, individuals in the helping professions would report even higher rates of calling orientation, particularly those in training to practice, or who already practice, psychotherapy. Over the years I have observed that, generally speaking, highly effective therapists demonstrate a calling or vocation orientation.

STAGES OF EXPERTISE IN PSYCHOTHERAPISTS

Another factor that appears to influence the extent of effectiveness is level or stage of expertise that a professional has achieved. Being a competent professional involves the capacity to appropriately and effectively utilize the knowledge, skills, and attitudes necessary to perform a wide range of professional activities, including the therapeutic and other clinical tasks associated with the practice of psychotherapy. Becoming a competent professional involves the acquisition of the core competencies of that profession, which is a developmental process. This process has been described in terms of five developmental stages of expertise across the various professions (Dreyfus & Dreyfus, 1986). A description of these stages has been modified to reflect training for practicing, and the practice of, psychotherapy (Sperry, 2010).

Beginner

At this stage, trainees possess a limited knowledge and understanding of how to analyze problems and intervene. Such trainees are reliant on basic principles and techniques, are rule-bound, and are usually too inexperienced to flexibly apply these principles and techniques.

Advanced Beginner

In this stage, trainees possess a limited capacity for pattern recognition and application of interventions but have difficulty generalizing this capacity to different clients and new situations. Rules and principles previously learned now become guidelines. Trainees at this stage inevitably need considerable support and clinical supervision.

Minimally Competent

At this stage, psychotherapists can function independently, albeit at a minimal level of competence, which is the level required for licensure as an independent practitioner. Psychotherapists at this stage are likely to be consciously aware of long-range goals and plans for their clients and can adapt to the changes in their clients with appropriate changes in the intervention plan. They typically can recognize patterns more easily and begin to tailor intervention. They usually experience a feeling of mastery and are able to cope with and handle crises or other problems as they arise. Furthermore, they can more easily integrate theory and research into every aspect of their practice applications.

Proficient

At this stage, psychotherapists possess a more integrative understanding of their clients, and their performance is guided by flexibility and a clear understanding of the nuances of therapeutic interventions and the impact of the intervention on the client and others. At this stage, psychotherapists are typically able to effectively train and supervise others in intervention skills.

Table 15.1 Developmental Stages and Expected Level of Effectiveness

Developmental Stage	Expected Level of Therapeutic Effectiveness
Beginner/advanced beginner	Less effective therapy
Minimally competent	Less effective therapy to more effective therapy
Proficient	Effective therapy to more highly effective therapy
Expert (master therapist)	Highly effective therapy

Expert

At this stage, psychotherapists possess an intuitive grasp of clinical situations and can rapidly assess problems and design appropriate interventions. They quickly recognize, usually intuitively, when interventions and are not working and are able to modify treatment accordingly. Typically, these individuals have integrated their personal and professional lives, and are highly effective in their professional endeavor, be it therapy, consultation, or supervision. They are usually masterful in relating to others and value human relationships above personal needs. Not surprisingly, they are admired by their clients and are considered master therapists by their peers, even though they continue to be lifelong learners. Expert psychotherapists, also referred to as master therapists (Skovholt & Jennings, 2004), routinely practice highly effective therapy (Sperry, 2009). Table 15.1 summarizes this discussion and correlates stage with likely levels of therapeutic effectiveness.

LEARNING TO BECOME A HIGHLY EFFECTIVE THERAPIST

The process of developing core competencies can best be understood in terms of three kinds of learning: declarative, procedural, and reflective (Bennett-Levy, 2006; Binder, 1993, 2004). Each is briefly described.

Declarative learning involves conceptual, technical, and interpersonal knowledge. This kind of learning is largely facilitated by lectures, presentations, discussions, and reading. Declarative learning involves knowledge.

Procedural learning is the application of knowledge to the clinical practice and is largely facilitated by clinical experiences and supervision. It occurs when declarative knowledge is actualized and refined. Procedural learning is essentially skill-based, clinical learning.

238

Reflective learning differs markedly from declarative and procedural learning. It involves reflecting on declarative and procedural learning and coming to a decision about a course of action. Various processes are involved in this type of learning. They include analyzing experiences, comparing them with others, identifying a plan of action as necessary, and possibly changing previous information and insights in light of the analysis. In clinical training, the reflective system is mostly facilitated by client and supervisor feedback of therapist performance in addition to therapist self-evaluation (Bennett-Levy, 2006).

When it comes to developing competencies, all three types of learning are involved. In fact, research shows that the interaction of these three types of learning is required to develop and master a competency (Bennett-Levy & Thwaites, 2006).

This three-pronged view of learning further clarifies the difference between a skill and a competency. Skill learning involves primarily procedural learning, although some declarative learning may also be involved. In contrast, competency learning involves all three types of learning: knowledge (i.e., declarative learning), skills (i.e., procedural learning), and attitudes, values, and standards (i.e., reflective learning). It appears that reflective learning is essential to becoming a highly proficient and effective therapist (Bennett-Levy & Thwaites, 2006; Schön, 1983).

MODES OF PRACTICE

It has been noted that highly effective and competent therapists think, act, and reflect differently than less effective therapists (Binder, 2004; Sperry, 2010). The result of what is essentially a different mode of practice is evident in both therapeutic alliances and clinical outcomes achieved by highly effective therapists. These differences are increasingly being confirmed by research (Skovholt & Jennings, 2004). This section briefly summarizes these observations in terms of the characteristic way in which these therapists characteristically think, act, and reflect.

Think

So how do highly effective and competent therapists think differently? They seem to quickly and intuitively know if they are connecting with clients, and they are guided by cognitive maps that assist them in incisively assessing, conceptualizing, and planning intervention. In addition, they quickly and intuitively know if their case conceptualization is accurate. How is this possible? For one, highly effective therapists engage in more nonlinear thinking than linear thinking. Linear thinking is the familiar and characteristic thinking pattern in which an individual approaches life and problems. In a psychotherapeutic context, nonlinear thinking "requires therapists to see and understand the client's characteristic, old, 'personally' linear pattern; envision a new alternative way (or pattern) of seeing and behaving; and communicate that new way to the client" (Mozdzierz, Peluso, & Lisiecki, 2009, p. 5).

Act

Highly effective and competent therapists act differently than other therapists with regard to all the core competencies. That means they easily develop and maintain effective therapeutic alliances and work with clients in ways that are qualitatively different than beginning and minimally competent therapists. On observation, it becomes clear that they listen, respond, assess, formulate, plan interventions, and manage treatment issues differently than other therapists. Largely, this is because they are guided by cognitive maps in focusing and implementing treatment interventions. They continually seek feedback from clients by observation and questioning, and are more likely to assess progress with outcome measures. Thus, they quickly know if treatment is on target and change and modify it based on that feedback. It has been observed that master therapists easily and effortlessly are able to improvise and change therapeutic direction and methods as treatment circumstances change (Binder, 2004). As a result of these capabilities, highly effective and competent therapists rather consistently excel in dealing with complex clinical situations and difficult clients (Lambert & Okishi, 1997).

Reflect

Finally, highly effective and competent therapists reflect differently than other psychotherapists. Although the domain of reflection may seem subtler and more difficult to observe than thinking and action, it may well be that expertise in this domain actually inspires, drives, and gives direction to how these master therapists think and act. Reflective practice is a continuous process and involves the learner considering critical incidents in his or her life's experiences. As defined by Schön (1983), reflective practice involves thoughtfully considering one's own experiences in applying knowledge to practice while being coached by professionals in the discipline. It is the process by which therapists reflect on their own therapeutic methods in order to more fully understand the client and the optimal strategies and tactics for fostering goal attainment and client growth (Sutton, Townend, & Wright, 2007). Table 15.2 summarizes this discussion.

REFLECTION AND REFLECTIVE PRACTICE

Reflection, also called reflective practice, can be a threefold process for the psychotherapist. The therapist can self-reflect; reflect with a supervisor, peer, or consultant; or reflect with the client. Highly effective and competent therapists are likely to regularly engage in all three types of reflective practice, in contrast to less effective therapists. Over the years of being involved in the training and supervision of therapists, I have noted major differences have been found in reflection and reflective activity among trainees and practicing psychotherapists.

Supervisory Reflection

In terms of reflection within a supervisory context, some therapist trainees are highly involved in the supervisory process and consider it essential to their development as effective therapists. Accordingly, they are likely to carefully prepare case material, such as process notes, transcriptions, and tapes, and are eager to receive the supervisor's feedback. This responsiveness is also noted in receptivity to expert and peer consultation. Others reveal a more lackadaisical attitude and respond to supervision with less preparation and less enthusiasm for learning from supervisory feedback. It has also been my experience that these trainees are less likely to seek out expert and peer consultation.

Self-Reflection

Self-reflection, which is also referred to as self-supervision, can be done with or without a written account, such as a journal. Some trainees and practicing psychotherapists keep a journal of encounters with clients in

241

Table 15.2 Modes of Practice Among Less and More Highly Effective Therapists

Practice Mode	Less Effective Therapists	More Highly Effective Therapists
Thinking	Engages primarily in linear reasoning	Engages in linear & nonlinear reasoning
	Difficulty or slowness in accurate pattern recognition	Ease and quickness in accurate pattern recognition
Acting	Engages in linear interviewing	Engages in linear & iterative interviewing
	Uses linear questions & queries	Uses interventive questions & queries
	Difficulty in formulating and limited use of case conceptualizations	Ease in formulating and making maximum use of case conceptualizations in making tailored treatment interventions
	Unable to improvise when the need to modify the intervention plan arises	Easily and expertly improvises when the need to modify the intervention plan arises
	Seldom, if ever, seeks feedback	Actively seeks feedback, e.g., outcome instruments (SRS, ORS, OQ-45, etc.)
Reflecting	Engages in self-supervision seldom, if ever	Engages in self-supervision regularly
	Reactive use of supervision; little or no use of case consultation	Proactive use of supervision & case consultation
		Considered by others to be a "reflective practitioner"

which they reflect on what they have learned from their mistakes, implementation of their supervisor's suggestions and directives, countertransferences, and so forth. They are also likely to ponder client issues between sessions and to prepare themselves for subsequent sessions. In contrast, other trainees and practitioners demonstrate little or no interest in keeping such a reflection journal and are less likely to spend time contemplating client issues between sessions. These differences are noteworthy because research demonstrates that therapist self-reflection involving journal keeping translates to improved therapeutic alliances and clinical outcomes (Bennett-Levy & Thwaites, 2006).

I have noticed that highly effective and competent psychotherapists tend to regularly reflect on the details of their performance with one or all of their clients on a given day and are more likely to identify specific actions and alternate strategies for reaching their goals. They will focus on controllable factors such as "I probably should have done this instead of that," or "I forgot to do this and will do it next session." For example, "Instead of organizing today's session on his drinking behavior, it would have made more sense to focus on getting his driver's license back, because that's what he seems to be really concerned about. Next session, I'll focus on what the client really wants and then pursue that."

In contrast, when less effective psychotherapists reflect on a past session, they are more likely to attribute failure to external and uncontrollable factors: "This client is just not motivated to change," "She's just so resistant," "I guess I had a bad day," or "I wasn't feeling very well today." They are also more likely to focus on failed strategies, believing that an understanding of the reasons an approach did not work will lead to better outcomes. Subsequently, unlike highly effective therapists, they spend less time focusing on strategies that might have been more effective.

Reflection Involving Clients

In terms of therapists engaging in reflection with clients (i.e., seeking feedback from clients on the therapy process and progress as well as on the therapeutic relationship), differences among trainees are also evident. When therapists actively seek out such feedback verbally or with brief feedback instruments, the therapeutic alliance improves, as do treatment outcomes, and the likelihood of premature termination decreases significantly. My experience and that of other therapy trainers and supervisors match the findings of a growing body of research pointing to both statistical and clinically significant differences between therapists who engage in such feedback reflection with clients and those who do not (Reese, Usher, et al., 2009).

ILLUSTRATION: TWO THERAPISTS

Jefferson Kiley, Ph.D., has been licensed and in practice for the past 8 years, the past 5 as a psychologist in a large community mental health clinic. He is married with two children and has become active in the Rotary Club, and he is an assistant coach for the Little League team on which his son plays. He is comfortable with both his personal and professional life. Overall, Jeff's annual performance reviews are positive but not exceptional. He is content to practice the way he was taught in graduate school and resists "new approaches." Four years ago, he was asked to provide supervision for interns, but he declined, saying he "needed more time to get up to speed first." A year later, he was asked again and refused. The next time supervision assignments were made, the clinic's administrator assigned two interns to Jeff. After about 5 weeks, one intern complained that Dr. Kiley seemed uninterested in supervising her, and the other intern asked for a reassignment, effectively ending his short career as a supervisor. Completing continuing education requirements had become a challenge for him after the clinic's policy on continuing education units (CEUs) changed. Previously, staff could complete their hours on clinic time if they scheduled their time wisely. Now, the majority of hours had to be met on the staff member's personal time or on weekends and without clinic reimbursement. Last month he received a letter from the state licensing board requesting he verify 40 hours of CEUs over the past 2 years. He began to scramble looking for workshops since he could only log 6 hours of clinic workshops. His pride and joy is restoring old Corvettes, and he continually talks about the time he spends restoring and showing his cars at car shows and meets around the state. Of note is that he has one of the highest no-show rates for clients in his case load among all staff at the clinic. He has never been in personal therapy, although it had been recommended by more than one supervisor, and he sees no value in keeping a reflection journal, although it is a requirement for all interns and other trainees at the clinic. When one of Jeff's younger colleagues asked another staff member how long Jeff had been in practice, the tongue-in-cheek reply was "I believe it is 8 years. But I'm not sure if that is 8 years of progressive experience or 1 year repeated 8 times."

Jack Raskin, Ph.D., completed his Ph.D. degree a year before Jeff Kiley, although he was admitted into the same year and class as Jeff. In addition to having the same dissertation advisor, they had both completed their predoctoral internships at the same place. Jack began to distinguish himself during the internship and was the top recruit at the community mental health clinic, where he has worked for 9 years. A year later, he was asked to become the assistant training director. This meant he would not only supervise interns but also schedule weekly seminars and case conferences. He is married with two children. Over the years, Jack has been heavily involved in his work at the clinic and has taken great satisfaction in helping clients as well as mentoring interns and younger staff. He reads widely and writes a column on new techniques for the clinic's monthly newsletter. At the advice of his internship supervisor, Jack kept a reflection journal of his work with clients and continued with this practice because it seemed to make a difference in his work with clients. As a result of such reflection, he entered personal therapy for about 6 months to understand his countertransference issues. Today, his colleagues regularly seek him out to consult on their difficult cases. He remains an untiring advocate for wellness and self-care for psychotherapists, and 3 years ago he was appointed as a member of the state psychology licensing board with the charge to create a task force on psychologist self-care.

Case Commentary. Although Jeff and Jack completed the same internship and graduated from the same doctoral program, their professional lives have evolved along diverging developmental lines. Their priorities, work orientations, and commitments seem to be quite different. It appears that Jeff manifested a job orientation, whereas Jack manifested a calling orientation. In terms of levels of professional expertise, Jeff seemed to be functioning in the minimal competence stage, whereas Jack appeared to be functioning somewhere between the proficient and expert stages. It could also be inferred that there are differences between the two therapists in terms of their overall effectiveness, with Jeff likely to be providing lesser effective to effective therapy and Jack more likely to be providing effective to highly effective therapy.

CONCLUDING NOTE

Competency-based psychotherapy training and practice are beginning to define the way in which accountability is being framed today and vice versa. Effectiveness of psychotherapy practice is not simply a matter of the extent of the therapist's knowledge base and skill sets. Because effectiveness is a function of competency, the attitudinal component is as basic a consideration in determining effectiveness as the knowledge and skills components. The discussion of work orientation, stage of expertise, and mode of practice suggested that these factors reflect all the components of a competency and are useful markers in distinguishing lesser effective from more highly effective therapists. Be advised that these three factors are not absolute predictors of the level of therapeutic effectiveness, as context does matter. In the coming months and years, counseling and psychotherapy training programs, as well as licensure, certification, and accreditation boards, will undoubtedly become increasingly competency-based. Accordingly, it is likely that more highly effective therapy will be practiced.

BIBLIOGRAPHY

Accreditation Council for Graduate Medical Education (ACGME). (2007). *ACGME program requirements for graduate medical education in psychiatry.* Chicago: Author. Retrieved January 15, 2010, from http://www.acgme.org/acWebsite/downloads/RRC_progReq/400_psychiatry_07012007_u04122008.pdf

Accreditation of Counseling and Related Educational Programs. (2009). *CACREP accreditation manual* (3rd ed.). Alexandria, VA: Author.

Ackerman, S., & Hillensroth, M. (2003). A review of therapist characteristics and techniques positively impacting the therapeutic alliance. *Clinical Psychology Review, 23,* 1–33.

Alberti, R. (1977). *Assertiveness: Innovations, applications, and issues.* San Luis Obispo, CA: Impact Publications.

Alexander, F., & French, T. (1946). *Psychoanalytic therapy: Principles and applications.* New York: Ronald Press.

American Association of Marriage and Family Therapy (AAMFT). (2002). *Competencies task force: Scope and charge.* Alexandria, VA: Author.

American Association of Marriage and Family Therapy (AAMFT). (2004). *Marriage and family therapy core competencies.* Alexandria, VA: Author.

American Psychiatric Association. (2000). *Diagnostic and statistical manual of mental disorders* (4th ed., Text rev.; *DSM–IV–TR*). Washington, DC: Author.

Añez, L., Silva, M., Paris, M., & Bedregal, L. (2008). Engaging Latinos through the integration of cultural values and motivational interviewing principles. *Professional Psychology: Research and Practice, 39,* 153–159.

Anker, M., Duncan, B., & Sparks, J. (2009). Using client feedback to improve couple therapy outcomes: A randomized clinical trial in a naturalistic setting. *Journal of Consulting and Clinical Psychology, 77,* 693–704.

Antony, M., Ledley, D., & Heimberg, R. (Eds.). (2005). *Improving outcomes and preventing relapse in cognitive-behavioral therapy.* New York: Guilford Press.

Arkowitz, H., Westra, H., Miller, W., & Rollnick, S. (Eds.). (2007). *Motivational interviewing in the treatment of psychological problems.* New York: Guilford Press.

Arnkoff, D. (2000). Two examples of strains in the therapeutic alliance in an integrative cognitive therapy. *Journal of Clinical Psychology, 56,* 187–200.

Atkinson, D., Worthington, R., Dana, D., & Good, G. (1991). Etiology beliefs, preferences for counseling orientations, and counseling effectiveness. *Journal of Counseling Psychology, 38,* 258–264.

Aubuchon-Endsley, N., & Callahan, J. (2009). The hour of departure: Predicting attrition in the training clinic from role expectancies. *Training and Education in Professional Psychology, 3,* 120–126.

Ayd, F. (1995). *Lexicon of psychiatry, neurology, and the neurosciences.* Baltimore: Williams & Wilkins.

Beck, A. T., Rush, A. J., Shaw, B. F., & Emery, G. (1979). *Cognitive therapy for depression*. New York: Guilford Press.

Beck, J. (1995). *Cognitive therapy: Basics and beyond*. New York: Guilford Press.

Beck, J. (2005). *Cognitive therapy for challenging problems: What to do when the basics don't work*. New York: Guilford Press.

Beitman, B. (1999). Sex, love and psychotherapy. In B. Beitman & D. Yue (Eds.), *Learning psychotherapy: A time-efficient, research-based, and outcome-measured psychotherapy training program* (pp. 265–279). New York: Norton.

Beitman, B., & Yue, D. (1999). *Learning psychotherapy: A time-efficient, research-based, and outcome-measured psychotherapy training program*. New York: Norton.

Bellah, R., Madsen, R., Sullivan, W., Swidler, L., & Tipton, S. (1985). *Habits of the heart: Individualism and commitment in American life*. New York: Harper & Row.

Bender, D. (2005). The therapeutic alliance in the treatment of personality disorders. *Journal of Psychiatric Practice, 11*, 73–87.

Bennett-Levy, J. (2006). Therapist skills: A cognitive model of their acquisition and refinement. *Behavioural and Cognitive Psychotherapy, 34*, 57–78.

Bennett-Levy, J., & Thwaites, R. (2006). Self and self-refection in the therapeutic relationship. In P. Gilbert & R. Leahy (Eds.), *The therapeutic relationship in the cognitive behavioral psychotherapies* (pp. 255–282). London: Taylor & Francis.

Berg, I., & Miller, S. (1992). *Working with the problem drinker*. New York: Norton.

Berg, I., Sperry, L., & Carlson, J. (1999). Intimacy and culture: A solution-focused perspective—Interview. In J. Carlson & L. Sperry (Eds.), *The intimate couple* (pp. 33–40). New York: Brunner/Mazel.

Berger, R., & Hannah, M. T. (1999). *Preventive approaches in couples therapy*. Philadelphia: Brunner/Mazel.

Bhui, K., & Bhugra, D. (2004). Communication with patients from other cultures: The place of explanatory models. *Advances in Psychiatric Treatment, 10*, 474–478.

Bibring, E. (1954). Psychoanalysis and the dynamic psychotherapies. *Journal of the American Psychoanalytic Association, 2*, 745–770.

Binder, J. (1993). Is it time to improve psychotherapy training? *Clinical Psychology Review, 13*(4), 301–318.

Binder, J. (2004). *Key competencies in brief dynamic psychotherapy: Clinical practice beyond the manual*. New York: Guilford Press.

Binder, J., & Wechsler, F. (2009). The intervention competency. In M. Kenkel & R. Peterson (Eds.), *Competency-based education for professional psychology* (pp. 105–124). Washington, DC: American Psychological Association.

Bing, M., & Burroughs, S. (2001). The predictive and interactive effects of equity sensitivity in teamwork-oriented organizations. *Journal of Organizational Behavior, 22*, 271–290.

Blagys, M., & Hilsenroth, M. (2000). Distinctive features of short-term psychodynamic-interpersonal psychotherapy: A review of the comparative psychotherapy process literature. *Clinical Psychology: Science and Practice, 7*, 167–188.

248

Blagys, M., & Hilsenroth, M. (2002). Distinctive activities of cognitive-behavioral therapy: A review of the comparative psychotherapy process literature. *Clinical Psychology Review, 22,* 671–706.

Blatt, S., Sanislow, C., Zuroff, D., & Pilkonis, P. (1996). Characteristics of effective therapists: Further analysis of data from the National Institute of Mental Health Treatment of Depression Collaborative Research Program. *Journal of Consulting and Clinical Psychology, 64,* 1276–1284.

Bordin, E. (1979). The generalizability of the psychoanalytic concept of the working alliance. *Psychotherapy: Theory, Research, and Practice, 16,* 252–259.

Boscolo, L., Cecchin, G., Hoffman, L., & Penn, P. (1987). *Milan system family therapy.* New York: Basic Books.

Broadbent, E., Petrie, K., Main, J., & Weinman, J. (2006). The Brief Illness Perception Questionnaire (BIPQ). *Journal of Psychosomatic Research, 60,* 631–637.

Burnam, M., Hough, R., Karno, M., Escobar, J., & Telles, C. (1987). Acculturation and lifetime prevalence of psychiatric disorders among Mexican Americans in Los Angeles. *Journal of Health and Social Behavior, 28,* 89–102.

Butler, A., & Beck, J. (2000). Cognitive therapy outcomes: A review of meta-analyses. *Journal of the Norwegian Psychological Association, 37,* 1–9.

Callahan, J. L., Almstrom, C. M., Swift, J. K., Borja, S. E., & Heath, C. J. (2009). Exploring the contribution of supervisors to intervention outcomes. *Training and Education in Professional Psychology, 3,* 72–77.

Callahan, J. L., Aubuchon-Endsley, N., Borja, S. E., & Swift, J. K. (2009). Pretreatment expectancies and premature termination in a training clinic environment. *Training and Education in Professional Psychology, 3,* 111–119.

Campbell, A., & Hemsley, S. (2009). Outcome Rating Scale and Session Rating Scale in psychological practice: Clinical utility of ultra-brief measures. *Clinical Psychologist, 13*(1), 1–9.

Cardemil, E. (2008). Commentary: Culturally sensitive treatments: Need for an organizing framework. *Culture Psychology, 14,* 357–367.

Carlson, J., Sperry, L., & Lewis, J. (2005). *Family therapy techniques: Integrating and tailoring treatment.* New York: Routledge.

Carroll, K. M. (1996). Relapse prevention as a psychosocial treatment: A review of controlled clinical trials. *Experimental and Clinical Psychopharmacology, 4,* 46–54.

Cautela, J., & Wisocki, P. (1977). The thought-stopping procedure: Description, application, and learning theory interpretations. *Psychological Record, 1,* 255–264.

Celano, M. P., Smith, C. O., & Kaslow, N. J. (2010). A competency-based approach to couple and family therapy supervision. *Psychotherapy: Theory, Research, Practice, Training, 47,* 35-44. doi: 10.1037/a0018845

Chunbo, Li., & Yanling, H. (2008). Morita therapy for schizophrenia. *Schizophrenia Bulletin, 34,* 1021–1023.

Claes, R., & Ruiz-Quintanilla, S. (1994). Initial career and work meanings in seven European countries. *Career Development Quarterly, 42,* 337–352.

249

Clarkin, J., & Levy, K. (2003). Influence of client variables on psychotherapy. In M. Lambert (Ed.), *Handbook of psychotherapy and behavior change* (5th ed.). New York: Wiley.

Constantine, M., & Ladany, N. (2000). Self-report multicultural counseling scale: Their relationship to social desirability attitudes and multicultural case conceptualization abilities. *Journal of Counseling Psychology, 47,* 155–164.

Constantino, G., Malgady, R., & Rogler, L. (1986). Cuento therapy: A culturally sensitive modality for Puerto Rican children. *Journal of Consulting and Clinical Psychology, 54,* 639–645.

Cottone, R. R., & Tarvydas, V. M. (2003). *Ethical and professional issues in counseling* (2nd ed.). Upper Saddle River, NJ: Pearson.

Cottone, R. R., & Tarvydas, V. M. (2007). *Counseling ethics and decision making* (3rd ed.). Upper Saddle River, NJ: Pearson.

Council for Accreditation of Counseling and Related Educational Programs (CACREP). (2009). *CACREP accreditation procedures manual and application.* Alexandria, VA: Author.

Council on Social Work Education (CSWE). (2004). *Educational policy and accreditation standards.* Alexandria, VA: Author.

Cucciare, M., & O'Donohue, W. (2008). Clinical case conceptualization and termination of psychotherapy. In M. O'Donohue & W. Cucciare (Eds.), *Terminating psychotherapy: A clinician's guide* (pp. 121–146). New York: Routledge.

Cummings, N., & VandenBos, G. (1979). The general practice of psychology. *Professional Psychology: Research and Practice, 10,* 430–440.

Daley, D. C. (1989). *Relapse prevention: Treatment alternatives and counseling aids.* Blaze Ridge Summit, PA: TAB Books.

Dana, R. (1993). *Multicultural assessment perspectives for professional psychology.* Boston: Allyn & Bacon.

Davidson, J., & Caddell, D. (1994). Religion and the meaning of work. *Journal for the Scientific Study of Religion, 33,* 135–147.

Derogatis, L., & Cleary, P. (1977). Confirmation of the dimensional structure of the SCL-90: A study in construct validation. *Journal of Clinical Psychology, 33,* 981–989.

de Shazer, S. (1985). *Keys to solutions in brief therapy.* New York: Norton.

de Shazer, S. (1988). *Clues: Investigating solutions in brief therapy.* New York: Norton.

de Shazer, S. (1991). *Putting differences to work.* New York: Norton.

de Shazer, S. (1994). *Words were originally magic.* New York: Norton.

de Shazer, S., Dolan, Y., Korman, H., Trepper, T., McCullom, E., & Berg, I. (2007). *More than miracles: The state of the art of solution-focused brief therapy.* New York: Haworth.

Dik, B., Duffy, R., & Eldridge, B. (2009). Calling and vocation in career counseling: Recommendations for promoting meaningful work. *Professional Psychology: Research and Practice, 40,* 625–632.

Dinkmeyer, D., & Sperry, L. (2000). *Counseling and psychotherapy: An integrated, individual psychology approach.* Upper Saddle River, NJ: Prentice Hall.

Dobson, K. (Ed.). (2001). *Handbook of cognitive-behavioral therapies* (2nd ed.). New York: Guilford Press.

Dobson, K. S., & Haubert, L. C. (2008). Termination with persons with depressive disorders. In M. O'Donohue & W. Cucciare (Eds.), *Terminating psychotherapy: A clinician's guide* (pp. 303–324). New York: Routledge.

Dreyfus, H., & Dreyfus, S. (1986). *Mind over machine.* New York: Free Press.

Duckett, L., & Ryden, M. (1994). Education for ethical nursing practice. In J. Rest & D. Narcvaez (Eds.), *Moral development in the professions: Psychology and applied ethics* (pp. 51–70). Hillsdale, NJ: Erlbaum.

Duffy, R., & Sedlacek, W. (in press). The salience of a career calling among college students: Exploring group differences and links to religiousness, life meaning, and life satisfaction. *Career Development Quarterly, 43.*

Duncan, B., Miller, S., Parks, L., Claud, D., Reynolds, L., Brown, J., et al. (2003). The Session Rating Scale: Preliminary properties of a "working" alliance measures. *Journal of Brief Therapy, 3,* 3–12.

Eells, T. (Ed.). (2007). *Handbook of psychotherapy case formulation* (2nd ed.). New York: Guilford Press.

Eells, T., & Lombart, K. (2003). Case formulation and treatment concepts among novice, experienced, and expert cognitive-behavioral and psychodynamic therapists. *Psychotherapy Research, 13,* 187–204.

Eells, T., Lombart, K., Kendjelic, E., Turner, L., & Lucas, C. (2005). The quality of psychotherapy case formulations: A comparison of expert, experienced, and novice cognitive-behavioral and psychodynamic therapists. *Journal of Consulting and Clinical Psychology, 73,* 579–589.

Ellis, A. (1962). *Reason and emotion in psychotherapy.* New York: Lyle Stuart.

Ellis, A., & Harper, R. (1997). *A guide to rational living.* North Hollywood, CA: Melvin Powers.

Engels, D., Minton, C., Ray, D., & Associates. (2010). *The professional counselor: Portfolio, competencies, performance guidelines, and assessment* (4th ed.). Alexandria, VA: American Counseling Association.

Engle, D., & Arkowitz, H. (2006). *Ambivalence in psychotherapy: Facilitating readiness to change.* New York: Guilford Press.

Epstein, R., & Hundert, E. (2002). Defining and assessing professional competence. *Journal of the American Medical Association, 287,* 226–235.

Erickson, K. (Ed.). (1996). *The road to excellence: The acquisition of expert performance in the arts and sciences, sports and games.* Mahwah, NJ: Erlbaum.

Falender, C., & Shafranske, E. (2004). *Clinical supervision: A competency-based approach.* Washington, DC: American Psychological Association.

Falvey, J. (2001). Clinical judgment in case conceptualization and treatment planning across mental health disciplines. *Journal of Counseling and Development, 79,* 292–303.

Farber, E. W., & Kaslow, N. J. (2010). Introduction to the special section: The role of supervision in ensuring the development of psychothearpy competencies across diverse theoretical perspectives. *Psychotherapy: Theory, Research, Practice, Training, 47,* 1–2. doi: 10.1037/a0018850

Fisch, R., Weakland, J., & Segal, L. (1982). *The tactics of change.* San Francisco: Jossey-Bass.

Fleck-Hendersen, A. (1995). Ethical sensitivity: A theoretical and empirical study. *Dissertation Abstracts International, 56,* 2862B.

Fouad, N. A., Grus, C. L., Hatcher, R. L., Kaslow, N. J., Hutchings, P. S., Madson, M. B., et al. (2009). Competency benchmarks: A model for understanding and measuring competence in professional psychology across training levels. *Training and Education in Professional Psychology, 3,* S5–S26.

Frank, K. (1999). *Psychoanalytic participation.* Hillsdale, NJ: Analytic Press.

Frank, K., & Frank, J. (1991). *Persuasion and healing: A comparative study of psychotherapy* (3rd ed.). New York: Praeger.

Frayn, D. (2008). Premature termination issues involving psychoanalytic therapy. In M. O'Donohue & W. Cucciare (Eds.), *Terminating psychotherapy: A clinician's guide* (pp. 33–52). New York: Routledge.

Freeman, A., & McCluskey, R. (2005). Resistance: Impediments to effective psychotherapy. In A. Freeman (Ed.), *Encyclopedia of cognitive behavior therapy* (pp. 334–340). New York: Springer.

Freitas, G. (2002). The impact of psychotherapy supervision on client outcome: A critical examination of two decades of research. *Psychotherapy: Theory, Research, Practice, Training, 39,* 354–367.

Freud, A. (1936). The ego and the mechanisms of defense. In *The writings of Anna Freud* (Vol. 2, pp. 1–191). New York: International Universities Press.

Freud, S. (1940). *An outline of psychoanalysis.* London: Hogarth Press.

Gabbard, G. (1999). An overview of countertransference: Theory and technique. In G. Gabbard (Ed.), *Countertransference issues in psychiatric treatment* (pp. 1–25). Washington, DC: American Psychiatric Press.

Gabbard, G. (2004). *Long-term psychodynamic psychotherapy: A basic text.* Washington, DC: American Psychiatric Press.

GAP Committee on Cultural Psychiatry. (2002). *Cultural assessment in clinical psychiatry.* Washington, DC: American Psychiatric Press.

Garfield, S. (1994). Research on client variables in psychotherapy. In A. E. Bergin & S. L. Garfield (Eds.), *Handbook of psychotherapy and behavior change* (pp. 190–228). New York: Wiley.

Gehart, D. (2010). *Mastering competencies in family therapy: A practical approach to theories and clinical case documentation.* Belmont, CA: Brooks/Cole.

Gelso, C., & Hayes, J. (2007). *Countertransference and the therapist's inner experience: Perils and possibilities.* Mahwah, NJ: Erlbaum.

Gelso, C., Hill, C., Mohr, J., Rochlen, A., & Zack, J. (1999). Describing the face of transference: Psychodynamic therapists' recollections about transference in cases of successful long-term therapy. *Journal of Counseling Psychology, 46,* 257–267.

Gilbert, P., & Leahy, R. (2005). Introduction and overview: Basic issues in the thera-peutic relationship. In P. Gilbert & R. Leahy (Eds.), *The therapeutic relationship in the cognitive behavioral psychotherapies* (pp. 2–23). London: Routledge.

Gilbert, P., & Leahy, R. (Eds.). (2007). *The therapeutic relationship in the cognitive behavioral psychotherapies.* London: Routledge.

Gloaguen, V., Cottraus, J., Cucharet, M., & Blackburn, I. (1998). A meta-analysis of the effects of cognitive therapy in depressed patients. *Journal of Affective Disorders, 49,* 59–72.

Goldfried, M., & Davison, G. (1994). *Clinical behavior therapy* (Expanded ed.). New York: Wiley.

Goldfried, M., Raue, P., & Castonguay, L. (1998). The therapeutic focus in signifi-cant sessions of master therapists: A comparison of cognitive-behavioral and psychodynamic-interpersonal interventions. *Journal of Consulting and Clinical Psychology, 66,* 803–810.

Good, G., & Beitman, B. (2006). *Counseling and psychotherapy essentials: Integrating theories, skills, and practices.* New York: Norton.

Google. (2010). Web definitions for treatment failure. Retrieved March 11, 2010, from http://www.google.com/search?hl=en&rlz=1R2GGLL_en&defl=en&q=de fine:treatment+failure&ei=wF-ZS7j5HsiUtgej6eywCQ&sa=X&oi=glossary_ definition&ct=title&ved=0CAcQkAE

Greenberg, L., & Watson, J. (2006). *Emotion-focused therapy for depression.* Washington, DC: American Psychological Association.

Greenson, R. (1967). *The technique and practice of psychoanalysis* (Vol. 1). New York: International Universities Press.

Haley, J. (1976). *Problem-solving therapy.* San Francisco: Jossey-Bass.

Haley, J. (1984). *Ordeal therapy.* San Francisco: Jossey-Bass.

Haley, J., & Richeport-Haley, M. (2007). *Directive family therapy.* New York: Hawthorne.

Hampson, R., & Beavers, R. (2004). Observational assessment of couples and fami-lies. In L. Sperry (Ed.), *Assessment of couples and families: Contemporary and cutting edge strategies* (pp. 91–116). New York: Routledge.

Hanna, S., & Brown, J. (1999). *The practice of family therapy: Key elements across mod-els.* Pacific Grove, CA: Brooks/Cole.

Hannan, C., Lambert, M., Harmon, C., Nielsen, S., Smart, D., & Shimokawa, K., (2005). A lab test and algorithms for identifying clients at risk for treatment failure. *Journal of Counseling Psychology, 50,* 155–163.

Hansen, N., Randazzo, K., Schwartz, A., Marshall, M., Kalis, D., Fraziers, R., et al. (2006). Do we practice what we preach? An exploratory survey of mul-ticultural psychotherapy competencies. *Professional Psychology: Research and Practice, 337,* 66–74.

Hardy, G., Cahill, J., & Barkham, M. (2007). Active ingredients of the therapeutic relationship that promote client change: A research perspective. In P. Gilbert & R. Leahy (Eds.), *The therapeutic relationship in the cognitive behavioral psycho-therapies* (pp. 24–42). London: Routledge.

Harmon, C., Hawkins, E., Lambert, M., Slade, K., & Whipple, J. (2005). Improving outcomes for poorly responding clients: The use of clinical support tools and feedback to clients. *Journal of Clinical Psychology, 61,* 175–185.

Hayes, S., Follette, V., & Linehan, M. (Eds.). (2004). *Mindfulness and acceptance: Expanding the cognitive-behavioral tradition.* New York: Guilford Press.

Haynes, R., Corey, G., & Moulton, P. (2003). *Clinical supervision in the helping professions: A practical guide.* Pacific Grove, CA: Brooks/Cole.

Hays, P., & Iwanasa, G. (Eds.). (2006). *Culturally responsive cognitive-behavioral therapy: Assessment, practice, and supervision.* Washington, DC: American Psychological Association.

Heaton, J. (1998). *Building basic therapeutic skills: A practical guide for current mental health practice.* San Francisco: Jossey-Bass.

Hill, C. (2004). *Helping skills: Facilitating exploration, insight, and action* (2nd ed.). Washington, DC: American Psychological Association.

Hill, C. (2005). Therapist techniques, client involvement, and the therapeutic relationship: Inextricably intertwined in the therapy process. *Psychotherapy: Theory, Research, Practice, Training, 42,* 431–442.

Hoge, M., Paris, M., Adger, H., Collins, F., Finn, C., Fricks, L., et al. (2005). Workforce competencies in behavioral health: An overview. *Administration and Policy in Mental Health and Mental Health Services Research, 32*(5–6), 593–631.

Holtzworth-Munroe, A., Jacobson, N., DeKlyen, M., & Whisman, M. (1989). Relationship between behavioral marital therapy outcome and process variables. *Journal of Consulting and Clinical Psychology, 57,* 658–662.

Horvath, A., & Greenberg, L. (1989). Development and validation of the Working Alliance Inventory. *Journal of Counseling Psychology, 36,* 223–233.

Horvath, A., & Symonds, B. (1991). Relationship between working alliance and outcome in psychotherapy: A meta-analysis. *Journal of Counseling Psychology, 38,* 139–149.

Howard, K., Kopta, S., Krause, M., & Orlinsky, D. (1986). The dose-effect relationship in psychotherapy. *American Psychologist, 41,* 159–164.

Howard, K., Lueger, R., Maling, M., & Martinovich, Z. (1993). A phase model of psychotherapy: Causal mediation of outcome. *Journal of Consulting and Clinical Psychology, 61,* 678–685.

Hubble, A., Duncan, B., & Miller, S. (1999). *The heart and soul of change.* Washington, DC: APA Books.

Institute of Medicine. (2003). *Health professions education: A bridge to quality.* Washington, DC: National Academies Press.

Jennings, L., & Skovholt, T. (1999). The cognitive, emotional and relational characteristics of master therapists. *Journal of Counseling Psychology, 46,* 3–11.

Johnson, S. (2004). *The practice of emotionally focused marital therapy: Creating connections* (2nd ed.). New York: Brunner/Routledge.

Jongsma, A., Peterson, L., & Bruce, Y. (2006). *The complete adult psychotherapy treatment planner* (4th ed.). New York: Wiley.

254

Jonsen, A., Siegler, M., & Winslade, W. (1986). *Clinical ethics: A practical approach to ethical decisions in clinical medicine* (2nd ed.). New York: Macmillan.

Kabat-Zinn, J. (1994). *Wherever you go, there you are: Mindfulness meditation in everyday life.* New York: Hyperion.

Kanfer, F. (1970). Self-monitoring: Methodological limitations and clinical applications. *Journal of Consulting and Clinical Psychology, 35,* 148–152.

Kaslow, N. (2004). Competencies in professional psychology. *American Psychologist, 59,* 74–781.

Kaslow, N. (2009). President's column. *Psychotherapy Bulletin, 44*(3), 2–5.

Kaslow, N. J., & Bell, K. D. (2008). A competency-based approach to supervision. In C. A. Falendar & E. P. Shafranske (Eds.), *Casebook for clinical supervision: A competency-based approach* (pp. 17–38). Washington D.C.: American Psychological Association.

Kaslow, N. J., Borden, K. A., Collins, F. L., Forrest, L., Illfelder-Kaye, J., Nelson, P. D., et al. (2004). Competencies Conference: Future directions in education and credentialing in professional psychology. *Journal of Clinical Psychology, 80,* 699-712. doi: 10.1002/jclp.20016

Kaslow, N. J., Celano, M. P., & Stanton, M. (2005). Training in family psychology: A competencies-based approach. *Family Process, 44,* 337–353. doi: 10.1111/j.1545-5300.2005.00063.x

Kaslow, N. J., Dunn, S. E., & Smith, C. O. (2008). Competencies for psychologists in academic health centers (AHCs). *Journal of Clinical Psychology in Medical Settings, 15,* 18-27. doi: 10.1007/s10880-008-9094-y

Kaslow, N. J., Grus, C. L., Campbell, L. F., Fouad, N. A., Hatcher, R. L., & Rodolfa, E. R. (2009). Competency assessment toolkit for professional Psychology. *Training and Education in Professional Psychology, 3,* S27–S45. doi: 10.1037/a0015833

Kaslow, N. J., & Ingram, M. V. (2009). Board certification: A competency-based perspective. In C. M. Nezu, A. J. Finch & N. P. Simon (Eds.), *Becoming board certified by the American Board of Professional Psychology* (pp. 37–46). New York: Oxford University Press.

Kaslow, N. J., Rubin, N. J., Bebeau, M., Leigh, I. W., Lichtenberg, J., Nelson, P. D., et al. (2007). Guiding principles and recommendations for the assessment of competence. *Professional Psychology: Research and Practice, 38,* 441–451. doi: 10.1037/0735-7028.38.5.441

Kazantzis, N. (2005). Introduction and overview. In N. Kazantzis, F. Deane, K. Ronan, & L. L'Abate (Eds.), *Using homework assignments in cognitive behavior therapy* (pp. 1–8). New York: Routledge.

Kendjelic, E., & Eells, T. (2007). Generic psychotherapy case formulation training improves formulation quality. *Psychotherapy: Theory, Research, Practice, Training, 44,* 66–77.

Kenkel, M., & Peterson, R. (Eds.). (2009). *Competency-based education for professional psychology.* Washington, DC: American Psychological Association.

Kitchner, K. (1984). Intuition, critical evaluation, and ethical principles: The foundation for ethical decisions in counseling psychology. *Counseling Psychologist, 12*, 43–55.

Klein, M. (1975). *Envy and gratitude and other works, 1946-1963.* New York: Free Press.

Kleinman, A. (1988). *Rethinking psychiatry: From cultural category to personal experience.* New York: Free Press.

Kohut, H. (1977). *The restoration of the self.* New York: International Universities Press.

Kuyken, W. (2004). Cognitive therapy outcome: The effects of hopelessness in a naturalistic outcome study. *Behavior Research and Therapy, 42*, 631–646.

Lambert, M. (1992). Psychotherapy outcome research: Implications for integrative and eclectic therapists. In J. Norcross & M. Goldfried (Eds.), *Handbook of psychotherapy* (pp. 94–129). New York: Basic Books.

Lambert, M. (2010). *Prevention of treatment failure: The use of measuring, monitoring, and feedback in clinical practice.* Washington, DC: American Psychological Association.

Lambert, M., Morton, J., Hatfield, D., Harmon, C., Hamilton, S., & Reid, R. (2004). *Administration and scoring manual for the Outcome Questionnaire-45.* Orem, UT: American Professional Credentialing Services.

Lambert, M., & Ogles, B. (2004). The efficacy and effectiveness of psychotherapy. In M. Lambert (Ed.), *Bergin and Garfield's handbook of psychotherapy and behavior change* (5th ed., pp. 139–193). New York: Wiley.

Lambert, M., & Okishi, B. (1997). The efficacy and effectiveness of psychotherapy supervision. In C. Watkins (Ed.), *Bergin and Garfield's handbook of psychotherapy and behavior change* (4th ed., pp. 139–193). New York: Wiley.

Lambert, M., Whipple, J., Hawkins, E., Vermeersch, D., Nielsen, S., & Smart, D. (2003). Is it time for clinicians to routinely track patient outcomes? A metaanalysis. *Clinical Psychology: Science and Practice, 10*, 288–301.

Lambert, M., Whipple, J., Smart, D., Vermeersch, D., Nielsen, S., & Hawkins, E. (2001). The effects of providing therapists with feedback on patient progress during psychotherapy: Are outcomes enhanced? *Psychotherapy Research, 11*(1), 49–68.

La Roche, M., & Christopher, M. (2008). Culture and empirically supported treatments: On the road to a collision? *Culture and Psychology, 14*, 333–356.

Lazarus, A. (1966). Behavioral rehearsal vs. non-directive therapy vs. advice in effective behavior change. *Behavior Research and Therapy, 4*, 209–212.

Leahy, R. (2003). *Cognitive therapy techniques: A practitioner's guide.* New York: Guilford Press.

Ledley, D., Marx, B., & Heimberg, R. (2005). *Making cognitive-behavioral therapy work: Clinical process for new practitioners.* New York: Guilford Press.

Levenson, H. (1995). *Time-limited dynamic psychotherapy: A guide to clinical practice.* New York: Basic Books.

Levenson, H. (2004). Time-limited dynamic psychotherapy: Formulation and intervention. In M. Dewan, B. Steenbarger, & R. Greenberg (Eds.), *The art and science of brief psychotherapies: A practitioner's guide* (pp. 157–187). Washington, DC: American Psychiatric Press.

Levenson, H., & Strupp, H. H. (2007). Cyclical maladaptive patterns in time-limited dynamic psychotherapy. In T. Eells (Ed.), *Handbook of psychotherapy case formulation* (pp. 164–197). New York: Guilford Press.

Leventhal, H., Diefenbach, M., & Leventhal, E. (1992). Illness cognition: Using common sense to understand treatment adherence and affect in cognitive interactions. *Cognitive Therapy and Research, 16*, 143–163.

Li, C., & He, Y. (2008). Morita therapy for schizophrenia. *Schizophrenia Bulletin, 34*, 1021–1023.

Linehan, M. (1993). *Cognitive-behavioral treatment of borderline personality disorder.* New York: Guilford Press.

Ludgate, J. (1995). *Maximizing psychotherapeutic gains and preventing relapse in emotionally distressed clients.* Sarasota, FL: Professional Resource Press.

Madanes, C. (1981). *Strategic family therapy.* San Francisco: Jossey-Bass.

Magnavita, J. J. (1997). *Restructuring personality disorders: A short-term dynamic approach.* New York: Guilford Press.

Marlatt, G. A., & Gordon, J. R. (1985). *Relapse prevention: Maintenance strategies in the treatment of addictive behaviors.* New York: Guilford Press.

Marra, T. (2005). *Dialectic behavior therapy in private practice: A practical and comprehensive guide.* Oakland, CA: New Harbinger Publications.

Martinez-Taboas, A. (2005). The plural world of culturally sensitive psychotherapy: A response to Castro-Blanco's comments. *Psychotherapy: Theory, Research, Practice, Training, 42*(1), 17–19.

Martinez-Taboas, A. (2005). Psychogenic seizures in an *espiritismo* context: The role of culturally sensitive psychotherapy. *Psychotherapy: Theory, Research, Practice, Training, 42*, 6–13.

McClelland, D. (1973). Testing for competence rather than intelligence. *American Psychologist, 28*, 1–14.

McCullough, J. (2000). *Treatment for chronic depression: Cognitive behavioral analysis system of psychotherapy.* New York: Guilford Press.

McCullough, J. (2005). *Treating chronic depression with disciplined personal involvement.* New York: Springer.

McWilliams, N. (2004). *Psychoanalytic psychotherapy: A practitioner's guide.* New York: Guilford Press.

Meichenbaum, D. (1977). *Cognitive behavior modification: An integrative approach.* New York: Plenum.

Meichenbaum, D., & Turk, D. (1987). *Facilitating treatment adherence: A practitioner's guide.* New York: Plenum.

Meissner, W. (1980). A note on projective identification. *Journal of the American Psychoanalytic Association, 28*, 43–67.

Mellman, L., & Beresin, E. (2003). Psychotherapy competencies: Development and implementation. *Academic Psychiatry, 27,* 149–153.

Miller, J., Todahl, J., & Platt, J. (2010). The competency movement in marriage and family therapy: Key considerations from other disciplines. *Journal of Marital and Family therapy, 36,* 59–70.

Miller, S., & Duncan, B. (2000). *The Outcomes Rating Scale.* Chicago: Author.

Miller, S., Duncan, B., Brown, J., Sorrell, R., & Chalk, M. (2006). Using outcome to inform and improve treatment outcomes: Making ongoing, real-time assessment feasible. *Journal of Brief Therapy, 5,* 5–23.

Miller, S., Duncan, B., & Hubble, M. (1997). *Escape from Babel: Toward a unifying language for psychotherapy practice.* New York: Norton.

Miller, S., Duncan, B., Sorrell, R., &, Brown, J. (2005). The partners for change outcome management system. *Journal of Clinical Psychology, 61,* 199–208.

Miller, W., & Rollnick, S. (2002). *Motivational interviewing: Preparing people for change* (2nd ed.). New York: Guilford Press.

Minuchin, S. (1974). *Families and family therapy.* Cambridge, MA: Harvard University Press.

Minuchin, S., & Fishman, H. (1981). *Family therapy techniques.* Cambridge, MA: Harvard University Press.

Minuchin, S., & Nicols (1981).

Mondofacto Online Medical Dictionary. (2010). Treatment failure. *Mondofacto Online Medical Dictionary.* Retrieved March 11, 2010, from http://www.mondofacto.com/factsdictionary?treatment+failure

Moore, B., & Fine, B. (1968). *A glossary of psychoanalytic terms and concepts.* New York: American Psychoanalytic Association.

Mours, J. M., Campbell, C. D., Gathercoal, K. A., & Peterson, M. (2009). Training in the use of psychotherapy outcome assessment measures at psychology internship sites. *Training and Education in Professional Psychology, 3,* 169–176.

Mozdzierz, G., Peluso, P., & Lisiecki, J. (2009). *Principles of counseling and psychotherapy: Learning the essential domains and nonlinear thinking of master practitioners.* New York: Routledge.

Myers, R., & Smith, J. (1995). *Clinical guide to alcohol treatment.* New York: Guilford Press.

Nelson, P. (2007). Striving for competence in the assessment of competence: Psychology's professional education and credentialing journey of public accountability. *Training and Education in Professional Psychology, 1,* 3–12.

Nelson, T., Chenail, R., Alexander, J., Crane, D., Johnson, D., & Schwallie, L. (2007). The development of core competencies for the practice of marriage and family therapy. *Journal of Marital and Family Therapy, 33,* 417–438.

Neufield, S., E. Pinterits, E., Moleiro, C., Lee, T., Yang, P., & Brodie, R. (2006). How do graduate student therapists incorporate diversity factors in case conceptualizations? *Psychotherapy: Theory, Research, Practice, Training, 43,* 464–479.

Norcross, J. (2002). Empirically supported therapy relationship. In J. Norcross (Ed.), *Psychotherapy relationships that work: Therapist contributions and responsiveness to patients* (pp. 3–16). New York: Oxford University Press.

Norcross, J. (Ed.). (2002). *Psychotherapy relationships that work: Therapist contributions and responsiveness to patients.* New York: Oxford University Press.

Norcross, J. (2005). A primer on psychotherapy integration. In J. Norcross & M. Goldfried (Eds.), *Handbook of psychotherapy integration* (2nd ed., pp. 3–23). New York: Oxford University Press.

Ochoa, E., & Muran, J. (2008). A relational take on termination in cognitive-behavioral therapy. In W. T. O'Donohue & M. A. Cucciare (Eds.), *Terminating psychotherapy: A clinician's guide* (pp. 183–204). New York: Routledge.

O'Donohue, W., & Cucciare, M. (2008). Introduction. In M. O'Donohue & W. Cucciare (Eds.). *Terminating psychotherapy: A clinician's guide* (pp. xv–xxvi) New York: Routledge.

O'Hanlon, B., & Beadle, S. (1999). *A guide to possibilityland: Possibility therapy methods.* Omaha, NE: Possibility Press.

O'Hanlon, B., & Weiner-Davis, M. (1989). *In search of solutions: A new direction in psychotherapy.* New York: Norton.

Okazaki, S. (2000). Assessing and treating Asian Americans: Recent advances. In I. Cuellar & F. Paniagua (Eds.), *Handbook of multicultural mental health: Assessment and treatment of diversion populations* (pp. 171–193). New York: Academic Press.

Orlinsky, D., Grawe, K., & Parks, B. (1994). Process and outcome in psychotherapy. In A. Bergin & S. Garfield (Eds.), *Handbook of psychotherapy and behavior change* (4th ed., pp. 270–376). New York: Wiley.

Orlinsky, D., Ronnestad, M., & Willutzi, U. (2004). Fifty years of psychotherapy process-outcome research: Continuity and change. In M. Lambert (Ed.), *Bergin and Garfield's handbook of psychotherapy and behavior change* (5th ed., pp. 307–389). New York: Wiley.

Ornstein, E., & Ganzer, C. (2005). Relational social work: A model for the future. *Families in Society, 86,* 565–572.

Paniagua, F. (2005). *Assessing and treating culturally diverse clients: A practical guide* (3rd ed.). Thousand Oaks, CA: Sage.

Paul, G. (1969). Outcome of systematic desensitization. In C. Franks (Ed.), *Behavior therapy: Appraisal and status.* New York: McGraw-Hill.

Penn, Scheon, & Berland Associates. (2004). [Survey for the American Psychological Association] "Mental Illness the Need for Health Care Access Reform". Unpublished survey.

Perry, S., Cooper, A., & Michels, R. (1987). The psychodynamic formulation: Its purpose, structure, and clinical application. *American Journal of Psychiatry, 144,* 543–551.

Persons, E. (1989). *Cognitive therapy in practice. A case formulation approach.* New York: Norton.

Persons, J. (2007). Psychotherapists collect data during routine clinical work that can contribute to knowledge about mechanisms of change in psychotherapy. *Clinical Psychology: Science and Practice, 14*, 244–246.

Piercy, F., & Sprenkle, D. (1986). *Family therapy sourcebook*. New York: Guilford Press.

Pine, F. (2003). *Diversity and direction in psychoanalytic technique* (2nd ed.). New York: Other Press.

Plakun, E. (2008). *The Y-model for teaching psychotherapy competencies*. Stockbridge, MA: Austen Riggs Center. Retrieved January 15, 2010, from http://www.austenriggs.org/continuing_education/ymodel

Plakun, E., Sudak, D., & Goldberg, D. (2009). The Y model: An integrated, evidence-based approach to teaching psychotherapy competencies. *Journal of Psychiatric Practice, 15*(1), 5–11.

Prochaska, J., DiClementi, C., & Norcross, J. (1992). In search of how people change. *American Psychologist, 47*, 1102–1114.

Rest, J. (1994). Background: Theory and research. In J. Rest & D. Narcvaez (Eds.), *Moral development in the professions: Psychology and applied ethics* (pp. 1–26). Hillsdale, NJ: Erlbaum.

Quick, E. K. (2008). *Doing what works in brief therapy: A strategic solution focused approach* (2nd ed.). Burlington, MA: Academic Press.

Reese, R., Norsworthy, L., & Rowlands, S. (2009). Does a continuous feedback system improve psychotherapy outcome? *Psychotherapy: Theory, Research, Practice, Training, 46*, 418–431.

Reese, R., Usher, E., Bowman, D., Norsworthy, L., Halsted, J., Rowlands, S., et al. (2009). Using client feedback in psychotherapy training: An analysis of its influence on supervision and counselor self-efficacy. *Training and Education in Professional Psychology, 3*, 157–168.

Reis, B., & Brown, L. (1999). Reducing psychotherapy dropouts: Maximizing perspective convergence in the psychotherapy dyad. *Psychotherapy: Theory, Research, Practice, Training, 36*, 123–136.

Ridley, C., & Kelly, S. (2007). Multicultural considerations in case formation. In T. Eells (Ed.), *Handbook of psychotherapy case formulation* (2nd ed., pp. 33–64). New York: Guilford Press.

Roberts, L., & Dyer, A. (2004). *Concise guide to ethics in mental health care*. Washington, DC: American Psychiatric Press.

Rogers, C. (1961). *On becoming a person*. Boston: Houghton Mifflin.

Rowa, K., Bieling, P., & Segal, Z. (2005). Depression. In M. Antony, D. Ledley, & R. Heimberg (Eds.), *Improving outcomes and preventing relapse in cognitive-behavioral therapy* (pp. 204–245). New York: Guilford Press.

Safran, J., & Muran, J. (2000). *Negotiating the therapeutic alliance: A relational treatment guide*. New York: Guilford Press.

Samstag, C., Muran, J., & Safran, J. (2003). Defining and identifying alliance ruptures. In D. Chairman (Ed.), *Core processes in brief dynamic psychotherapy: Advancing effective practice* (pp. 182–214). New York: Erlbaum.

Safran, J., Muran, J., Samstag, C., & Stevens, C. (2002). Repairing alliance ruptures. In J. Norcross (Ed.), *Psychotherapy relationships that work: Therapist contributions and responsiveness to patients* (pp. 235–254). New York: Oxford University Press.

Schön, D. (1983). *The reflective practitioner*. New York: Basic Books.

Segal, Z., Williams, J., Teasdale, J., & Williams, M. (2004). Mindfulness-based cognitive therapy: Theoretical and empirical status. In S. Hayes, V. Follette, & M. Linehan (Eds.), *Mindfulness and acceptance: Expanding the cognitive-behavioral tradition* (pp. 45–65). New York: Guilford Press.

Seligman, L. (2005). *Conceptual skills for mental health professionals*. Columbus, OH: Merrill.

Shapiro, D. (1989). *Psychotherapy of neurotic character*. New York: Basic Books.

Shapiro, F. (2001). *Eye movement desensitization and reprocessing: Basic principles, protocols, and procedures* (2nd ed.). New York: Guilford Press.

Sherman, R., Oresky, P., & Rountress, Y. (1991). *Solving problems in couples and family therapy*. New York: Brunner/Mazel.

Sim, K., Gwee, K., & Bateman, A. (2005). Case formulation in psychotherapy: Revitalizing its usefulness as a clinical tool. *Academic Psychiatry, 29*, 289–292.

Skovholt, T., & Jennings, L. (2004). *Master therapists: Exploring expertise in therapy and counseling*. Boston: Allyn & Bacon.

Slade, K., Lambert, M., Harmon, C., Smart, D., & Bailey, R. (2008). Improving psychotherapy outcome: The use of immediate electronic feedback and revised clinical support tools. *Clinical Psychology & Psychotherapy, 15*, 287–303.

Smith, M., Glass, G., & Miller, T. (1980). *The benefits of psychotherapy*. Baltimore: Johns Hopkins Press.

Sotsky, S., Galss, D., & Shea, M. (1991). Patient predictors of response to psychotherapy and pharmacotherapy: Findings in the NIMH treatment of depression collaborative research program. *American Journal of Psychiatry, 148*, 997–1008.

Sperry, L. (1997). The rediscovery of interventive interviewing. In J. Carlson & S. Slavik (Eds.), *Techniques in Adlerian psychology* (pp. 107–110). Washington, DC: Taylor & Francis.

Sperry, L. (2005a). Case conceptualization: A strategy for incorporating individual, couple, and family dynamics in the treatment process. *American Journal of Family Therapy, 33*, 353–364.

Sperry, L. (2005b). Case conceptualizations: The missing link between theory and practice. *The Family Journal: Counseling and Therapy for Couples and Families, 13*, 71–76.

Sperry, L. (2006). *Psychological treatment of chronic illness: The biopsychosocial therapy approach*. Washington, DC: American Psychological Association.

Sperry, L. (2007a). *Dictionary of ethical and legal terms and issues: The essential guide for mental health professionals*. New York: Routledge.

Sperry, L. (2007b). *The ethical and professional practice of counseling and psychotherapy*. Boston: Allyn & Bacon.

Sperry, L. (2009). *Treatment of chronic medical conditions: Cognitive-behavioral therapy strategies and integrative treatment protocols.* Washington, DC: American Psychological Association.

Sperry, L. (2010). *Highly effective therapy: Developing essential clinical competencies in counseling and psychotherapy.* New York: Routledge.

Sperry, L., Brill, P., Howard, K., & Grissom, G. (1996). *Treatment outcomes in psychotherapy and psychiatric interventions.* New York: Brunner/Mazel.

Sperry, L., Carlson, J., & Kjos, D. (2003). *Becoming an effective therapist.* Boston: Allyn & Bacon.

Sperry, L., Gudeman, J., Blackwell, B., & Faulkner, L. (1992). *Psychiatric case formulation.* Washington, DC: American Psychiatric Press.

Sperry, L., Lewis, J., Carlson, J., & Englar-Carlson, M. (2003). *Health promotion and health counseling: Effective counseling and psychotherapeutic strategies.* Boston: Allyn & Bacon.

Spruill, J., Rozensky, R., Stigall, T., Vasquez, M., Bingham, R., & Olvey, B. (2004). Becoming a competent clinician: Basic competencies in intervention. *Journal of Clinical Psychology, 60,* 741–754.

Strupp, H., & Binder, J. (1984). *Psychotherapy in a new key.* New York: Basic Books.

Sue, D., & Zane, N. (1987). The role of culture and cultural technique in psychotherapy: A critique and reformulation. *American Psychologist, 59,* 533–540.

Sutton, L., Townend, M., & Wright, J. (2007). The experiences of reflective learning journals by cognitive behavioural psychotherapy students. *Reflective Practice: International and Multidisciplinary Perspectives, 8,* 387–404.

Swift, K., & Callahan, J. (2009). The impact of client treatment preferences on outcome: A meta-analysis. *Journal of Clinical Psychology, 65,* 368–381.

Talmon, M. (1990). *Single-session therapy.* San Francisco: Jossey-Bass.

Tarrier, N., & Calam, R. (2002). New developments in cognitive-behavioral case formulation. Epidemiological, systemic and social context: An integrative approach. *Cognitive and Behavioral Psychotherapy, 30,* 311–328.

Taymor, J. (Director). (2007). *Across the universe* [Motion picture]. United States: Revolution Studios.

Thwaites, R., & Bennett-Levy, J. (2007). Conceptualizing empathy in cognitive behavior therapy: Making the implicit explicit. *Behavioral and Cognitive Psychotherapy, 35,* 591–612.

Tomm, K. (1987a). Interventive interviewing: Part I. Strategizing as a fourth guideline for the therapist. *Family Process, 26,* 3–13.

Tomm, K. (1987b). Interventive interviewing: Part II. Reflexive questioning as a means to enable self-healing. *Family Process, 26,* 167–183.

Tomm, K. (1988). Interventive interviewing: Part III. Intending to ask lineal, circular, strategic, or reflective questions? *Family Process, 27,* 1–16.

Urbain, E., & Kendall, P. (1980). Review of social-cognitive problem solving interventions with children. *Psychological Bulletin, 88,* 109–143.

VandenBos, G. (Ed.). (2007). *APA dictionary of psychology.* Washington, DC: American Psychological Association.

Viamontes, G., & Beitman, B. (2006). Neural substrates of psychotherapeutic change, Part II: Beyond default mode. *Psychiatric Annals, 36*, 239–246.

Vollmer, B., Grote, J., Lange, R., & Walter, C. (2009). A therapy preference interview: Empowering clients by offering choices. *Psychotherapy Bulletin, 44*(2), 33–37.

Wachtel, P. (1993). *Therapeutic communication: Principles and effective practice.* New York: Guilford Press.

Walter, J., & Peller, J. (1992). *Becoming solution-focused in brief therapy.* New York: Brunner/Mazel.

Watson, J., & Greenberg, L. (2000). Alliance ruptures and repairs in experiential therapy. *Journal of Clinical Psychology, 56*(2), 175–186.

Weber, M. (1958). *The Protestant ethics and the spirit of capitalism.* New York: Scribners.

Weddington, W., & Cavenar, J. (1979). Termination initiated by the therapist: A countertransference storm. *American Journal of Psychiatry, 136*, 1302–1305.

Weinman, J., Petrie, K., Moss-Morris, R., & Horne, R. (1996). The Illness Perception Questionnaire: A new method of assessing illness perceptions. *Psychology and Health, 11*, 431–446.

Weiss, J. (1994). *How psychotherapy works: Process and technique.* New York: Guilford Press.

Westra, H. (2004). Managing resistance in cognitive behavioural therapy: The application of motivational interviewing in mixed anxiety and depression. *Cognitive Behaviour Therapy, 33*, 161–175.

Weissman, M., Verdeli, H., Gameroff, M., Bledsoe, S., Betts, K., Mufson, L., et al. (2006). National survey of psychotherapy training in psychiatry, psychology, and social work. *Archives of General Psychiatry, 63*, 925–934.

Whipple, J., Lambert, M., Vermeersch, D., Smart, D., Nielsen, S., & Hawkins, E. (2003). Improving the effects of psychotherapy: The use of early identification of treatment and problem-solving strategies in routine practice. *Journal of Counseling Psychology, 50*, 59–68.

White, M., & Epston, D. (1990). *Narrative means to therapeutic ends.* New York: Norton.

Wierzbicki, M., & Pekarik, G. (1993). A meta-analysis of psychotherapy dropout. *Professional Psychology: Research and Practice, 24*, 190–195.

Wilson, P. H. (Ed.). (1992). *Principles and practice of relapse prevention.* New York: Guilford Press.

Wolpe, J. (1969). *The practice of behavior therapy.* New York: Pergamon.

Wolpe, J. (1990). *The practice of behavior therapy* (4th ed.). New York: Pergamon.

Wright, J., Basco, M., & Thase, M. (2006). *Learning cognitive-behavior therapy: An illustrated guide.* Washington, DC: American Psychiatric Press.

Wrzesniewski, A., McCaukley, C., Rozin, P., & Schwartz, B. (1997). Jobs, careers, and callings: People's relations to their work. *Journal of Research in Personality, 31*, 21–33.

Young, J. (1999). *Cognitive therapy for personality disorders: A schema-focused approach* (3rd ed.). Sarasota, FL: Professional Resource Press.

Young, J., Klosko, J., & Weishaar, M. (2003). *Schema therapy: A practitioner's guide.* New York: Guilford Press.

INDEX